21st Century
REVELATION

World Wars, Iraq Wars & End Wars

Creation to Laodicea

Robert Cook

Xulon PRESS

21st Century Revelation: World Wars, Iraq Wars & End Wars
Creation to Laodicea
by Robert Cook

Printed in the United States of America

ISBN 9781625097927

Unless otherwise indicated, Bible quotations are taken from The Authorized King James Version.

www.xulonpress.com

Dedication

One day
I asked God
to love His Word more.
God revealed Himself,
His Word,
His Time
and His plan for our time.

This book is dedicated
to God the Father,
my Savior and Lord Jesus Christ
and the Holy Spirit
who reveals truth
from the Word of God
for the Church
about God's plan
for our time.

This book is written
for the Church.
Wake up,
draw near to God,
study God's Word,
grow within a local church,
make disciples
and together
do the work of the kingdom
until the Feast of Trumpets
when Jesus Christ calls us home.

The Revelation of Jesus Christ,
which God gave
unto him,
to show
unto his servants
things which must shortly come
to pass;
and he sent
and signified it
by his angel
unto his servant John:
Who bare record
of the word of God,
and of the testimony
of Jesus Christ,
and of all things
that he saw.

Blessed is
he that reads,
and they that hear the words
of this prophecy,
and keep those things
which are written therein:
for the time is at hand
(Revelation 1:1-3).

Contents

God's Plan for Our Time

Midway

Appendix

Preface

End Time prophecy is the most misunderstood part of the Bible. Many views describe all kinds of theories of how the world ends. Which one is correct? After having a growing relationship with God and connecting with His people in a local church, End Time prophecy is the most relevant part of the Bible, because it describes our time.

Scripture predicts the First Coming of Jesus Christ. It describes the events in His life from the day and place of His birth to the day and year of His death, burial and resurrection. Jesus Christ, the Son of God, literally fulfilled every prophecy by His life and redemption of humanity. The people of His time heard the message, saw the great miracles, knew His life and understood His claims to be the Messiah. They should have accepted Him with open arms yet the majority of people rejected Him. Even His disciples did not understand at the time. They failed to recognize the prophecies of His First Coming, understand the symbols that pointed to their Messiah and to recognize the signs of the times. They did not put it all together.

Prophecies are being unsealed, fulfilled and revealed today.

Scripture predicts that Jesus Christ is coming again. End Time prophecies go into greater detail about events that precede the Rapture and Second Coming. Because of reliance on traditional views and older commentaries, many current details are overlooked. Key events are happening now before the Tribulation begins.

Do you recognize the signs of the times? In the last one hundred years, we have seen the World Wars, the Cold War and the Iraq Wars. Most people say these are more of the same. Even Christians say they are just "wars and rumors of wars." "No one knows the day or the hour" is another excuse to avoid Bible prophecy. If we cannot know and understand, why did God give us so much prophecy about His plan for our time? He wants us to know.

The Word of God is alive and relevant for today. Through prophecies of our time, God is revealing key events to His people. These events are occurring right before our eyes. Most scholars agree that the 1948 rebirth of Israel is a super sign, a key prophecy fulfilled before the Rapture of the Church. However, there are over twenty precise super signs that occur before we leave. Many of these signs include America. Prophecies are being fulfilled today.

> Blessed are the eyes which see the things that you see. For I tell you, that many prophets and kings have desired to see those things which you see, and have not seen them; and to hear those things which you hear, and have not heard them (Luke 10:23-24).

Why another End Time Book?

Bookstores, libraries and the internet are filled with millions of End Time books, commentaries, sermons and articles explaining all types of views. Most books and commentaries are written by pastors, evangelists and prophecy teachers with lifetimes of Bible study and biblical teaching experience. Without a doubt, these authors know so much more about the Bible than I do. Further, they are better writers and speakers. However, they come up with little more than commentaries which were written fifty or five hundred years earlier. While some parts are correct, other parts are missing and do not help us know and understand our time. As a result, more symbolism exists than solutions and more confusion rather than clarity.

There has to be a twenty-first century understanding of prophecy.

Although the Bible is new every time it is read, most prophecy books rewrite the same thing from older commentaries and ignore what is happening now. In the last ten years, the world has drastically changed and the knowledge of prophecy changed exponentially. I would not write this book if it did not add a clear, current and unique twenty-first century understanding necessary for our time.

Churches are not teaching the complete story of God's time and God's plan. All too often the same mistakes are made. Although God's time and plan are inseparable, most views explain God's plan but fail to understand God's time. Other interpretations confuse Israel and the Church, the Rapture and Second Coming or events before and during the Tribulation. Some writers avoid Jewish culture. One traditional view is taken from a commentary written sixteen hundred years ago, which only began to be fulfilled sixty years ago.

The major problem is that a clear understanding of Scripture could not be revealed until after many recent prophecies were fulfilled. We could not understand these prophecies two hundred or even twenty years ago. These missed details do not create any great heresies but rather they prevent us from hearing God's clear message. They leave us in a fog of confusion about what is going on in our world.

I am not a prophet. I do not have a monopoly on truth and I do not know all the answers. However, I have the same Holy Spirit and the same Word of God as these great scholars. I take a current look at traditional Protestant views and hold them up to Scripture. When they agree with the Bible, they are accepted but when they conflict with the Bible, they are rejected.

The order of the Rapture, followed by the Tribulation, Second Coming and Millennium is correct but it only tells half the story. Another fifteen percent comes from a better understanding of Jewish culture and God's timing. This gives the structure of God's plan. Because we have the advantage of 20/20 hindsight, about twenty-five percent comes from understanding history, which includes key super signs of the last one hundred years.

**The closer we get to the end of the age,
the clearer the picture becomes.**

After clearly understanding God's time and God's plan, many answers fall into place. More is revealed before the Tribulation begins. This view of prophecy still leaves unanswered questions but it brings us light years ahead of what was previously written.

Evaluating views on End Time prophecy requires God's Word to discern what is true. Breaking through the symbols and restudying old traditions reveal new insights into God's plan. Matching prophecies with many of the events of our time brings our amazing God to the forefront of our lives.

Can you find the prophecies of the United States in the Bible? How about America in Iraq? They are right there in Daniel and Revelation. Daniel, John and the other prophets saw visions of our past, present and future. The rise and fall of the United States is described in over one hundred prophetic symbols, events and dates. The Jewish calendar tells us when. Over sixty prophecies have been fulfilled in recent history or current events. Why is the United States a superpower during the End Times but not the Tribulation? What final event brings the judgment of God against America? God tells us before it happens.

**Bible prophecy tells us Israel is the destination
but three Iraq Wars bring us to the Tribulation.**

Amazing but true, one quarter of events mistakenly assigned to the Tribulation occur before the Rapture. Most of these events are already complete. We are living the events as the visions are fulfilled. Three Iraq Wars change the balance of power so America falls and the European Union rules the world.

Basic Prophecy Principles

Before beginning this study, here are a few basic principles.

1. The Bible is the inspired Word of God and the ultimate authority for truth. Through a proper understanding of Scripture, prophecy is revealed.
2. Studying prophecy is a pursuit of truth. This will require rejecting a few traditional views and denominational teachings that conflict with the Bible.
3. End Time prophecy is not a salvation issue. We may have different views but only one way to God exists: grace through faith in Jesus Christ alone.
4. Like the rest of the Bible, End Time prophecy can be understood. Just as humanity complicates God's simple plan of salvation, we also complicate prophecy.
5. Unlike other doctrines of the Bible, End Time prophecy is changing with time. When one prophecy is unsealed, fulfilled and revealed, other prophecies are better understood.
6. To know and understand End Time prophecy is good but it is worthless unless we allow the Holy Spirit to change our hearts and our lives to impact our churches, our communities, our nation and the world.
7. Knowing God's plan for our time decreases our fear and increases our faith and boldness. We cannot hide in a bunker or sit on a hill to wait out the clock. We must wake up the Church and make disciples to spread the Gospel to our families, our neighbors, our cities, our nation and throughout our world.

   For now we see through a glass, darkly; but then face to face: now I know in part; but then shall I know even as also I am known (1 Corinthians 13:12).

21st Century Revelation: World Wars, Iraq Wars & End Wars

A current understanding of God's plan for our time:

1. Creation to Laodicea
2. America & the Rapture
3. Tribulation

God

The book, *21st Century Revelation*, is a three part comprehensive study that goes beyond symbols and traditions. Prophecy is all about the character and nature of God. First, God reveals Himself and then He reveals prophecy.

God's Word

The foundation of this book is the Word of God. About twenty percent of this book is quotes of relevant Scripture verses. How do you study prophecy? Follow basic principles to know Scripture and decipher symbols. Then take a current but literal, twenty-first century understanding to gain a clear picture of God's view of the world. This ancient book comes alive and becomes a guide to our past and our future.

God's Time

The disciples asked Jesus, "When?" and time gives the structure of prophecy. God's time is revealed through creation, Jewish culture and history, Daniel's seventy weeks, the life of Christ and Bible chronology. The Jewish feast and fast days are fulfilled in Jesus Christ and these days predict many key events of the End Times. Specific prophecies have been fulfilled and are being fulfilled before the Tribulation starts. Time is about up.

God's Plan for Our Time

The rest of the study examines events from the Church Age, End Times, Rapture, Tribulation, Second Coming, Millennium and beyond. Each chapter explains Bible prophecies and uses the works of past and present Bible scholars. Mistakes are corrected while adding Jewish culture, world history and current events to understand clearly God's plan for our time and the time to come.

As a result of this message, prophecy becomes history and current events as we witness what is occurring in the world. This book tells exactly when and where we are and what happens next. God's Word is current, dependable, relevant and powerful in our lives, in our churches and in our world knowing our time is the End Times.

Anybody here expect not to die?

We live in exciting times. First, God the Father gave us Jesus Christ for redemption, the Holy Spirit for guidance and the Word of God for instruction. Then God surrounds us with other believers to grow in our relationship with God and fellowship with other Christians as we minister together. Beyond that, we have been chosen to be the End Time people that witness many Scriptures fulfilled. Finally, like Enoch and Elijah, we are given the opportunity to avoid death and go from life to eternal life. Oh, glorious day!

The story of our redemption through Jesus Christ is the greatest story ever told. This book describes the greatest ending of the greatest story.

Introduction

Chapter 1

Does Prophecy Matter?

Prophecy does not matter
if there is no God,
if God is not sovereign over all His creation,
if God is not personally involved in the lives of His people,
if God did not send His Son to redeem us,
if Jesus Christ did not rise from the dead
or if He will not come again.

Prophecy does not matter
if God did not give us the Holy Spirit,
if God did not give us His Word,
if God's Word is not true,
if we cannot know God's Word
or if we cannot understand God's Word.

Prophecy does not matter
if we cannot get beyond the symbolism,
if we do not realize we are living in the End Times
or if we do not know Jesus Christ is coming again in our lifetime.

Prophecy does not matter
if we do not believe God,
if we do not apply the truth
or if the truth does not change our hearts and lives.

However,
Prophecy does matter
because there is a God

who is sovereign over all His creation,
who is personally involved in the lives of His people,
who sent His Son to redeem us,
whose Son, Jesus Christ, arose from the dead
and who is coming again.

Prophecy does matter
because God gave us the Holy Spirit,
God gave us His Word
and His Word is true.
We can know God's Word
and understand God's Word.

Prophecy does matter
because we can get beyond the symbolism
so we realize we are living in the End Times
and we know Jesus Christ is coming again in our lifetime.

Prophecy does matter
because we can believe God
and apply the truth
and truth will change our hearts and lives.

In the fall of 2002 during the Iraq War debate, my pastor taught a Revelation Bible study. This was my first pastor to teach a complete study of the book. I became interested in prophecy when I was in the sixth grade. I read Revelation a few times, stumbling over those bizarre symbols. This class was my first in-depth study of the book.

By watching the news, I saw the signs of the times. America was headed for war with Iraq. This was not Armageddon, since the Tribulation had not started. Was this just another war or a sign from God? Was Iraq the catalyst that grows into a larger Middle East war leading to the Tribulation?

Four years later, I found the answer. Iraq did not spill into Israel like I initially thought but rather Iraq is much more than just another war. Hidden within those strange symbols of Revelation are specific prophecies of two World Wars, the Cold War and three Iraq Wars.

The Persian Gulf War caused the Iraq War which brought the United States to the banks of the Euphrates River and into Iraq War III. These wars require a twenty-first century understanding of Bible prophecy.

Most Christians believe in the "pan" theory of Bible prophecy—it will all "pan" out in the end. It's more of a confession of "I don't know and I can't know, so I don't care." Those who believe this hinder God's ability to reveal Himself and His plan for the world to His people.

Generally speaking, prophecy is declaring the Word of God. All Scripture is prophecy. Specifically in 8,352 of 31,124 verses, God reveals the future.[1] We cannot neglect over a quarter of the Bible. God does not give us His Word and then make it impossible to know. The "pan" theory discloses our relationship with God. How much do we really want to know God and His Word?

Prophecy Fulfilled in Jesus Christ's First Coming

Every time you refer to the death, burial and resurrection of Jesus Christ, you speak of Bible prophecy. In Jesus Christ's first coming, 360 prophecies are literally fulfilled as written, proving we can know and understand prophecy.[2]

Worship God: for the testimony of Jesus is the spirit of prophecy (Revelation 19:10).

Did anyone know of Jesus Christ's first coming? In Matthew 2, wise men had access to the book of Daniel and the signs in the sky. They traveled from the Babylon/Persia area to Bethlehem and witnessed prophecy fulfilled. In Luke 2, Simeon and Anna were searching for the salvation of Israel. Their prayers were answered the day Joseph and Mary dedicated Jesus Christ at the temple. In John 4, the woman at the well knew the Messiah was coming but He found her first. After Jesus Christ was resurrected, He appeared to the disciples and to more than five hundred people. The risen Messiah is the fulfillment of prophecy.

However, the political and religious leaders of the day had the same Scripture, saw the same signs, knew the same man, heard of the same miracles and yet because of their religious beliefs and traditions, they failed to put the prophecies and signs together.

Will your religious beliefs, denominational teaching and neglect of Scripture make you overlook God's message for you? Will you apply Scripture to current times and see God at work? Will you minister to the Church and be a witness to your community until He comes?

Prophecy Fulfilled in Jesus Christ's Second Coming

History is past, current events are present and prophecy is future. "God speaks by the Holy Spirit through the Bible, prayer, circumstances and the Church to reveal Himself, His purposes and His ways."[3] God is at work to build relationships with people.

Frequently in Scripture, our all-knowing God reveals future events before they happen to display His character of a sovereign, all-powerful God who has everything under control. This was a great comfort to His people Israel when they were captive in Babylon or ruled by Greek and Roman tyrants. It is an even greater comfort to Christians who are living in the End Times.

> Behold, the former things are come to pass, and new things do I declare: before they spring forth I tell you of them (Isaiah 42:9).

Why Study End Time Prophecy?[4]

1. To Know God

> That I may know him, and the power of his resurrection, and the fellowship of his sufferings, being made conformable unto his death (Philippians 3:10).

2. To Know God's Word

> All scripture is given by inspiration of God, and is profitable for doctrine, for reproof, for correction, for instruction in righteousness (2 Timothy 3:16).

3. To Know God's Time

> So Christ was once offered to bear the sins of many; and unto them that look for him shall he appear the second time without sin unto salvation (Hebrews 9:28).

4. To Know God's Purpose and Plan

> "For I know the plans I have for you," declares the Lord, "plans to prosper you and not to harm you, plans to give you hope and a future" (Jeremiah 29:11 NIV).

5. To Prove God Is True to His Word

According to the faith of God's elect, and the acknowledging of the truth which is after godliness; in hope of eternal life, which God, that cannot lie, promised before the world began (Titus 1:1-2).

6. To Worship God

That at the name of Jesus every knee should bow and that every tongue should confess that Jesus Christ is Lord, to the glory of God the Father (Philippians 2:10-11).

7. To Have Hope in God

Being confident of this very thing, that he which has begun a good work in you will perform it until the day of Jesus Christ (Philippians 1:6).

8. To Build Our Faith in God

Now faith is the substance of things hoped for, the evidence of things not seen. But without faith it is impossible to please him: for he that comes to God must believe that he is, and that he is a rewarder of them that diligently seek him (Hebrews 11:1, 6).

9. To Recognize God Is Always at Work in the Middle of Our Trials

On the left hand, where he does work, but I cannot behold him: he hides himself on the right hand, that I cannot see him: but he knows the way that I take: when he has tried me, I shall come forth as gold (Job 23:9-10).

10. To Wake Up

And that, knowing the time, that now it is high time to awake out of sleep: for now is our salvation nearer than when we believed (Romans 13:11).

11. To Discern Between Truth and Error, Sound Doctrine and Apostasy

When he, the Spirit of truth, is come, he will guide you into all truth: for he shall not speak of himself; but whatsoever he shall hear, that shall he speak: and he will show you things to come (John 16:13).

12. To Transform Knowledge and Understanding into a Changed Life

I beseech you therefore, brethren, by the mercies of God, that you present your bodies a living sacrifice, holy, acceptable unto God, which is your reasonable service. And be not conformed to this world: but be transformed by the renewing of your mind, that you may prove what is that good, and acceptable, and perfect, will of God (Romans 12:1-2).

13. To Act on the New Understanding

But be doers of the word, and not hearers only, deceiving your own selves (James 1:22).

14. To Disciple and Equip the Church for Ministry

And he gave some, apostles; and some, prophets; and some, evangelists; and some, pastors and teachers; for the perfecting of the saints, for the work of the ministry, for the edifying of the body of Christ (Ephesians 4:12).

15. To Share the Gospel with Others

You shall receive power, after that the Holy Spirit is come upon you: and you shall be witnesses unto me both in Jerusalem, and in all Judea, and in Samaria, and unto the uttermost part of the earth (Acts 1:8).

16. To Remind Us that Jesus Christ Wins

And the seventh angel sounded; and there were great voices in heaven, saying, The kingdoms of this world are become the kingdoms of our Lord, and of his Christ; and he shall reign for ever and ever (Revelation 11:15).

17. To Receive God's Blessings for Reading, Hearing and Applying Prophecy

Blessed is he that reads, and they that hear the words of this prophecy, and keep those things which are written therein: for the time is at hand (Revelation 1:3).

18. To Know Our Time Is the End Times

> You can discern the face of the sky; but can you not discern the signs of the times (Matthew 16:3)?

God's Plan for Us

What does Iraq have to do with Bible prophecy? Plenty! Throughout the years, all wars have been fought over politics, religion or economics. The Iraq Wars are part of a bigger conflict between Capitalism, Communism and Islam. The American versus European argument over Iraq was about who controls the world.[5] For the sake of peace, the Quartet on the Middle East will divide Israel and cause the fall of the United States and the Tribulation.[6] Red China's economic rise and hunger for power will lead to a confrontation with America.[7] Then the Russian-Islamic alliance will fight Israel.[8] Although Israel is the final destination, Iraq is the catalyst for three End Wars that end with Armageddon.

God's plan for the world is so precise yet His plan for our individual lives is just as precise. God deals with people individually and collectively. First, He brings a person into a relationship with Himself. Then He unites individual believers in local churches for encouragement and training to do God's work.

The knowledge of End Time prophecy has a powerful effect on Christians. It is not required for salvation but seeing when and where we are in time builds confidence in God and makes the Word of God Monday-morning relevant. Our eyes are open to see God at work in light of current events. We mature our relationship with God, build our faith in God, expand our personal ministry and in the middle of this global crisis, live what we believe as witnesses to a lost world. When the truth of God is revealed, our hearts and lives must change.

> Let us hold fast the profession of our faith without wavering; (for he is faithful that promised); and let us consider one another to provoke love and to good works: not forsaking the assembling of ourselves together but exhorting one another: and so much the more, as you see the day approaching (Hebrews 10:23-25).

Does prophecy matter to you?

Chapter 2

End Times Defined

B efore studying the End Times, it is important to define some basic terms.[1] This will help those new to End Time prophecy and make sure everyone begins at the same place.

There is a God in heaven that reveals secrets, and makes known to the king Nebuchadnezzar what shall be in the latter days (Daniel 2:28).

Prophecy Terms

1. Redemption

Jesus Christ died, was buried and rose again to save us from our sins. This is the good news of the Gospel and first part of God's plan of salvation.

> Being justified freely by his grace through the redemption that is in Christ Jesus (Romans 3:24).

2. Return

Jesus Christ is about to call His people home, restore Israel and reign over the earth. These events are fulfilled in the End Times. This is the second part of God's plan of salvation.

> Then comes the end, when he [Jesus Christ] shall have delivered up the kingdom to God, even the Father; when he shall have put down all rule and all authority and power (1 Corinthians 15:24).

3. Last Days

The period covered in the New Testament starts with Christ's First Coming and all future events. This includes the Church Age, Tribulation and Millennium. Over a quarter of the Bible deals with the future.[2]

> God, who at sundry times and in diverse manners spoke in time past to the fathers by the prophets, has in these last days spoken to us by his Son, whom he has appointed heir of all things, by whom also he made the worlds (Hebrews 1:1-2).

4. Eschatology

As part of a study of God's Word, prophecy describes future events of the last days. Topics include the Church Age, End Times, Rapture, Tribulation, Second Coming, Millennium, judgment and life after death. It is not "the end of the world" but rather a transition from human rule to God's rule.

> And as he sat upon the mount of Olives, the disciples came unto him privately, saying, Tell us, when shall these things be? and what shall be the sign of thy coming, and of the end of the world (Matthew 24:3)?

5. Church Age

The Church Age begins at Pentecost and ends at the Rapture. God, the Holy Spirit, dwells within Christians and works through the Church to spread the Gospel. The Church has endured for almost two thousand years.

> John to the seven churches which are in Asia: Grace be unto you, and peace, from him which is, and which was, and which is to come (Revelation 1:4).

6. Laodicean Period

Revelation 2-3 describes characteristics of seven local first century churches. The churches predict seven periods during the Church Age. The seventh church is the lukewarm Laodicean church. Starting about 1900, this period is when Christians are half-hearted about their faith but God works to wake up His Church and prepares the world for the Tribulation. We have been in the End Times for one hundred years.

I [Jesus Christ] know your works, that you [Laodicean church] are neither cold nor hot: I would you were cold or hot. So then because you are lukewarm and neither cold nor hot, I will spew you out of my mouth (Revelation 3:15-16).

7. End Times

Future prophetic events are focused on the Laodicean period and the Tribulation. It is important to separate events before the Tribulation from events during the Tribulation. For Christians, anything past the Rapture is not the end but rather the beginning of our new and glorious lives with God.

And he said, Go your way, Daniel: for the words are closed up and sealed till the time of the end (Daniel 12:9).

8. Super Sign

Prophecies fulfill specific events. The most important super sign occurred in 1948. After two thousand years of Gentile control, Israel became an independent nation. During the last one hundred years, the Bible describes over twenty super signs fulfilled before the Rapture. These include the World Wars, Iraq Wars and rise and fall of the United States and European Union.

Who has heard such a thing? who has seen such things? Shall the earth be made to bring forth in one day? or shall a nation be born at once? for as soon as Zion [Israel] travailed, she brought forth her children (Isaiah 66:8).

9. End Time Powers & End Wars

China, the European Union, India, Islam, Israel, Russia, the United Nations and the United States are End Time powers. Iraq War III, Russian-Islamic War and Armageddon are three End Wars. The End Time powers lead three World Wars. By the Second Coming, all nations fall except Israel.

I beheld, and the same horn [Antichrist] made war with the saints, and prevailed against them; Until the Ancient of days came, and judgment was given to the saints of the most High; and the time came that the saints possessed the kingdom (Daniel 7:21-22).

10. Rapture

At the sound of the trumpet, Jesus Christ calls His children home. The dead in Christ are resurrected to life and all believers meet Jesus Christ in the air.

> For the Lord himself shall descend from heaven with a shout, with the voice of the archangel, and with the trump of God: and the dead in Christ shall rise first: Then we which are alive and remain shall be caught up [raptured] together with them in the clouds, to meet the Lord in the air: and so shall we ever be with the Lord (1 Thessalonians 4:16-17).

11. Tribulation

The last seven years of human rule is described by Daniel's seventy weeks. God restores Israel but pours out wrath on those who reject His mercy and grace and rebel against His sovereignty over the world. The second half of the Tribulation is the Great Tribulation or "Jacob's trouble."

> For then shall be great tribulation, such as was not since the beginning of the world to this time, no, nor ever shall be (Matthew 24:21).

12. Confirmation of the Covenant

The Antichrist confirms the Israel-Palestine peace treaty that takes the West Bank from Israel. The covenant begins and causes the Tribulation. Judea and Samaria are the Israeli term for the West Bank of Jordan.[3]

> And he [Antichrist] shall confirm the covenant with many for one week [seven]: and in the midst of the week he shall cause the [Jewish] sacrifice and the offerings to cease (Daniel 9:27).

13. Antichrist

A man empowered by Satan claims to be the promised Messiah. He leads a political, religious and economic world government during the last half of the Tribulation. His character and purpose is opposite Jesus Christ and he fights God's people. He is the "Man of Sin," "Little Horn" and he leads the Beast.

Little children, it is the last time: and as you have heard that antichrist shall come, even now are there many antichrists; whereby we know that it is the last time (1 John 2:18).

14. The Beast

Sometimes synonymous with the man, Antichrist, the Beast describes a ten-nation supranational government. These national leaders give power and allegiance to the Antichrist. He leads this empire and rules the world.

And the ten horns which you saw are ten kings, which have received no kingdom as yet; but receive power as kings one hour with the beast. These have one mind, and shall give their power and strength unto the beast (Revelation 17:12-13).

15. False Prophet

Many false prophets exist but this man is a great religious leader. Through many wonders, he leads the world in worship of the Antichrist. He looks like a lamb but speaks like a dragon and leads the second beast.

And he exercises all the power of the first beast before him, and causes the earth and them which dwell therein to worship the first beast. And he does great wonders, so that he makes fire come down from heaven on the earth in the sight of men (Revelation 13:12-13).

16. Whore of Babylon

As the Antichrist leads the political system (the beast), the False Prophet leads the religious system (woman). The Bible depicts true religion as the Bride of Christ and false religion as the Whore of Babylon.

I saw a woman sit upon a scarlet colored beast, full of names of blasphemy, having seven heads [kings] and ten horns [nations] (Revelation 17:3).

17. Abomination of Desolation

In the middle of the Tribulation, the Antichrist begins his reign. He will disrupt Jewish worship, sit in the third Jewish temple, claim to be God and demand worship from all.

Let no man deceive you by any means: for that day shall not come, except that man of sin be revealed, the son of perdition; who opposes and exalts himself above all that is called God, or that is worshipped; so that he as God sits in the temple of God, showing himself that he is God (2 Thessalonians 2:3-4).

18. Armageddon

Near the end of the Tribulation, all nations gather their armies at the valley of Megiddo in northern Israel and then invade Jerusalem. This begins the final battle between Israel and the world.

And he [Antichrist] gathered them together into a place called in the Hebrew tongue Armageddon (Revelation 16:16).

19. Second Coming

Jesus Christ returns to earth, restores Israel, defeats His foes and begins His one thousand year reign on earth.

And I saw heaven opened, and behold a white horse; and he that sat upon him was called Faithful and True, and in righteousness he does judge and make war. And he has on his robe and on his thigh a name written, KING OF KINGS, AND LORD OF LORDS (Revelation 19:11, 16).

20. Millennium Reign of Jesus Christ

After the Tribulation, Jesus Christ reigns over all the people of earth for one thousand years. The earth will be restored, sin will be restrained and true peace will exist on earth. This is called the Day of the Lord.

And they [martyred saints] lived and reigned with Christ a thousand years (Revelation 20:4).

21. Premillennium Pretribulation

A view of End Time prophecy states the Rapture occurs before the seven years of Tribulation and one thousand year reign of Christ. This view is held by many Protestant

Premillennium Pretribulation Timeline[4]

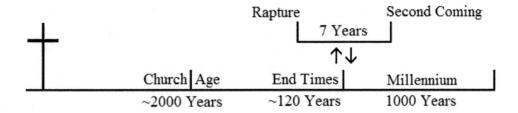

churches and prophecy preachers such as Billy Graham, Timothy LaHaye, Hal Lindsey, Perry Stone and Jack Van Impe. I agree with the Premillennium Pretribulation view. The End Times is the Laodicean period of the Church Age.

> For God has not appointed us to wrath, but to obtain salvation by our Lord Jesus Christ, Who died for us, that, whether we wake or sleep, we should live together with him (1 Thessalonians 5:9-10).

When in the World Are We?

Everyone watching for the end of time wants to know when we are. Despite views to the contrary, God's Word tells us when and where we are and describes specific details about our time. The book, *21st Century Revelation*, explains why we are so close to the Rapture and Tribulation.

1. God's character and nature gives man a choice and judgment day.
2. The Word of God reveals the time of God and the plan of God.
3. God's time is four thousand years before the cross and three thousand years after.
4. Bible chronology points to the end of man's six-thousand-year rule.
5. Key events of the last one hundred years occur on Jewish holy days.
6. The end of the Laodicean period is the end of the Church Age.
7. Seven End Time powers are ready for the Tribulation.
8. Four horses of the apocalypse are on the run today.
9. Seven wars of the seven trumpets occur in a 120-year period.
10. The United States is described in over one hundred Bible prophecies.

Over Twenty Super Signs

We have been in the End Times for about one hundred years. Wars reconfigure the world's political, religious and economic systems in preparation for the Tribulation. Super signs before the Tribulation include the World Wars and Iraq Wars. They are a part of God's unsealed, fulfilled and revealed plan. These super signs are more than just generic "wars and rumors of wars" since Scripture gives specific details. God tells us events before they happen so we know the signs of the times, encourage and work with one another and prepare to meet our Lord.

> Now learn a parable of the fig tree; When his branch is yet tender, and puts forth leaves, you know that summer is nigh: So likewise when you shall see all these things, know that it is near, even at the doors (Matthew 24:32-33).

The birth of the United States is a super sign that occurs before 1900 and fulfills five Bible prophecies. There are more than twenty super signs that occur between 1900 and the Rapture. Each super sign has a corresponding Scripture passage.

Super Signs of the End Times

Year	Fulfillment	Prophecy	Scripture
1776	Birth of the United States		
~1900	End Times Begin		
1914 -1918	World War I		
1917	Rise of the United States		
1917	Rise of Communism		
1938 -1945	World War II		
1945	Germany Divided		
1948	Israel Reborn		
1950	European Union (Revived Roman Empire)		
1957	Germany Joins EU		
1967	Jerusalem Reunited		

1973	United Kingdom Joins EU		
1979	Rise of Islam		
1945 -1989	Cold War		
1986	Chernobyl Accident		
1989	Iron Curtain Falls Russia Hibernates		
1990 -1991	Iraq War I (Persian Gulf War)		
1990	Reunification of Germany		
1997	EU-Russia Partnership		
2000	Israel Associate Member of EU		
2002	The Quartet on the Middle East (European Union, Russia, United Nations, United States)		
2003 -2010	Iraq War II Saddam Hussein		
20??	English Official Language of European Union		
20??	Iraq War III		
20??	Rapture		
20??	Tribulation Begins Israel Joins EU		
20??	Israel Builds Temple		
20??	Fall of the United States		
20??	Russia Joins EU		
20??	EU & United Nations Merge		
20??	Apostasy & False Religions Merge		
20??	World Political, Religious, & Economic System		
20??	False Religion and European Union		

20??	Russian-Islamic War		
20??	Battle of Armageddon		
20??	Second Coming		
20??	Reign of Christ		

Prophecy Unsealed, Fulfilled and Revealed

Our amazing God tells us we are living in amazing times. Studying End Times is challenging but life-changing. Before starting, know basic End Time prophecy terms. From a Christian perspective, the End Times is the Laodicean period. Many key historical events of the last one hundred years are precise, fulfilled prophecies. What Scriptures predict events of the last 120 years of human rule?

When studying End Time prophecy, it is important to understand the background before digging into the details. This study of the Bible begins with the character and nature of God.

Section 1

God

Chapter 3

The Throne of God

S cripture reveals God in many ways. We see His character of holiness, unconditional love, mercy and grace, Savior and Messiah. These characteristics are seen in the End Times. However, the emphasis of prophecy is on an exalted God. He reveals Himself as the Lord God Almighty, Ancient of Days, Sovereign of the Universe, Alpha and Omega, Protector of His people, Victor over His enemies, King of Kings and Lord of Lords.

> Looking unto Jesus the author and finisher of our faith; who for the joy that was set before him endured the cross, despising the shame, and is set down at the right hand of the throne of God (Hebrews 12:2).

Before given prophecy, a prophet saw a glimpse of God the Father on His throne, high and lifted up and Jesus Christ worthy of praise and glory. That is the Almighty God that we serve.

Visions of God the Father

1. Daniel—The Ancient of Days

> I beheld till the thrones were cast down, and the Ancient of days did sit, whose garment was white as snow, and the hair of his head like the pure wool: his throne was like the fiery flame and his wheels as burning fire. A fiery stream issued and came forth from before him: thousand thousands ministered unto him, and ten thousand times ten thousand stood before him: the judgment was set, and the books were opened (Daniel 7:9-10).

In Daniel's vision, the Ancient of Days is God the Father.[1] The white garment symbolizes His righteousness and white hair depicts His wisdom and authority. The fire from the throne represents His righteous judgment. Many angels ministered to Him, while many people were judged before Him.

This vision is of the Great White Throne. Revelation 21 tells of the judgment of humanity at the end of the Millennium. The Lamb's Book of Life lists the redeemed and the Book of Remembrance lists peoples' good and bad deeds. If a person does not accept Jesus Christ's pardon for sin, he is judged by works which fall short of perfection. Daniel sees God on the throne in Heaven as sovereign judge of humanity.

2. Isaiah—God upon the Throne

> In the year that king Uzziah died I saw also the Lord sitting upon a throne, high and lifted up, and his train filled the temple. Above it stood the seraphims: each one had six wings; with two he covered his face, and with two he covered his feet, and with two he did fly. And one cried unto another, and said, Holy, holy, holy, is the Lord of hosts: the whole earth is full of his glory (Isaiah 6:1-3).

The prophet Isaiah sees our exalted God on His throne.[2] Despite circumstances on the earth, God is sovereign over all. The length of robe describes a king's importance. He is surrounded by angels. Cherubim serve God while seraphim worship God around the throne. Two wings cover their eyes from God's glory, two wings cover their feet for humility and two wings fly as they serve God.

One seraph witnesses God's glory and proclaims God's nature. All of God's moral characteristics originate from His holiness. Christians were created in the image of God, were given the righteousness of God and have fellowship with God because God is holy. In the Hebrew language, repetition intensifies the description. God is three times holy. It also refers to the Trinity: God the Father, Son and Spirit are holy. God is exalted above all angels, humans and other created beings.

When Isaiah saw God as holy, he saw himself as a sinner. He repented and was restored to a right relationship with God. Then God called Isaiah to minister to His people. When we truly see God, it changes our hearts, our lives and our ministry.

3. John the Disciple—The Throne in Heaven

> And immediately I was in the spirit: and, behold, a throne was set in heaven, and one sat on the throne. And he that sat was to look upon like a jasper and

sardine stone: and there was a rainbow round about the throne, in sight like unto an emerald (Revelation 4:2-3).

John the disciple witnesses a glorious view of God in Heaven. First, he saw God Almighty seated on the throne. Revelation refers to the throne of God forty times.[3] John does not describe His physical form but rather His glory as jasper and sardine, the first and last gems in the priestly breastplate.[4] An emerald rainbow is God's unbroken covenant of redemption, which surrounds the throne to display His eternal rule. Although sovereign over Heaven and earth, God is limited by His Word. Because He is truth, He fulfills His promises.[5]

> And round about the throne were twenty-four seats: and upon the seats I saw twenty-four elders sitting, clothed in white raiment; and they had on their heads crowns of gold. And out of the throne proceeded lightnings and thunderings and voices: and there were seven lamps of fire burning before the throne, which are the seven Spirits of God. And before the throne there was a sea of glass like unto crystal: and in the midst of the throne, and round about the throne, were four living creatures full of eyes before and behind (Revelation 4:4-6).

Twelve represents government and twenty-four is God's government. There were twelve sons of Jacob and twelve disciples of Jesus Christ. Aaron was the grandfather of twenty-four men and twenty-four priestly divisions that led worship in the Jewish temple.[6] The elders are dressed in white robes and gold crowns as God gave them His righteousness and authority to reign.

Lightning and thunder illustrate God's power. In Exodus 19, God displays His presence at Mt. Sinai. In Job 38-40, God questions Job on His sovereignty, using many wonders of nature. Seven golden lampstands or sevenfold Spirits of God surround the throne.[7] The sea is smooth as glass which describes God's reign over a world at peace.

> And the spirit of the Lord shall rest upon him, the spirit of wisdom and understanding, the spirit of counsel and might, the spirit of knowledge and of the fear of the Lord (Isaiah 11:2).

The four living creatures are four cherubim. Both angels and humans are created to glorify God. These four angels give glory, honor and thanksgiving and the twenty-four elders worship God.

Direct Access to God

Most people lack direct access to their king, president or prime minister but some people are a part of the inner circle. There is a picture of US President John Kennedy working in the oval office while his son, John-John, plays underneath.

As the children of God, we have direct access to God through prayer, Bible study and fellowship with other Christians. We can appeal directly to our Daddy or just stop by to praise and worship our great God. What a wonderful reminder of our relationship with God.

> Let us therefore come boldly unto the throne of grace, that we may obtain mercy, and find grace to help in time of need (Hebrews 4:16).

Visions of Jesus Christ

1. Daniel—Son of Man

> I saw in the night visions, and, behold, one like the Son of man came with the clouds of heaven, and came to the Ancient of days, and they brought him near before him. And there was given him dominion, and glory, and a kingdom, that all people, nations, and languages, should serve him: his dominion is an everlasting dominion, which shall not pass away, and his kingdom that which shall not be destroyed (Daniel 7:13-14).

Daniel sees God the Father as the Ancient of Days, then sees Jesus Christ, the Son of Man. Because of Calvary, the Father gives His Son power and authority to govern earth. At the Second Coming, Antichrist is conquered, world government is overthrown and all people worship God the Father and the Lamb on the throne. Then Jesus Christ reigns over an eternal kingdom.

> And the kingdom and dominion, and the greatness of the kingdom under the whole heaven, shall be given to the people of the saints of the most High, whose kingdom is an everlasting kingdom, and all dominions shall serve and obey him (Daniel 7:27).

Daniel was troubled by the vision but we are encouraged. Even though the enemies of God control the earth, it will be temporary. In the final chapter, Jesus Christ conquers His enemies and reigns forever.

2. John the Disciple—Revealer of Prophecy

> And in the midst of the seven candlesticks one like unto the Son of man, clothed with a garment down to the foot, and girded about the chest with a golden belt. His head and his hairs were white like wool, as white as snow; and his eyes were as a flame of fire; And his feet like unto fine brass, as if they burned in a furnace; and his voice as the sound of many waters. And he had in his right hand seven stars: and out of his mouth went a sharp two-edged sword: and his countenance was as the sun shines in his strength (Revelation 1:13-16).

John knew Jesus. Along with the other disciples, He lived with Him and saw Him as both man and God throughout His ministry. For one short moment, John saw the full glory of Jesus Christ.[8] Yet this was a different view of the Son of God.

In the center of seven lampstands or seven churches is One like the Son of Man. God became man to be the Savior of humanity. Jesus Christ is the High Priest in the middle of His churches caring for their needs. His long robe describes His authority.[9] His gold belt shows He is greater than the High Priest. His hair is white depicting wisdom. His eyes are like fire as He is our righteous judge. As human, He experienced the fiery trials of life but as God, He possesses confidence and authority.[10]

Jesus Christ has seven stars in His hand which show his personal care for the pastors of the seven churches.[11] Out of His mouth is a sharp two-edged sword which is the Word of God. Ephesians 6 describes the armor of God. Truth is our powerful offensive weapon. His countenance reveals His glory. This was no human Jesus Christ whose glory was hidden by a human body but rather our exalted Savior and Lord.

> The mystery of the seven stars which you saw in my right hand, and the seven golden candlesticks. The seven stars are the angels [messengers] of the seven churches: and the seven candlesticks which you saw are the seven churches (Revelation 1:20).

John saw the vision of God the Son but was overwhelmed and fainted. Jesus Christ restored John and calmed his fears. Jesus Christ overcame death and Hell. He tells John to write Revelation: the past vision of Jesus Christ, the present churches of Asia Minor and the future events of the End Times.

3. John the Disciple — Victor on the White Horse

> And I saw heaven opened, and behold a white horse; and he that sat upon him was called Faithful and True, and in righteousness he does judge and make war. His eyes were as a flame of fire, and on his head were many crowns; and he had a name written, that no man knew, but he himself. And he was clothed with a robe dipped in blood: and his name is called The Word of God (Revelation 19:11-13).

Many descriptions of Jesus Christ are found in the Bible but here He is Victor over His enemies. Revelation 19 is the climactic chapter of human history. In the middle of the greatest battle ever fought when Satan and Antichrist are about to annihilate Israel and win the war, John sees Heaven open. In the past, Jesus entered Jerusalem riding on a lowly donkey as a peaceful servant. Now at the Second Coming, He returns to Jerusalem riding a white horse as the conquering King of Kings.

Jesus Christ comes to judge the world but He is still called Faithful and True. God desires all people to come into a relationship. At this last moment, there is a final opportunity for salvation. Zechariah 12 says Israel sees their Messiah, immediately repents and is saved. Others who fight against Israel reject Jesus Christ for the last time and are destroyed.

Jesus Christ's eyes of fire see the heart and He judges justly. Previously, He was given a crown of thorns but now He takes the crowns of all kings. He has authority over all peoples, tribes, nations and languages and establishes His kingdom on earth.

John 1 calls Jesus Christ the Word of God and Revelation 19 calls Him King of Kings and Lord of Lords yet He has a name that no one knows: *YHWH*.[12] Only the High Priest spoke the name of God on the Day of Atonement. To know the God of the Bible takes a lifetime and yet, we will know much more when we see Him face-to-face. His robe is dipped in His blood for redemption and the blood of His enemies for justice.

> And the armies which were in heaven followed him upon white horses, clothed in fine linen, white and clean. And out of his mouth goes a sharp sword, that with it he should smite the nations: and he shall rule them with a rod of iron: and he treads the winepress of the fierceness and wrath of

Almighty God. And he has on his robe and on his thigh a name written, KING OF KINGS, AND LORD OF LORDS (Revelation 19:14-16).

The armies in Heaven are the Old Testament Saints and the Church clothed in the righteousness of God. We have the opportunity to witness this glorious day. The Son of God is the great General that leads His people into the fight but this battle is the Lord's and He receives all the glory. The God that spoke the world into existence became the Word that lived with humanity and personally speaks His children home, is now the Word that speaks judgment to His enemies. He judges with righteous indignation on the rebellious enemy who refuses His mercy and grace, steals His land, slaughters His people and challenges His authority over the earth.[13] He wins the victory then reigns for one thousand years with a rod of iron, a symbol of absolute power and authority.

God the Father gave His inheritance to Jesus Christ for His redemption of humanity. Jesus Christ shares His great victory with His people. His victory means we have victory over sin, death, Hell and gain a relationship with God and Heaven too.

We can know Jesus Christ as John saw Him. We can see John's vision of the future clearer than John could. God wants us to know about the End Times but it starts with a proper vision of God.

See the God of Prophecy

Some people go through End Time prophecy wanting to know signs and symbols but overlook God. Before God reveals prophecy to the prophets, God reveals Himself. See our Sovereign God as Holy Father and worthy Son, Jesus Christ. He loves us, He saves us, He won the victory and He is about to bring us home.

Blessing, and honor, and glory, and power, be unto him that sits upon the throne, and unto the Lamb for ever and ever (Revelation 5:13).

Before studying the End Times, do you clearly see and live knowing God is sovereign and on His throne?

Chapter 4

The Revelation of Jesus Christ

T he book of Revelation starts with the words "The Revelation of Jesus Christ." What a great way to begin. John the apostle starts with the true author and message—Jesus Christ. Understand that God's Word is not just another book of philosophy, positive thinking or good principles by which to live. Jesus Christ is more than a good teacher or prophet. He was and is God!

Before Abraham was, I am (John 8:58).

The Bible depicts God the Father, Son and Spirit by their acts of creation and interaction with people. When studying prophecy, do not get so consumed with the details that you do not experience God. Studying the Bible is about your relationship with God. Focus on God and He will reveal Himself and His Word.

Jesus Christ Reveals Himself

1. **Jesus Christ Reveals Himself as God.**

> In in the midst of the seven candlesticks one like unto the Son of man, clothed with a garment down to the foot, and girded about the chest with a golden belt. His head and his hairs were white like wool, as white as snow; and his eyes were as a flame of fire; And his feet like unto fine brass, as if they burned in a furnace; and his voice as the sound of many waters (Revelation 1:13-15).

John was a disciple, apostle, pastor and writer. He was no stranger to Jesus Christ. John lived with Him, he was taught by Him, he saw His character and he saw His ministry. Additionally, he saw Jesus Christ betrayed, crucified and resurrected. However, for one short moment, John caught a glimpse of His glory as God.

Yet when John sees Jesus this time, He reveals Himself as the sovereign, all-powerful God. Daniel, John and other prophets see a glimpse of God, talk with angels and receive dreams and visions about events in the future. Being human, they are full of fear and are overcome with the majesty of God.

When we see these incredible events, we too are overwhelmed because they reveal the character and nature of God. Anytime we commune in prayer, encounter Him in Scripture or see His life displayed in other Christians, we have the opportunity to view the glory of God. These experiences change our hearts and lives as we truly see Jesus Christ as God.

2. Jesus Christ Reveals Himself as Savior.

Jesus or *Yeshua* literally means Savior.[1] He is the Lamb of God. He is worthy, because He was obedient to His Father's will, became a lowly servant and was sacrificed for the sins of the world. His blood shed on the cross cleanses us from all sin. All who believe in Jesus Christ and accept Him as Savior and Lord will be saved.

> And they sung a new song, saying, Thou are worthy to take the book, and to open the seals: for thou were slain, and have redeemed us to God by thy blood out of every kindred, and tongue, and people, and nation (Revelation 5:9).

3. Jesus Christ Reveals Himself as Prophet.

A prophet speaks more than future events. He speaks the Word of God to the people for instruction and correction. John declared that "the Word was made flesh." Jesus said, "I am the truth." The prophecy God gave to Moses was fulfilled in the greatest prophet, Jesus Christ.

> I will raise them up a Prophet from among their brethren, like unto you [Moses], and will put my words in his mouth; and he shall speak unto them all that I shall command him (Deuteronomy 18:18).

4. Jesus Christ Reveals Himself as Priest.

A prophet is a messenger from God to man but a priest is an intercessor from man to God. Jesus Christ became human and experienced the same trials as we do. He knows what we are going through and has compassion for us. He is our perfect High Priest who intercedes before God the Father on our behalf.

Seeing then that we have a great high priest, that is passed into the heavens, Jesus the Son of God, let us hold fast our profession. For we have not an high priest which cannot be touched with the feeling of our infirmities; but was in all points tempted like as we are, yet without sin. Let us therefore come boldly unto the throne of grace, that we may obtain mercy, and find grace to help in time of need (Hebrews 4:14-16).

5. Jesus Christ Reveals Himself as King of Kings.

During His first coming, Jesus Christ was the Savior of humanity. No other god, prophet, priest or king died for the sins of the world. No one else is worthy to be our Savior. During His Second Coming, He will be the victorious conqueror. No one else is worthy to be our King.

And I saw heaven opened, and behold a white horse; and he that sat upon him was called Faithful and True, and in righteousness he does judge and make war. And he has on his robe and on his thigh a name written, KING OF KINGS AND LORD OF LORDS (Revelation 19:11, 16).

6. Jesus Christ Reveals Himself as Righteous Judge.

Many people like the kind and gentle Jesus in the Gospels but cringe at the judgment in Revelation. God is the same in the Old Testament as in the New Testament and in the Gospels as in Revelation. The dual nature of the Lion and the Lamb is present throughout the Bible. Jesus is inclusive as Savior for all the world but He is exclusive as the only way, truth and life.[2] The character and nature of God gives man a choice and a judgment day. As Jesus Christ came to earth to redeem the world, soon He comes to judge the world.

[God] has appointed a day, in which he will judge the world in righteousness by that man whom he has ordained [Jesus Christ]; whereof he has given assurance unto all men, in that he has raised him from the dead (Acts 17:31).

Jesus Christ is righteous and holy, the perfect sacrifice for us and our way to a right relationship with God the Father. God gave Jesus Christ the authority to judge humanity. Because Jesus Christ was human, He judges us fairly according to Scripture. Those who accept mercy and grace through faith in Jesus Christ are accepted. Those who reject mercy and grace are rejected.

And I saw the dead, small and great, stand before God; and the dead were judged out of those things which were written in the books, according to their works (Revelation 20:12).

7. Jesus Christ Reveals His Mercy and Grace.

Revelation seems quite severe but mercy and grace are present. God has given everyone plenty of opportunities to know and accept God. In the book, repent or repentance is used twelve times.[3] God desires every person to come to Him by their own free will and not manipulated by intimidation or force. The Holy Spirit convicts of sin but we must respond to that conviction, acknowledge our sin and accept God's perfect gift of salvation.

For by grace are you saved through faith; and that not of yourselves: it is the gift of God (Ephesians 2:8).

Even during the End Times and Tribulation, we see God's mercy and grace. People have the opportunity to repent and follow God. We see some who accept Christ and stand strong through severe persecution. Despite astonishing events and terrible judgments, many people still reject God but mercy and grace are available until the end.

And the rest of the men which were not killed by these plagues yet repented not of the works of their hands, that they should not worship devils, and idols of gold, and silver, and brass, and stone, and of wood: which neither can see, nor hear, nor walk (Revelation 9:20).

8. Jesus Christ Reveals His Love to His Children.

God forgave our sins and so much more. He did not give us a religion filled with rules to follow. Christianity is based on a personal relationship. We are the children of God and He especially loves His own children.

Behold, what manner of love the Father has bestowed upon us, that we should be called the children of God (1 John 3:1).

9. Jesus Christ Reveals His Love to the World.

The End Times, Tribulation and Millennium have different purposes in God's plan but one purpose is consistent: the redemption of humanity. Many people come to Jesus

Christ for salvation before the Rapture but it does not stop there. Despite terrible persecution, some people accept Christ during the Tribulation. More people accept Christ during the reign of Christ. In each period, salvation is just a prayer away.

The most amazing picture of God's love is His relationship with the nation of Israel. The Jewish people have rejected God many times but God has never rejected His people. Even though they were scattered throughout the world, He gave Abraham an everlasting covenant. God uses the Tribulation to bring Israel back to Himself. What patience, longsuffering and unconditional love God has for Israel and the world.

> I will bring the third part through the fire, and will refine them as silver is refined, and will try them as gold is tried: they shall call on my name, and I will hear them: I will say, It is my people: and they shall say, The Lord is my God (Zechariah 13:9).

10. Jesus Christ Reveals His Patience.

Although Christians are ready to leave the world and go home, God is patient. He gives every person the opportunity to accept salvation. That is one reason for the delay. God is waiting for the last person to be saved. Additionally, He is waiting for you and me to tell them. Like Jonah and Philip, it takes more effort to send Christians to the harvest than it takes for the lost to be found. Although God delays His return and judgment, do not take God's patience for granted.

> The Lord is not slack concerning his promise, as some men count slackness; but is longsuffering to us, not willing that any should perish, but that all should come to repentance (2 Peter 3:9).

11. Jesus Christ Reveals His Purpose and Plan.

God told the disciples and us His plan for the world in one key verse.

> For God so loved the world that he gave his only begotten son that whosoever believes in him should not perish but have everlasting life (John 3:16).

God reveals His character and two-part plan. Jesus Christ's First Coming is for redemption. Our responsibility is to accept the free gift but there are consequences if we reject God. Jesus Christ's Second Coming is for our eternal life.

12. Jesus Christ Reveals His Blessings.

God desires us to know Himself, His purpose and His plan. He has given special blessings to those who read, hear and keep what is written in Revelation. Despite this troubled world, this message builds confidence in God. We are blessed by prophecy.

> The Revelation of Jesus Christ, which God gave unto him, to show his servants things which must shortly come to pass. Blessed is he that reads, and they that hear the words of this prophecy, and keep those things which are written there: for the time is at hand (Revelation 1:1, 3).

Jesus Christ Reveals Prophecy

As prophecy reveals God, then God reveals prophecy. Through the Holy Spirit, He reveals His Word to His children who seek Him.

> I [Jesus Christ] thank thee, O Father, Lord of heaven and earth, that thou has hid these things from the wise and prudent, and has revealed them unto babes: even so, Father; for so it seemed good in thy sight (Luke 10:21).

1. Prophecy Hidden from the World

If you talk about Bible prophecy, most people, including many Christians, will be fearful instead of encouraged. People see the storm clouds on the horizon. Some are overwhelmed by false fears while others fear a future nuclear war and for good reason. God is sending warning signs. Most people do not need a discussion of End Time events. They just need to know Jesus Christ.

> But the natural man receives not the things of the Spirit of God: for they are foolishness unto him: neither can he know them, because they are spiritually discerned (1 Corinthians 2:14).

2. Prophecy Revealed to God's Children

Christians know and understand Scripture by the Holy Spirit through a personal and collective study within the Church. The more we study the Word, the more truth the

Spirit of God uncovers. God reveals knowledge to Babylonian king Nebuchadnezzar but He reveals understanding to Daniel.[4]

> There is a God in heaven that reveals secrets, and makes known to the king Nebuchadnezzar what shall be in the latter days (Daniel 2:28).

3. Prophecy Revealed to the Humble

Studying prophecy starts with humility. In a maturing relationship, we realize that we need God and need to know His Word more. A personal desire is present to spend time alone with God. We can know God's Word with help from the Holy Spirit. God is searching for people with teachable hearts.

With Christians, no one is at the same spiritual level. Some are new Christians while others have a good understanding of Scripture. Each person has a different set of spiritual gifts but we are mutually dependent on each other. End Time prophecy has many differing views and no view is completely correct. One must discern what is true, what is false, what is known and what is unknown. It all starts with humility.

> All of you be subject one to another, and be clothed with humility: for God resists the proud, and gives grace to the humble (1 Peter 5:5).

If you are new to prophecy, you can still understand. A good knowledge of the Gospels and overview of the entire Bible are the basics. God is more concerned with your desire and action to seek truth than how much you know.

> And he [Jesus Christ] said unto them [disciples], Unto you it is given to know the mystery of the kingdom of God: but unto them that are without, all these things are done in parables (Mark 4:11).

4. Prophecy Revealed Before the Crisis

America was founded on the freedom to worship God. In the name of tolerance and political correctness, culture is removing God from public society. Bible reading, prayer, Christmas nativity scenes and displays of the Ten Commandments are banned from government property. However, during a national crisis such as a school shooting or 9/11, people return to God with public church services and candlelight memorials. It is sad when it takes a national emergency to move people back to God. Instead of seeking God in a crisis, seek Him now before the crisis.

> Seek the Lord while he may be found, call upon him while he is near (Isaiah 55:6).

5. Prophecy Revealed to Those Who Seek Understanding

Daniel purposed in his heart to honor God instead of being defiled by the king's meat. He set a good example for his friends and the people around him. God made Daniel prosper in pagan kings' palaces and made him steward of God's people. Daniel prayed consistently despite consequences. As a result, God gave Daniel some of the greatest prophecies of the Bible. Daniel had a vision of future Israel.[5] He was deeply concerned about his people so he humbled himself, fasted and got down to serious praying. However, God wanted Daniel to understand the prophecy more than Daniel.

> Then he [the angel] said unto me, Fear not, Daniel: for from the first day that you set your heart to understand, and to humble yourself before your God, your words were heard, and I am come for your words (Daniel 10:12).

Throughout the Bible, those who sought God, not only found God but had a uniquely personal and deeply spiritual experience with God. Enoch walked with God and went to Heaven without dying.[6] Abraham was about to sacrifice his son Isaac but God provided a lamb.[7] Before Jacob met his brother Esau, he spent the night wrestling with God.[8] Moses sought God on Mt. Sinai where he experienced the burning bush.[9] Elijah was raptured without dying and Elisha received a double blessing because he was faithful to God's minister.[10]

Peter was the only disciple to walk on water with Jesus Christ.[11] Although he sank into the Sea of Galilee and sank even deeper at the cross, God chose him to preach at Pentecost. Peter, James and John were Christ's closest disciples and they experienced the glory of God.[12] Paul was raptured into the third Heaven for a special revelation.[13] In many examples, those who faithfully sought God, abundantly found God in amazing ways.

You decide how much of a relationship you have with God. Three choices are available: coldhearted, halfhearted or wholehearted. How diligently we seek God is how much God reveals of Himself and His Word to us.

You shall seek me, and find me, when you shall search for me with all your heart (Jeremiah 29:13).

6. Prophecy Revealed Because God Desires Us to Know

God desires us to know His character and nature and then know the future. God gave Daniel, Ezekiel, Zechariah, John and other prophets a glimpse of the future world—especially for people who live during the end of the age—us. We have the unique privilege to live in the End Times and the responsibility to know the Word of God as it describes these last years. This is God's wake-up call for the Church. Our focus is not about what happens in the Tribulation but what happens now. While we are here on earth, we can make a difference. Seek God and fulfill God's plan during this critical time.

Eye has not seen, nor ear heard, neither have entered into the heart of man, the things which God has prepared for them that love him. But God has revealed them to us by his Spirit: for the Spirit searches all things, the deep things of God (1 Corinthians 2:9-10).

Prophecy Reveals God Then God Reveals Prophecy

Prophecy is all about God. While studying the End Times, first see how Jesus Christ is revealed as God, Savior, Prophet, Priest, King and Righteous Judge. Know His mercy and grace, His love for His children, Israel and the world. Understand His patience, purpose and plan, timing and blessings for us. Go beyond the prophecies to genuinely see God.

God reveals prophecy by the Holy Spirit to Christians who desire a deeper relationship with God and hunger for understanding of His Word, seek God with humility, prayer and their whole hearts. The Holy Spirit personally reveals spiritual truths. You will be blessed because you experience God in amazing ways.

Do you see and experience the character and nature of God through your relationship with God?

Section 2

God's Word

Chapter 5

Study the Bible

After focusing on God, it is important to know how to study the Bible and especially prophecy. God is pursuing a relationship with humanity through Jesus Christ as promised in the Old Testament and fulfilled in the New Testament. He communicates this message of unconditional love, complete forgiveness, perfect redemption and personal communion so we know God and apply His Word to our lives. We learn the Bible within the local church. However, God also wants us to study the Bible alone with Him.

Scripture is our greatest weapon but throughout the years, it has been the target of the spiritual battle. First, Satan limits access to Bibles by destroying copies, limiting translations, hindering reading skills and keeping Bibles from the people. When the Word is available, it is attacked directly through false doctrine, apostasy and flawed interpretations. Then congregations rely on preachers and teachers to feed them, which minimizes power and stunts maturity. Finally, our own pride and selfishness, ignorance and apathy, worldliness and busyness hinder our private studies. A personal study of the Bible helps us grow closer to God, teach and encourage other Christians and prepare for the spiritual battles ahead.

During Paul's second missionary journey, he came to the city of Berea in Greece. The Bereans were no secondhand Christians. They eagerly took what was given and compared it against the Bible. Even Paul's words were tested. We too must examine Scripture to see if what is preached, taught, written and believed is true. With End Time prophecy, we must shine the light of God's Word against our personal beliefs and actions, understanding of symbols, religious traditions, denominational teachings and established interpretations. The main reasons to study prophecy are to experience God and attain the truth.

[The Bereans] received the word with all readiness of mind, and searched the scriptures daily, whether those things were so (Acts 17:11).

Respect the Word

A man wanted to know God's will. He decided to open his Bible and randomly point to a verse.[1]

> Judas went and hanged himself (Matthew 27:5).

Then he thought he better try again.

> Go, and do likewise (Luke 10:37).

Maybe a third verse could clarify the message.

> That you do, do quickly (John 13:27).

Silly but many false teachings use this technique to teach all kinds of manmade doctrines. That goes double for prophecy. A message may look good on the surface but can it survive a proper study of the Bible? God gave us His Word to know and apply to our lives. We must respect Scripture by following a few basic principles to arrive at the truth.

Studying the Bible requires daily time, work and commitment. It is more than just reading the Bible but that is a good start. The best place to begin is with the Gospels and then the rest of the New Testament. After you read a passage, dig deeper, ask questions, use study techniques that work for you, get contrary views, discern the truth and get answers. Topical studies are good for going deeper and verse-by-verse book studies hit every topic. Even with a daily study, it takes a lifetime to begin to know God and His Word, so start today!

> The Bible is a literal treasure chest of the "wisdom of God" for everyday living, but most Christians do not know the book sufficiently to provide that wisdom when they need it. Intensive Bible study, along with repetition and Scripture memorization, will give you a thorough grasp of the Bible in a relatively short period of time.
> —Tim LaHaye, *How to Study the Bible*[2]

Bible study is about knowledge, understanding and response to God's Word.[3] First is knowledge. What is the passage saying? Understanding follows. What does it mean today? Finally, is our response. How do I apply it to my life? God gave King Nebuchadnezzar of Babylon a prophecy.[4] After the king learns the interpretation of the dream, he is overcome by pride. Then he misapplies Scripture by making an idol in his image, bringing judgment from God. Knowledge and understanding are worthless without correctly applying what is learned to our hearts and our lives.

Seven C's of Bible Study[5]

Part of learning Scripture is applying seven principles to Bible study. This is a review to many Christians but it exposes many flawed views when studying prophecy.

1. Communion

Bible study is about our relationship with God. It begins with prayerful communion. We must learn how to listen to the Holy Spirit and receive His instruction. Even with different maturity levels and spiritual gifts, every Christian starts with the same Holy Spirit, the same Bible and the same purpose: to know, understand and apply the Word of God.

> But the Comforter, which is the Holy Spirit, whom the Father will send in my name, he shall teach you all things, and bring all things to your remembrance, whatsoever I have said unto you (John 14:26).

2. Content

Bible study clarifies the meaning of the passage. Read the text and ask questions. Translations may sometimes interpret Scripture. With the internet, plenty of study tools are available. You can even look up words in the original Greek and Hebrew text. It helps to consult various translations to clarify words and get the clear meaning of the content.

- Who is the writer of the book? Who is the audience? Who are the people mentioned in the passage?
- What is the message of the passage? What does it mean then? What does it mean now? What does it mean to me? What is the reason for the message? What does it tell us about God and humanity?
- Where was it written? Where does it take place?
- When was it written? When does it occur? Is it history, current events or prophecy? Has it already been fulfilled or is it still future?
- Why do we need to know? Why is this passage included in Scripture?
- How do we know, understand and apply it to our lives?

Study to show yourself approved unto God, a workman that needs not to be ashamed, rightly dividing the word of truth (2 Timothy 2:15).

3. Context

Bible study considers the context of the passage. Do not take verses out of context. Each book is written as a whole. Chapters, verses and punctuation are not Scripture and may confuse the flow of a thought. Chapter introductions in Psalms are part of the original text but chapter titles and study notes are not. Events may not be in sequence. Understand the verse, chapter and book as it relates to the rest of Scripture. Read and study the passage first before going to study notes and consulting with commentaries.

- Before—What is written before this chapter or verse?
- After—What is written after this chapter or verse?

All scripture is given by inspiration of God, and is profitable for doctrine, for reproof, for correction, for instruction in righteousness: That the man of God may be perfect, thoroughly furnished unto all good works (2 Timothy 3:16-17).

4. Comparison

Bible study compares Scripture with Scripture. The Bible does not contradict itself but rather will clarify and interpret using other passages. Paul emphasizes faith while James emphasizes works. Both are a part of our Christian walk. Prophecy depends on a basic knowledge of the entire Bible. John the Apostle wrote Revelation with many references to various Old and New Testament passages. Comparing Scripture is critical to the study of prophecy.

Knowing this first, that no prophecy of the scripture is of any private inter-pretation. For the prophecy came not in old time by the will of man: but holy men of God spoke as they were moved by the Holy Spirit (2 Peter 1:20-21).

5. Culture

Bible study benefits from knowing the history and culture of the persons, times and places involved in the passage. Do not ignore the culture or apply our culture to a passage. Put yourself in their lives and understand the Word from their perspective.

Knowing some background of the people, culture, geography, history and language will overcome many obstacles.[6]

With Bible prophecy, it is critical to know the culture, traditions and history. The Hebrew people, the Jewish race, the Israeli nation and Judaism are interwoven yet form our Christian heritage. Knowing how the Egyptians, Canaanites, Philistines, Assyrians, Babylonians, Persians, Greeks and Romans interact with Israel adds depth. Knowing world history of the last one hundred years discloses fulfilled prophecy.

Many misinterpretations of Scripture occur. Most errors are from the lack of knowledge of Scripture or from following traditional or religious teachings. Even great scholars misinterpret prophecy by not understanding Jewish figures-of-speech. Breaking the rule of culture happens without a second thought. Studying the descendants of Abraham, Isaac and Jacob provides a wealth of information that reduces confusion and clarifies the passage.

> And these words, which I command you this day, shall be in your heart: And you shall teach them diligently to your children, and shall talk of them when you sit in your house, and when you walk by the way, and when you lie down, and when you rise up (Deuteronomy 6:6-7).

6. Consultation

Rely on instruction by the Holy Spirit and text of the Word of God when you use the first five C's. Then, Bible study benefits from consultation with other Bible scholars through commentaries, books, articles and sermons. Do not put the words or books of men higher than the Word of God or you end up following a man or denomination.

Now through the internet, a variety of resources are available. Many Bible translations, commentaries and dictionaries are available but discernment is critical. You will need to research the denomination (Catholic, Protestant, cult or humanist), the philosophy of Scripture (conservative or liberal), application of prophecy (figurative or literal), basis of prophecy (Tribulation and Millennium) and world views (Christian, religious or secular) on the information given. This will disclose how much you can rely on the interpretation and how much it is biased toward a specific religious teaching. For example, *Wikipedia* is a good source for history but not Christian faith. Every teacher and writing will have some truth, error and bias.

To study various opposing views on prophecy is helpful. Discernment is required. Is that what Scripture is saying? Which rules of Bible study do they follow? Which rules do they break? Sometimes an alternative view gives a different perspective, provides additional insight, requires further study or strengthens your original belief. At times, you will get more questions than answers. After studying a passage thoroughly, take note of various opinions. If you are still not ready to decide on an answer, then return later. "I don't know" is better than accepting a wrong answer.

> For the word of God is quick, and powerful, and sharper than any two edged sword, piercing even to the dividing asunder of soul and spirit, and of the joints and marrow, and is a discerner of the thoughts and intents of the heart (Hebrews 4:12).

7. Communication

Bible study includes communicating what is learned. Don't just feed yourself or feed people but teach, encourage and inspire other people. Knowing and understanding Scripture leads to sharing, teaching, challenging, growing and encouraging others to study God's Word.

> For this cause also thank we God without ceasing, because, when you received the word of God which you heard of us, you received it not as the word of men, but as it is in truth, the word of God, which effectively works also in you that believe (1 Thessalonians 2:13).

The Bible: Written by God, Revealed by God

Through the prophets, the Holy Spirit gave us the Bible to teach us all things. Now we are responsible to study the Word and use basic principles of communion, content, contrast, comparison, culture, consultation and communication to know, understand and respond by applying truth to our hearts and lives. Seek and keep on seeking God's Word and you will not only find God but you also will experience Him.[7]

Like the Bereans of Acts 17:11, are you studying the Word for yourself to discern what is true?

Chapter 6

Symbols Revealed

W ithout a doubt, the first barrier of studying prophecy is symbols. However, symbols are not just in prophecy but are found throughout the entire Bible. God gives us hundreds of simple word pictures that explain complex ideas in His Word. The Bible and symbols are intertwined. You cannot know the Bible without knowing symbols.

Common Symbols

Some symbols are quite familiar. The Lamb of God is Jesus Christ and the dragon is Satan. Most symbols are not a problem in the majority of the Bible. Even in prophecy you may know more than you think.

- Lamb: Jesus Christ
- Body and Blood: Christ's Life and Death
- Shepherd: Christ
- Under Shepherd: Pastor
- Sheep: God's People
- Goats: Not God's People
- Serpent or Dragon: Satan
- Mount Sinai: Law
- Mount of Olives: Grace
- Body of Christ: Church
- Riding a Donkey: Humble Servant
- Riding a White Horse: Conquering King

Because it is given unto you to know the mysteries of the kingdom of heaven, but to them it is not given. But blessed are your eyes, for they see: and your ears, for they hear (Matthew 13:11, 16).

Types of Jesus Christ

Throughout the Bible, people, places and things are symbols of Jesus Christ's life or describe His work of redemption.

*   People: Adam, Seth, Noah, Abraham, Melchizedek, Isaac, Joseph, Moses, Joshua, Boaz, David, Solomon, Elijah, Jonah, Ezra, Nehemiah
*   Places: Bethlehem, Jerusalem, Judea, Mount of Olives, Mount Sinai, Nazareth
*   Things: Ark of the Covenant, Baptism, Brazen Serpent, Bread, Communion, Manna, Passover Lamb, Tabernacle, Temple, Water, Wine

For as Jonah was three days and three nights in the whale's belly so shall the Son of man be three days and three nights in the heart of the earth (Matthew 12:40).

Apocalyptic Writings

Apocalypse
1 a: one of the Jewish and Christian writings of 200 B.C. to A.D. 150 marked by pseudonymity, symbolic imagery, and the expectation of an imminent cosmic cataclysm in which God destroys the ruling powers of evil and raises the righteous to life in a messianic kingdom
b capitalized: Revelation
—*Merriam-Webster's Online Dictionary*[1]

Apocalypse simply means revelation. Some scholars put the books of Daniel and Revelation in the category of apocalyptic literature. This is because of the extensive use of symbolism, visions, angelic messengers, the final battle between God and Satan and a focus on the end of the age.[2]

However, Daniel, Revelation and other prophecy books are different than apocalyptic literature. These books are part of the inspired Word of God. They can be understood by a literal interpretation of Scripture. Revelation refers to many Old Testament passages, depicts Christ's work of salvation and tells of specific future events. Although written during times of exile and suffering, the writers are optimistic that God will restore His people and conquer

His enemies. The prophetic message encourages Christians to stand strong in our faith and live righteous lives despite the world's attacks as God fulfills His plan.[3]

Daniel and Revelation should not be categorized as apocalyptic writings. Jesus Christ describes Daniel as a prophet. Nineteen times Revelation says it is prophecy. They are interpreted as genuine Scripture. When symbols are understood, the World Wars and Iraq Wars are not just historic events but fulfilled prophecy.

Prophecy Symbols

Getting beyond symbols is challenging but not impossible. Many people get overwhelmed by the symbols. The seven this, that and the others with the four who's and the ten what's are confusing, just like the Abbot and Costello radio play: "Who's on First?"[4] We stumble with the symbols and strike out before understanding the passage. Man complicates God's message of salvation and the future. Even Bible scholars do not interpret all symbols correctly. This requires an up-to-date study to review traditional interpretations of prophecy to get a clear and current understanding of our time.

Symbols in the Bible[5]

- Animals: Ant, Bear, Beast, Bull, Eagle, Deer, Donkey, Dove, Dragon, Fox, Goat, Horse, Lamb, Leopard, Lion, Locust, Ox, Serpent, Wolf, Worm
- Colors: Black, Blue, Green, Purple, Red, White, Yellow
- Directions: North, South, East, West
- Heavens: Sun, Moon, Stars, Planets, Comets
- Materials: Gold, Silver, Bonze, Brass, Wood, Hay, Stubble
- Numbers: 1, 2, 3, 4, 5, 6, 7, 8, 9, 10, 11, 12, 24, 40, 70, 120, 490, 666
- Objects: Blood, Candlesticks, Crown, Incense, Sword, Trumpet, Water
- Revelation Sevens: Angels, Blessings, Bowls/Vials, Churches, Crowns, Eyes, Golden Lampstands, Heads, Hills, Horns, Kings, Lamps, Mountains, Plagues, Seals, Spirits of God, Stars, Thousands of People, Thunders, Trumpets, Years

Numbers in the Bible[6]

1. Unity: God, Israel, the Church
2. Diversity: God & Man, Man & Woman, Good & Evil, Old & New Testaments, Judah & Israel, Jews & Gentiles, Saved & Lost

3. Trinity, Society's Order: Father, Son & Holy Spirit, Satan, Antichrist & False Prophet, Past, Present & Future, Politics, Religion & Economics
4. Wholeness: Creation, Direction, Gospels, Horses
5. Covenant: The Law, Grace, Love
6. Humanity: Man, Sin, Falling Short, Human Rule
7. Perfection: Jesus Christ, God's Plan, Sabbaths of Rest
8. Completion: New Beginning, 8th Day
9. Finality: Judgment, Fruit of the Spirit
10. Judgment: Commandments, Egyptian Plagues, Kings
11. Incomplete: Sons of Jacob, Faithful Disciples
12. Government: Jacob's Sons, Israel's Tribes, Disciples, Heaven

Without understanding, prophecy is a bunch of pieces of a puzzle—more confusion than revealed truth. Many people get frightened or frustrated and do not study these books. However, God gave us His Word because He wants us to know. He has given us the Holy Spirit to reveal the mysteries of prophecy.

Guide to Know Symbols[7]

1. Apply the Seven C's

- Content & Context: Symbols may be interpreted by the passage. Daniel 7 contains a prophecy of four beasts. Later in the same chapter, an interpretation of the passage is given.
- Comparison: Check other Scriptures for an interpretation of Scripture. Revelation 13 and 17 further describes the symbols and prophecy from Daniel 7.
- Culture: Many symbols are hidden in Jewish culture and language. The basis of Jewish culture is the Law: Genesis through Deuteronomy. Many symbols are part of worship in the Jewish tabernacle and temples. Other symbols describe our recent history and current events.

2. Consistency

Certain symbols are consistent throughout the Bible but others are different depending on the context. Except Revelation 13, the symbol of a lamb is Jesus Christ. However, a lion has nine meanings in the New Testament.

Lions in the New Testament[8]

- Out of the Mouth of the Lion: God's Protection (2 Timothy 4:17)
- Stopped the Mouths of Lions: Literal Lions (Hebrews 11:33)
- As a Roaring Lion: Satan (1 Peter 5:8)
- Like a Lion: Angel of Matthew (Revelation 4:7)
- Lion of the Tribe of Judah: Jesus Christ (Revelation 5:5)
- As the Teeth of Lions: Air War (Revelation 9:8)
- As the Heads of Lions: Ground War (Revelation 9:17)
- When a Lion Roars: Angel's Voice (Revelation 10:3)
- As the Mouth of a Lion: Language (Revelation 13:2)

3. Description

Some passages are a description of the future. If a symbol is preceded by "like" or "as," the writer is using a simile which should not be taken literally or figuratively. Consider the context. For example: the United States eagle.

- The United States is not literally an eagle.
- The United States is not figuratively an angel.
- An eagle is the national symbol of the United States.

4. Specific

When interpreting Scripture, symbols have a specific meaning. Do not settle for some vague answer. Allow the pieces of the puzzle to fit. When describing God and Heaven, some flexibility exists. Prophecies that describe historical events, such as the Iraq Wars, are exact. These verses could not be understood by commentaries written more than twenty years ago.

> We have also a more sure word of prophecy; where you do well that you take heed, as unto a light that shines in a dark place, until the day dawn, and the day star arise in your hearts (2 Peter 1:19).

5. Reality

No matter how great the symbol, it is a shadow of the original. The Jewish temple on earth describes God's throne in Heaven. The lion and lamb do not compare to the majesty of Jesus Christ.

Whereby, when you read, you may understand my knowledge in the mystery of Christ which in other ages was not made known unto the sons of men, as it is now revealed unto his holy apostles and prophets by the Spirit (Ephesians 3:4-5).

Break Through the Symbolism

In the fall of 2002 during the Iraq War debate, my pastor taught a Revelation Bible study. A personal breakthrough came at Revelation 4 and the four living creatures. Here is a practical application of the rules on symbols.

And before the throne there was a sea of glass like unto crystal: and in the midst of the throne, and round about the throne, were four living creatures full of eyes before and behind. And the first living creature was like a lion, and the second living creature like a calf, and the third living creature had a face as a man, and the fourth living creature was like a flying eagle. And the four beasts had each of them six wings about him; and they were full of eyes within: and they rest not day and night, saying, Holy, holy, holy, Lord God Almighty, which was, and is, and is to come (Revelation 4:6-8).

Our pastor gave the traditional Protestant view. My notes from class describe the four living creatures as the highest rank of angels called cherubim who serve at the throne of God. The lion represents strength, the ox represents service, the man represents intelligence and the eagle represents swiftness.[9]

I was underwhelmed. The description was figurative not literal. When an interpretation goes figurative, it is a red flag that the interpretation does not fit the symbol. I went home thinking about the creatures but I had plenty of questions. Why are there four? Why are the symbols a lion, ox, man, and eagle? What did the living creatures describe? Something about those living creatures sounded familiar. After a week, I remembered. My eleventh-grade Bible class studied the life of Jesus Christ. The class went sequentially through the Gospels (Matthew, Mark, Luke, John) from birth, ministry, redemption and resurrection. My teacher, Mr. Weathers, began with an introduction.

The Gospel of Jesus Christ

The Gospels are written by four different men inspired by God to describe the life of Jesus Christ with four unique perspectives and purposes. Each book is linked to a living creature. The four Gospel cherubim worship and glorify God while they serve by the throne of God and endlessly proclaim the Gospel of Jesus Christ.[10] Even in this description of the throne of God, symbols have a specific meaning.

Four Gospels—Four Living Creatures[11]

Author Creature	Theme	Recipient	Color	Tribe
Matthew—Lion	Jesus the King	Jews	Purple	Judah—East
Mark—Ox (Peter)	Jesus the Servant	Romans	Red	Ephraim—West
Luke—Man (Paul)	Jesus, Son of Man	Gentiles	White	Reuben—South
John—Eagle	Jesus, Son of God	Christians	Blue	Dan—North

() Writer influenced by apostle

Content of the Gospels[12]

	Matthew	Mark	Luke	John
Miracles	29	23	23	7
Parables	31	13	37	3
Sermons	10	5	13	8
OT Quotes	45	23	23	13
Key Words	Kingdom, Fulfill	Immediately	Son of Man	Believe, Life, Father, Son, Word
Teaching Style	Kingdom Principles	Miracles	Parables	Conversation Discourse

The Gospels match the living creature in Revelation 4. The key verse of each Gospel reinforces the theme of the book.[13]

1. Matthew—Lion—Jesus the King

Matthew, a disciple of Jesus Christ, writes of the Lion of the tribe of Judah. The book starts with the Jewish royal genealogy from Abraham and David to Joseph and has the most Old Testament quotes. It is written for Jewish people to understand that the prophecies of the Messiah are fulfilled in Jesus Christ. Matthew describes the King and His Kingdom.

> Think not that I am come to destroy the law, or the prophets: I am not come to destroy, but to fulfill (Matthew 5:17).

2. Mark—Ox—Jesus the Servant

John Mark, an evangelist with Peter, writes of the Ox. While Matthew has the genealogy of the King, no genealogy exists for a servant. Although it is the shortest book of the Gospels and the writing is direct, it contains more miracles per chapter. John Mark describes a busy servant.

> For even the Son of man came not to be ministered unto, but to minister, and to give his life a ransom for many (Mark 10:45).

3. Luke—Man—Jesus the Son of Man

Dr. Luke, a missionary with Paul, writes of the Son of Man. He gives more information of Jesus Christ as human and the historical background. This genealogy traces Mary's descendants back through David to Adam and God. The book includes events of Christ's birth and uses many parables to teach of Jesus Christ's humanity as the Son of Man.

> For the Son of man is come to seek and to save that which was lost (Luke 19:10).

4. John—Eagle—Jesus the Son of God

John, a disciple of Jesus Christ, writes of the Son of God. The book describes the direct genealogy as the Word is God. John uses conversations, key miracles and details of the Holy Week to prove that Jesus Christ is God.

> But these are written, that you might believe that Jesus is the Christ, the Son of God; and that believing you might have life through his name (John 20:31).

Ezekiel's Vision of the Throne of God

Understanding prophecy requires a good understanding of the rest of Scripture. The living creatures of Revelation 4 are originally described in Ezekiel 1 and 10.

> As for the likeness of their faces, the four had the face of a man, and the face of a lion, on the right side: and the four had the face of an ox on the left side; the four also had the face of an eagle (Ezekiel 1:10).

During Ezekiel's call to ministry, he sees a similar vision of the throne of God. A four-sided structure with wheels is present. The man's face was in front with the lion's face on the right, the ox's face on the left and the eagle's face in back.

The Tabernacle and Temple

God's heavenly throne is reflected in symbols on earth. The Jewish tabernacle and temples were replicas of the throne in Heaven. The color of the temple curtains are purple, red, white and blue. Those colors correspond to the four Gospels. When Christ died, the curtain in the temple was torn apart so that through His sacrifice, we can boldly come into the presence of God.

> Moreover you shall make the tabernacle with ten curtains of fine wined linen, and blue, and purple, and scarlet: with cherubims of cunning work shall you make them (Exodus 26:1).

During the forty years in the wilderness, the tribes of Israel were arranged in a symbolic pattern. Levi was in the center of the people with the tabernacle. The other tribes of Israel were organized into four groups.[14] Jewish tradition says a lion was on the banner of Judah, an ox was on the banner of Ephraim, a man was on the banner of Ruben and an eagle was on the banner of Dan.[15] Like Ezekiel and Revelation, the tabernacle was surrounded by the four living creatures. The layout of the tribes forms a cross.

> [The priests] serve the example and shadow of heavenly things, as Moses was admonished of God when he was about to make the tabernacle (Hebrews 8:5).

It is amazing when God reveals a truth which uncovers a glimpse of God's glory. First, I read Scripture, then others supply parts of the story but the Holy Spirit put it all together.

Arrangement of Israeli Tribes

North

	Eagle Dan Asher Naphtali	
Ox Ephraim Benjamin Manasseh	Levi Tabernacle	**Lion** Judah Issachar Zebulun
	Man Ruben Gad Simeon	

Later, I verified this with other sources that confirm the four creatures refer to the Gospels. I broke through the symbolism to get to the truth.

Truth Beyond the Symbols

To understand the Bible, you must go beyond symbols. The four living creatures are a good example of that. Instead of passing by, accepting a random commentary or not knowing the answer, God gives a multidimensional view. The four living creatures of Ezekiel and Revelation, the four colors in the temple curtains and the layout of the tribes in the wilderness lead back to the four Gospels and the cross. The cross points to our redemption and forward to Jesus Christ's return.

Are the symbols in the Bible stumbling blocks that trip you up or stepping stones to the truth?

Chapter 7

Prophets and Prophecy

G od gives His message in sixty-six books through a diverse group of men. The prophet declares God's message to the people and tells events in the future.[1] To insure integrity of His Word, God set up rules for prophets.

All preachers, priests and popes are fallible and speak truth with error. Cult leaders and fortune tellers, including Mohammad, Nostradamus, Joseph Smith, Charles Russell, Jean Dixon, Jim Jones and David Koresh are false prophets. Because we are close to the Rapture, false preachers and prophets have increased. To test all messages in order to discern the truth is critical.

> For there shall arise false Christs, and false prophets, and shall show great signs and wonders; that, if it were possible, they shall deceive the very elect (Matthew 24:24).

Requirements for a Prophet[2]

1. A true prophet speaks in the name of God not in another god or his own name.

> For the prophecy came not in old time by the will of man: but holy men of God spoke as they were moved by the Holy Spirit (2 Peter 1:21).

2. A true prophet acts within the will and approval of God.

> I will raise them up a Prophet [Jesus Christ] from among their brethren, like you [Moses], and will put my words in his mouth; and he shall speak unto them all that I shall command him. But the prophet, which shall presume to speak a word in my name, which I have not commanded him to speak, or that shall speak in the name of other gods, even that prophet shall die (Deuteronomy 18:18, 20).

3. A true prophet recognizes the divinity and humanity of Jesus Christ, His life and redemption of humanity.

Beloved, believe not every spirit, but try the spirits whether they are of God: because many false prophets are gone out into the world. Therefore know the Spirit of God: Every spirit that confesses that Jesus Christ is come in the flesh is of God: And every spirit that confesses not that Jesus Christ is come in the flesh is not of God: and this is that spirit of antichrist, whereof you have heard that it should come; and even now already is it in the world (1 John 4:1-3).

4. A true prophet is in complete agreement with Scripture.

To the law and to the testimony: if they speak not according to this word, it is because there is no light in them (Isaiah 8:20).

5. A true prophet does not give his own interpretation of prophecy.

Knowing this first, that no prophecy of the scripture is of any private interpretation (2 Peter 1:20).

6. A true prophet will not add or subtract from God's Word.

If any man shall add unto these things, God shall add unto him the plagues that are written in this book: And if any man shall take away from the words of the book of this prophecy, God shall take away his part out of the book of life, and out of the holy city, and from the things which are written in this book (Revelation 22:18-19).

7. A true prophet confronts peoples' sins and speaks the truth in love.

Cry aloud, spare not, lift up your voice like a trumpet, and show my people their transgression, and the house of Jacob their sins (Isaiah 58:1).

8. A true prophet warns the people of God's coming judgment.

Fear God, and give glory to him; for the hour of his judgment is come: and worship him that made heaven, and earth (Revelation 14:7).

9. A true prophet delivers God's message despite consequences.

And [Ahab] the king of Israel said unto Jehoshaphat [king of Judah], There is yet one man, Micaiah by whom we may inquire of the Lord: but I hate him; for he does not prophesy good concerning me, but evil (1 Kings 22:8).

10. A true prophet builds up the church, counsels and advises in religious matters.

He that prophecies speaks unto men to edification, and exhortation, and comfort.... He that prophecies edifies the church (1 Corinthians 14:3-4).

11. A true prophet does not lie. His predictions will be fulfilled.

The prophet which prophecies of peace, when the word of the prophet shall come to pass, then shall the prophet be known, that the Lord has truly sent him (Jeremiah 28:9).

12. A true prophet can be recognized by the results of his work.

Beware of false prophets, which come to you in sheep's clothing, but inwardly they are ravening wolves. A good tree cannot bring forth evil fruit, neither can a corrupt tree bring forth good fruit. Wherefore by their fruits you shall know them (Matthew 7:15, 18, 20).

Through following the rules of Bible study and knowing the Word of God, we can test a prophet or preacher in order to discern truth. When a true prophet speaks, the congregation is responsible for the truth given.

Unseal Prophecy

The Words Are Sealed

And he said, Go your way, Daniel: for the words are closed up and sealed till the time of the end (Daniel 12:9).

Daniel was told to seal the book of Daniel but John was told to not seal Revelation. A practical reason to seal the book was to prove a prophet.[3] When a prophet completes a book, the scroll was sealed. Later, the prophet's writings were unsealed and tested. This guarded against false prophets who wrote history and then claimed it was prophecy.

Bind up the testimony, seal the law among my disciples (Isaiah 11:16).

Are older views of prophecy better than newer views? No. End Time prophecy is the only doctrine of the Bible that gets clearer the closer we get to the Rapture. Much has been unsealed, fulfilled and revealed in the last one hundred years.

Figurative or Literal?

Should prophecy be taken figuratively or literally? Liberal churches take prophecy figuratively. If a passage was not fulfilled during the first century, they find some spiritual fulfillment. This leads to many strange interpretations. Conservative churches take prophecy literally when possible.[4] Even with symbols in Revelation, a literal approach is best unless it conflicts with common sense.

Scripture tells us Jesus Christ was literally born, performed miracles, fulfilled prophecy, was crucified, buried and resurrected. Prophecies about Jesus Christ's First Coming literally came true. Yet, would you interpret the Rapture, Tribulation, Second Coming and Millennium figuratively? No reason exists to interpret Revelation differently from Matthew. The only choice is to interpret prophetic events of Christ's First and Second Coming in the same literal way. This makes the interpretation clear, consistent and relevant.

Or Descriptive?

Sometimes a passage should not be taken literally or figuratively. We know a literal lamb did not die on a tree. The sacrificial lambs in the Jewish temple are symbols pointing to Christ. The prophecy came true when the Lamb of God was crucified on a cross at Passover.

A writer uses symbols and figures-of-speech to describe something quite literal but foreign to his time. Wars of the twenty-first century are difficult to explain using first-century language. Daniel and Revelation tell of nightmare scenarios of modern wars. Before the twentieth century, most people never witnessed the horrors of war. Now on television, we can watch wars around the world live twenty-four hours a day.

Understand Prophecy

Over a quarter of the Bible is prophetic.[5] Although prophecy is concentrated in prophetic books, prophecy is found in sixty-four of sixty-six books.[6] Over three hundred prophecies deal with Jesus Christ's First Coming but there are about three times the prophecies dealing with the events surrounding Jesus Christ's Second Coming.

> And the vision of all is come to you as the words of a book that is sealed, which men deliver to one that is learned, saying, Read this, I pray: and he said, I cannot; for it is sealed (Isaiah 29:11).

Prophecy can be like a sealed scroll or a closed book. We study prophecies as they relate to the rest of Scripture. Understand the culture and confront misinterpretations, incorrect religious traditions, flawed denominational teachings and false doctrines. We study to find the truth. Great joy is present when the Holy Spirit reveals a truth so that a piece of the puzzle fits in place. Then we clearly see and experience God working in our world.

> [He gave the church body spiritual gifts so] that we are no more children, tossed to and fro, and carried about with every wind of doctrine, by the sleight of men, and cunning craftiness, whereby they lie in wait to deceive (Ephesians 4:14).

Guide to Study Bible Prophecy[7]

1. Apply the Seven C's

With prophecy, like all Scripture, apply the seven C's of communion, content, context, comparison, culture, consultation and communication.

- Content & Context: In Daniel 7, Revelation 13 and 17, the chapters explain horns as kings, beasts as kingdoms and heads as dynasties of kingdoms. Instead of seeing monsters, look at the world's top ten most powerful countries on a map.
- Comparison: Some passages tell a similar story, give more information and clarify the passage. Of Revelation's 404 verses, 278 verses are from the Old Testament.[8]

Revelation Cross Reference

- Two Lampstands & Olive Trees (Zechariah 4, Revelation 1)
- Sevenfold Spirit (Isaiah 11, Revelation 1)
- Throne of God (Isaiah 6, Revelation 4)
- Four Living Creatures (Ezekiel 1, 10, Revelation 4)
- Four Horses of the Apocalypse (Zechariah 1, 6, Matthew 24, Revelation 6)
- Jewish Temple (Daniel 9, 11, Matthew 24, 2 Thessalonians 2, Revelation 11)
- Two Witnesses (Zechariah 4, Revelation 11)
- The Woman Israel (Genesis 37, Revelation 12)
- Four Beasts (Daniel 7, Revelation 13, 17)
- Antichrist (Daniel 2, 7, 11, Revelation 13)
- Abomination of Desolation (Daniel 9, 11, Matthew 24, Revelation 13)
- Gog and Magog (Ezekiel 37-38, Daniel 11, Revelation 15-19)
- Seven Bowls (Exodus 7-11, Revelation 16)
- Peoples, Multitudes, Nations and Languages (Daniel 7, Revelation 17)
- Armageddon (Daniel 11, Zechariah 12-14, Revelation 15-19)
- Second Coming (Zechariah 12-14, Matthew 24, Revelation 19)
- Millennium (Isaiah 11, 65, Zechariah 14, Revelation 20)

- Hebrew Culture: In 1 Corinthians 15, Paul uses the term "Last Trump." He refers to Leviticus and not Revelation. The Jewish culture explains "First Trump" and "Last Trump."
- Current Culture: The United States is the current world superpower that prepares the world for the Tribulation. Prophecy refers to the United States over one hundred times, including our rise-and-fall by date.

2. Take Prophecy Literally When Possible

Interpret prophecy literally unless content includes figures of speech or the context suggests a different approach. Even then, the writer may describe something quite literal. Most scholars go figurative when they do not know. Logic, reason and common sense apply when studying the Bible.

If common sense makes good sense, seek no other sense.
—Jack Van Impe, *Dictionary of Prophecy Terms*[9]

Revelation 9 describes locusts, horses, man's face, women's hair, lion's teeth, chariot noise and scorpion-like creatures. John is familiar with locusts and demons. Instead, he describes a thing that is literal and known in our time.

3. Interpret Prophecy Consistently

No reason exists to interpret prophecy of Christ's Second Coming differently from the First Coming. This takes the mystery and confusion away to give a clear message for today's Church.

4. Timing Matters

Put events in order to understand the sequence. For example, the United States cannot be the only superpower while a ten-nation alliance rules the world. Other passages are fulfilled in two or more parts of "now and not yet."[10]

Are events in sequence? Daniel chapters 7-8 are before Daniel 5. Revelation is generally in order but critical exceptions exist. In Matthew 24, Jesus refers to the End Times, Rapture, Tribulation and Second Coming. Daniel 11:36-45 summarizes the Great Tribulation, while Ezekiel 37-38 and Revelation 16-19 fill in the details. God's time includes the period from Adam to the Millennium which puts the Bible in a proper historical perspective.

5. Israel and the Church

Know God's plan for Israel and His plan for the Church. Although salvation makes Jewish and Gentile Christians one in Jesus Christ, God has a different plan for Israel and the Church. If Christians replace the Jews or live through the Tribulation, no need exists for 144,002 witnesses. Confusing Jews and Christians confuses God's purpose. If a prophecy is fulfilled during the Church Age, it does not belong in the Tribulation.

6. General or Specific

Some prophecies are a summary, while other passages tell specific details. In 2 Peter 3:10, Jesus Christ returns and the earth burns up. One view uses this verse to disprove the one thousand year reign of Jesus Christ on earth. Peter gave a quick summary of events. Other passages fill in the details without contradicting Scripture.

7. Specific Fulfillment

Specific prophecies describe specific events. A proper noun describes an exact person, place or thing. These passages are fulfilled in God's time as written. The prophets may not understand the prophecies given to them but we can. Fulfilled prophecy improves our understanding of unfulfilled prophecy. When Israel became a nation and Jerusalem became its undivided capital, other prophecies came to light.

8. Simple Before the Complex

Study the simple before the complex. The first part of *21st Century Revelation* deals with Bible basics such as God, God's Word and God's time. This builds the foundation for God's plan for our time. Whether you are new to prophecy or have studied this topic for years, this book covers each event step by step. See the God of prophecy and then know His Word and timing before learning His plan. After the basics are covered, the events of the End Times, Rapture, Tribulation, Second Coming and Millennium are explained.

Prophecy Preserved

God preserves His Word through prophets and declares His Word through preachers and teachers so we can know the truth. Many views exist of End Time prophecy. Which one is true? I have not found anyone with all the answers, let alone all the right answers. Christians are responsible to discern what is true. The Holy Spirit guides us into all truth. Many errors of interpretation follow traditional or denominational teachings which break Bible study rules. Sometimes mistakes can be corrected by simply reading the text. Other information is buried in Jewish culture and traditions.

Some people say we cannot know what will happen and we will be gone before the Tribulation takes place. Because three Iraq Wars begin before the Rapture, we can know what happens and when. With the Holy Spirit and a genuine effort to seek the truth, we can understand these passages as more pieces of the puzzle fall into place.

Have you been in the Word enough so you can discern the differences between truth and error, true prophets and false prophets?

Chapter 8

Prophecy Fulfilled

N ow that Bible study, symbols and prophecy rules have been explained, it is time to apply them. In the previous chapter "Symbols Revealed," an example was given of knowing symbols to interpret a passage. Here is an example of knowing history to interpret a passage, making it easier to understand a fulfilled prophecy. Once history and symbols are identified, the rest of Daniel and Revelation can be understood in the same literal way.

Daniel 11 is the greatest chapter of fulfilled prophecy. Liberal scholars who deny God's omniscience and supernatural revelation claim Daniel was written about 165 BC.[1] They group it into apocalyptic literature which undermines the book and makes Daniel a fraud. No true prophet manipulates Scripture and writes history as if it were prophecy. Jesus Christ calls Daniel a prophet. This certifies that Daniel fulfilled all Old Testament requirements for a prophet and his writings are true.

> When you therefore shall see the abomination of desolation, spoken of by Daniel the prophet, stand in the holy place, ... (Matthew 24:15).

The book of Daniel was written between 605-530 BC.[2] The best proof of a true prophet is that his prophecies come true. Daniel describes key events of the Babylonian, Media-Persian, Greek and Roman empires that include Greek kings Alexander the Great and Antiochus IV. Daniel's seventy weeks predicts the exact year of the death, burial and resurrection of Jesus Christ. Then Daniel describes three powerful nations that merge and lead during the Tribulation.[3]

Daniel 8 and 11 describes the Greek victory over Media-Persia. According to historian Flavius Josephus, in 332 BC, Alexander the Great received a copy of Daniel after he captured Jerusalem.[4] During the time of Ptolemy III, the Hebrew Bible, including Daniel, is translated into the Greek Septuagint.[5]

During the reign of Cyrus the Great of Media-Persia, God gave Daniel a vision of 350 years of history that directly affected the Jewish people. Chapter 11 is the most detailed prophecy in the entire Bible. The first thirty-five verses contain 135 specific prophecies fulfilled during the Media-Persian and Greek empires.[6] When God tells prophecy, He gives history before it happens.

Here is a literal interpretation of Daniel 11:1-35 using history. It explains key events during the intertestamental period, the four hundred years between the Old and New Testaments. God uses these events to prepare the way for the Messiah.

Media-Persian History

> Behold, there shall stand up yet three kings in Persia; and the fourth shall be far richer than they all: and by his strength through his riches he shall stir up all against the realm of Greece (Daniel 11:2).

Daniel writes chapter 11 during the reign of Cyrus the Great. The king merged the Meads and Persians together and conquered the Babylonians.[7] The three kings are Cambyses II, Smerdis and Darius I. The fourth king is Ahasuerus or Xerxes, the husband of Queen Esther. In 580 BC during the Second Persian War, he attacked Greece and burned the temples in Athens.[8]

- **Kings of Media-Persia**: Cyrus II the Great, Cambyses II, Bardiya (Smerdis), Darius I, Xerxes (Ahasuerus), Artaxerxes I, Xerxes II, Darius II, Artaxerxes II, Artaxerxes III, Artaxerxes IV, Darius III[9]

The Bible is not a history book but when it explains historical events, the events are accurate. Scripture only shares events God considers relevant. There is a 150-year gap between verses 2 and 3. Because of somewhat peaceful times for Judah, the prophecy skips to the last Media-Persian king and the king of Greece.[10]

Greek History

> And a mighty king shall stand up, that shall rule with great dominion, and do according to his will (Daniel 11:3).

Daniel 8 describes a two-horned ram of Media-Persia and one-horned goat of Greece. Ahasuerus destroyed Athens 150 years earlier so Alexander the Great sought revenge. In eight years, he defeated King Darius III and conquered the Media-Persian Empire. He ruled from Greece to Egypt to western India.

> The ram which you saw having two horns are the kings of Media and Persia. And the rough goat is the king of Greece: and the great horn that is between his eyes is the first king [Alexander the Great]. Now that being broken, whereas four stood up for it, four kingdoms shall stand up out of the nation, but not in his power (Daniel 8:20-22).

> And when the Book of Daniel was showed him [Alexander the Great] wherein Daniel declared that one of the Greeks should destroy the empire of the Persians, he supposed that himself was the person intended.
> —Flavius Josephus, *The Antiquities of the Jews*, 94 AD[11]

Alexander began the war with Media-Persia in 334 BC. Exactly 2300 years later, Jerusalem is reunited by Israel in 1967.

- **Kings of United Greece**: Alexander III the Great, Philip III, Alexander IV[12]

After Alexander's death, the Greek Empire divided into four regions governed by Alexander's four generals. Through the Wars of Diadochi or succession, the generals fought the regent and ruled these four regional kingdoms. The civil war lasted for about twenty-five years.

Greece Divided[13]

- Greece—Lysimachus
- Asia Minor—Cassander
- Syria/Babylon/Persia—Seleucus (North)
- Egypt—Ptolemy (South)

Daniel's prophecies focus on the Seleucid Kingdom of Syria and Babylon (north) and Ptolemaic Kingdom of Egypt (south). Why does the Bible mention these events? Over a one hundred year period, these two Greek empires fought six wars for the land between Syria and Egypt, most importantly Judea. Greek Egypt started with control of the region.

After these wars, Greek Syria controlled the region. Later, Judah gained a brief period of independence.

Throughout Daniel, God tells the people of Judea about their future to remind them of His sovereignty. Despite the Babylonian captivity, Media-Persian and Greek conquests, wars between the two Greek empires and severe religious persecution of Antiochus IV, God will not abandon His people to these Gentile nations. Instead, God prepared the Jews for their Messiah.

Because of many details, historical names and explanations are included in the passage for clarity. Daniel 11:4-20 describes the Greek civil wars between Seleucid (North) and Ptolemy (South) and is in Appendix C. As a reader, you have the option to read that section now or advance to Daniel 11:21.

Syrian War VI & Antiochus IV Epiphanes

And in his [Seleucus IV of Greek Syria] estate shall stand up a vile person, to whom they shall not give the honor of the kingdom: [In 175 BC, rightful heir Demetrius I, son of Seleucus IV, is held prisoner in Rome for tribute owed. His infant brother Antiochus is king. Uncle Mithradates, son of Antiochus III the Great and brother of Seleucus IV, led a coup to become regent with his nephew Antiochus. He has Antiochus killed and changes his name to the infamous Antiochus IV Epiphanes.[14] The name Epiphanes means shining one but his opponents called him Epimanes or madman] but he shall come in peaceably and obtain the kingdom by flatteries. [He gained power by using diplomacy with the king of Pergamus in Asia Minor and by giving overdue tribute to Rome] (Daniel 11:21).

And with the arms of a flood shall they [Greek Egypt] be overflown from before him [Ptolemy VI], and shall be broken; yea, also the prince of the covenant. [In 170 BC, Antiochus replaces Jewish High Priest Onias III. Antiochus attempts to abolish Judaism and Hellenize the Jews by force.[15]] And after the league made with him he shall work deceitfully: [Alexandria, Egypt rejects Ptolemy VI as king in favor of sister/wife Cleopatra II and brother Ptolemy VII so he and uncle Antiochus IV make a treaty[16]], for he shall come up and shall become strong with a small people. He shall enter peaceably even upon the fattest places of the province [Antiochus IV of Syria and Ptolemy VI of Egypt meet together]; and he shall do that which his fathers have not done, nor his fathers' fathers he shall scatter among them the prey, and spoil, and riches: [Antiochus IV shares the spoils of war to bribe his generals and the people], and he shall forecast his devices against the strongholds, even for a time. [He plans for war against Egypt] (Daniel 11:22-24).

And he [Antiochus IV] shall stir up his power and his courage against the king of the south [Ptolemy VI of Egypt] with a great army; and the king of the south shall be stirred up to battle with a very great and mighty army but he [Ptolemy VI] shall not stand: for they [his sister/wife and brother] shall forecast devices against him. Yea, they that feed of the portion of his meat shall destroy him [they co-rule with Ptolemy VI and oust him], and his army shall overflow: and many shall fall down slain. And both of these kings' hearts shall be to do mischief, and they shall speak lies at one table [In 168 BC, Antiochus IV conquers most of Egypt and captures Ptolemy VI. This develops into a deceitful alliance as both want to take Alexandria from Ptolemy VII[17]]; but it shall not prosper: for yet the end shall be at the time appointed. [Neither one captures Alexandria.] Then shall he [Antiochus IV] return into his land with great riches, and his heart shall be against the holy covenant; and he shall do exploits and return to his own land. [In 169 BC, the Jews heard a rumor that Antiochus was killed in battle. Former High Priest Jason took control of Jerusalem. Returning to Syria, Antiochus IV attacked Jerusalem, plundered the temple and massacred 40,000 people[18]] (Daniel 11:25-28).

At the time appointed [in 168 BC] he [Antiochus IV] shall return, and come toward the south [to fight Egypt]; but it shall not be as the former, or as the latter. [Circumstances have drastically changed. Ptolemy VI reconciled with his sister/wife and brother and Egypt became a protectorate of Rome.[19]] For the ships of Chittim [Cyprus] shall come against him: [When Antiochus IV goes to Egypt, the Roman Commander Popillius Laenas drew a circle in the sand and forced him to surrender];[20] therefore he shall be grieved, and return, and have indignation against the holy covenant: so shall he do; [Humiliated and angry, he attacked Judea and devout Jews.] he shall even return, and have intelligence [or favor] with them that forsake the holy covenant. [Because of the Hellenistic culture and persecution, many Jews rejected God and worshiped Greek gods. Antiochus IV attempted to convert the remaining Jews by force] (Daniel 9:29-30).

Jewish Temple Desecrated

And arms shall stand on his [Antiochus IV] part, and they shall pollute the sanctuary of strength [Jewish temple], and shall take away the daily sacrifice, and they shall place the abomination that makes desolate. [His army destroyed much of

Jerusalem. On the 15th of *Kislev* (December), 168 BC, the army set up an image of the Greek pagan god Zeus in the Jewish temple and sacrificed pigs.] And such as do wickedly against the covenant shall he corrupt by flatteries. [Hellenized Jews ate the pig sacrificed to Zeus but those that refused are killed]: but the people that do know their God shall be strong and do exploits. [Jewish priest Mattathias refused to sacrifice pigs to Zeus and he threatened to kill priests that would.[21] This began the Jewish struggle for independence from Greek Syria] (Daniel 11:31-32).

Hanukkah and Independence

And they that understand among the people shall instruct many: yet they shall fall by the sword, and by flame, by captivity, and by spoil, many days. [Despite severe persecution, Mattathias and his son, Judas Maccabeus, revolted against the armies.] Now when they shall fall, they shall be defending with a little help: but many shall cleave to them with flatteries. [The bravery of devout Jews encouraged others to follow.] And some of them of understanding shall fall, to try them, and to purge, and to make them white, even to the time of the end: because it is yet for a time appointed. [The defiled temple lasted for 1150 days.[22] From the 15th of *Kislev*, 168 BC to the 25th of *Kislev*, 165 BC is three years of 360 days, two leap months and ten days (1080+60+10). The Jewish temple is rededicated on the first day of *Hanukkah*] (Daniel 11:33-35).

Antiochus IV left to confront the Parthians in Persia (Iran). His general, Lysias, remained to fight Judea.[23] By 165 BC, Judea recaptured their temple and the altar rededicated. In 164 BC, Antiochus IV dies from disease in Persia. Later in 141 BC, the Jewish people began seventy-eight years of independence during the reign of priests in the Hasmonean Kingdom.

In 63 BC, Rome intervened in a religious civil war between Pharisees and Sadducees and captured Judea.[24] With the loss of independence and Roman persecution, Jews sought a political messiah like Judas Maccabeus during Jesus Christ's ministry. In 70 AD, the Jews expected God to deliver them like He did with the Greeks but Rome crushed the rebellion and the Jews scatter.

Daniel 11:36-45 is prophecy that is still future. A prophecy gap of over 2175 years exists. Antiochus IV is a type of future Antichrist that will rule the world during the Great Tribulation. Both leaders persecute the Jewish people for three years but are eventually destroyed by the hand of God.

History Reveals Fulfilled Prophecy

Daniel 11 is a great example of a literal interpretation of prophecy. God gave the prophecy to Daniel, which was precisely fulfilled and verified by history without a figurative interpretation. Those who knew Daniel's writings and were living during the Media-Persian and Greek empires interpreted the signs of the times.

Understanding prophecy has more to do with understanding the last one hundred years. Knowing symbols, recent history and current events will be necessary to interpret passages in the same literal way.

Do you know enough American history and current events to understand the signs of the times?

Section 3

God's Time

Chapter 9

In the Beginning, God

A foundation is built on God and God's Word, then add time. The disciples asked Jesus Christ and we ask the same question today: "When?" Before jumping into prophecy, God's Word has plenty to say about God's time.

And as he sat upon the mount of Olives, the disciples came unto him privately, saying, Tell us, when shall these things be? and what shall be the sign of thy coming, and of the end of the world (Matthew 24:3)?

The End of the World

- Evolution states that the earth started from a big bang and will end with a big burn. It took billions of years to evolve and will take billions of years to end. Eventually, the sun will expand into a red giant star and earth will not sustain life because of the extreme heat.[1]
- Global warming is caused by humans polluting the earth. This results in a gradual warming of the seas until more and more ice melts. This will disrupt the natural flow of the ocean, plunging the earth into another ice age.[2]
- All wars are caused by national sovereignty, religious differences and economic inequalities. If society erases national borders, removes religions, shares resources and promotes tolerance of others, we will create a society that lives in mutual peace and harmony in this global village.[3]

The problem with these theories is they exclude God, God's Word, God's time and God's plan for our time. While most people believe the world will continue until we achieve utopia, humanity is quickly devolving and is about to abruptly and drastically change. This is no end of the world but God is going to overthrow the rule of man and inaugurate the rule of Jesus Christ.

For my thoughts are not your thoughts, neither are your ways my ways, says the Lord. For as the heavens are higher than the earth, so are my ways higher than your ways, and my thoughts than your thoughts (Isaiah 55:8-9).

WARNING
Specific years are mentioned in this book. This is not a prediction of the year of the Rapture or Second Coming. Put all of what is written in context with the rest of the book. After God's time, seven churches, four horses, seven trumpets and other End Time prophecies are combined, we can better understand God's plan for our time.

Most Bible scholars skip a complete explanation of time when discussing End Time prophecy. Scripture answers many questions about "when." A good reason exists as to why so much prophecy is occurring. It's about time for Jesus Christ.

Like King Nebuchadnezzar of Babylon, knowledge and understanding are worthless without the appropriate change in our hearts and lives.[4] The point of prophecy is not to pick a year but rather to make prophecy relevant, wake up the Church, prepare for Jesus Christ's return and work together for His kingdom until He calls us home.

The Great Disappointment

Throughout the Church Age, many have predicted the Rapture and Second Coming. Baptist preacher William Miller narrowed the Rapture from March 21, 1843 to March 21, 1844.[5] Many people believed him, stopped working and gathered together to wait. After the dates passed, he predicted April 18, 1844 but nothing happened. This prediction became known as the Great Disappointment. Scoffers point to these false predictions.

> Knowing this first, that there shall come in the last days scoffers, walking after their own lusts, And saying, Where is the promise of his coming (2 Peter 3:3-4)?

Why are these predictions wrong but the Rapture will happen during our lifetime within the next couple of decades? Why our time and not fifty or five hundred years earlier or later? Through a study of creation, Jewish feasts, American history, Jewish culture, the life of Christ and Bible chronology, Scripture gives the structure of time. God is sounding the trumpets but we are not listening.

Creation

In the beginning God created the heavens and the earth (Genesis 1:1).

Everything created by God has a beginning and end. Before creation, God had a plan of redemption. That plan has a specific start and stop date.

> To every thing there is a season, and a time to every purpose under the heaven: A time to be born, and a time to die (Ecclesiastes 3:1-2).

I am amused by evolutionists who say the universe is about 13.7 billion years old.[6] What great faith they have in science void of God. However, there is a margin of error of 13.7 billion years. The time from Adam to now is a little less than six thousand years. Even Christians have different views about creation and little information exists before Genesis 1:1. God created Adam and Eve not as infants but as adults. He created a mature universe to sustain life and confound the wise. The debate continues between young earth creationists and old earth evolutionists but the Bible is true from Genesis to Revelation.

> For the invisible things of him from the creation of the world are clearly seen, being understood by the things that are made, even his eternal power and Godhead; so that they are without excuse (Romans 1:20-21).

Like the atom, cell and universe, there is a pattern for time. God created the world in six days and rested on the seventh day. Seven is God's plan for time. Compare Genesis 1 to Bible chronology and the entire length of human history is given.

> For in six days the Lord made heaven and earth, the sea, and all that in them is, and rested the seventh day: wherefore the Lord blessed the sabbath day, and hallowed it (Exodus 20:11).

> But, beloved, be not ignorant of this one thing, that one day is with the Lord as a thousand years, and a thousand years as one day (2 Peter 3:8).

- Creation: 6 Days + 1 Day = 7 Days
- Humanity: 6000 Years + 1000 Years = 7000 Years

God's time is four thousand years before the cross and three thousand years after the cross. This timeline is a really bold message to some. The "can't know" people may disagree.

Seven Days—Seven Thousand Years

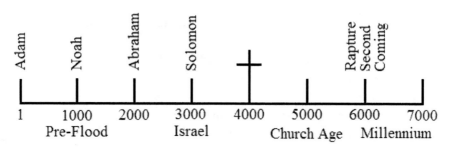

How can we know God's timing so clearly? The simple answer is the Bible tells me so. The Jewish feasts, Daniel's seventy weeks and Bible chronology answer many questions about time. The World Wars and Iraq Wars become God's alarm clock for His people.

Before the beginning of time, the plan of God was that Jesus Christ would die for our sins. God first told Adam and Eve about a Savior. Four thousand years later, Jesus Christ fulfilled that promise. About 1985 years after the cross, we watch for His return.

> And I will put enmity between you [serpent] and the woman, and between your seed and her seed; it shall bruise your head, and you shall bruise his heel (Genesis 3:15).

Jewish Sabbaths

Throughout the Bible, the number seven implies perfection and completion.[7] In the context of time, seven is the Sabbath rest. God designed the Jewish calendar with a Sabbath day, week, month, year, half-century and millennium rest.

Sabbaths in the Bible[8]

- 7 Days: Week
- 7th Day: Sabbath Day Rest for People
- 7 Weeks + 1 (50 Days): Weeks/Pentecost
- 7th Month *Nisan*: Civil Calendar
- 7th Month *Tishri*: Religious Calendar
- 7 Years: Sabbath Rest for Fields
- 7 X 7 Years + 1 (50 Years): Jubilee—Rest from Debt and Slavery
- 70 Years: Judgment

- 7 X 70 Years (490 Years): Redemption, Forgiveness
- 7th 1000: Millennium Reign of Christ
- 7000 Years: God's Complete Plan of Redemption

7th Day—Remember the sabbath day, to keep it holy. Six days shall you labor, and do all your work: But the seventh day is the sabbath of the Lord thy God: in it you shall not do any work (Exodus 20:8-10).

7th Year—Six years you shall sow your field, and six years you shall prune your vineyard, and gather in the fruit; but in the seventh year shall be a sabbath of rest unto the land, a sabbath for the Lord: you shall neither sow your field, nor prune your vineyard (Leviticus 25:3-4).

Jubilee Year—And you shall hallow the fiftieth year, and proclaim liberty throughout all the land unto all the inhabitants thereof: it shall be a jubilee unto you; and you shall return every man unto his possession, and you shall return every man unto his family (Leviticus 25:10).

Millennium Sabbath

The Jewish leaders said six thousand years of conflict would ensue, followed by one thousand years of peace.[9] They based their beliefs on creation.

The disciples of Elijah taught: The world will continue for six thousand years, the first two thousand of which were a chaos (Tahu), the second two thousand were of Torah, and the third two thousand are the days of the Messiah, and because of our sins many years of these have elapsed, still he has not come.
—*Babylonian Talmud*, Book 9, Chapter 1, 8th Century[10]

The early church adopted the Millennium Sabbath. In 341, support decreased when the Church adopted a figurative no millennium view of prophecy.

And 6,000 years must needs be accomplished, in order that the Sabbath may come, the rest, the holy day "on which God rested from all His works."
—Theologian Hippolytus, Rome, 3rd Century[11]

The Millennium Sabbath grew with the Protestant Reformation. Martin Luther's chronology estimates the Second Coming to be ~2040.[12] During the nineteenth and twentieth centuries, support increased when some Protestants moved back to a Second Coming before a Millennium view. Because of the imminent Rapture theory, some churches rejected the Millennium Sabbath view.

> For in so many days as this world was made, in so many thousand years shall it be concluded ... in six days created things were completed: it is evident that, therefore, they will come to an end after 6000 years.
> —Bishop Irenaeus, Gaul (France), 2nd Century[13]

Jewish Feasts

In Leviticus 23, God gave Israel seven Jewish feasts: Passover, Unleavened Bread, Firstfruits, Weeks, Trumpets, Atonement and Tabernacles. Like the many parts of Jewish worship, these feasts are symbols fulfilled in Jesus Christ.

> Let no man therefore judge you in meat, or in drink, or in respect of an holy day, or of the new moon, or of the sabbath days: Which are a shadow of things to come; but the body is of Christ (Colossians 2:16-17).

In Exodus 12, Israel celebrated the first Passover. On the 10th of *Nisan*, the Passover lamb was selected. On the 14th of *Nisan*, the lamb was slaughtered at twilight. The blood of the lamb was applied to the doorframe to protect the firstborn from the tenth plague. On the 15th of *Nisan*, the Feast of Unleavened Bread, the children of Israel left Egypt. On the Feast of Firstfruits, they crossed the Red Sea.

The Jewish feasts of Passover, Unleavened Bread and Firstfruits are prophecies fulfilled on the day of the death, burial and resurrection of Jesus Christ. According to the Gospels, Jesus Christ entered Jerusalem on a donkey and was presented to the Jewish people. On the 10th of *Nisan*, He was selected as the perfect sacrifice. He was crucified on Passover, buried by Unleavened Bread and rose again on Firstfruits. God's plan for creation, the Jewish feasts and life of Christ give us God's time.

Israel rejected Jesus Christ but God never breaks His covenant with Abraham. Hosea says two days later, God will revive Israel and on the third day, He will restore Israel. In 1948, God revived physical Israel.[14] At the beginning of the third day, Jesus Christ will return and Israel will be restored back to God.

Feasts, Passion Week and Chronology

Day/*Nisan*		Jewish Feasts	Jesus Christ	Chronology	Year
0	10	Select Lamb	Triumphal Entry	Creation	0
1	11			Noah	1000
2	12			Abraham	2000
3	13			Solomon	3000
4	14	Passover	Crucifixion	First Coming	4000
5	15	Unleavened Bread (Exodus)	Burial	Pentecost/ Church Age	5000
6	16	Firstfruits (Red Sea)	Resurrection Trumpets	Rapture/ Second Coming	6000
7	17		Atonement Tabernacles	Millennium Heaven	7000

Traditional Passion Week of Jesus Christ

> Come, and let us return unto the Lord: for he has torn, and he will heal us; he has smitten, and he will bind us up. After two days will he revive us: in the third day he will raise us up, and we shall live in his sight (Hosea 6:1-2).

Roman Years

In 532, Dionysius Exiguus (Dennis the Short) from Scythia Minor (Romania) calculated Easter dates.[15] He starts from the birth of Jesus Christ on December 25, in 1 BC. His work unintentionally led to the BC/AD format. BC is Before Christ and AD is *Anno Domini Nostri Jesu Christi* (In the Year of Our Lord Jesus Christ). Dennis was a little short calculating years.

Creation—Bible Chronologies[16]

- 4004 BC: James Ussher (1581-1656)
- 4000 BC: Dionysius Exiguus (470-544)
- 4000 BC: Isaac Newton (1643-1727)

- 3992 BC: Johannes Kepler (1571-1630)
- 3977 BC: Bill Bonnett (1967)
- 3952 BC: Venerable Bede (672-735)
- 3949 BC: Joseph Scaliger (1540-1609)
- 3929 BC: John Lightfoot (1602-1675)

In 1654, Anglican Archbishop James Ussher of Ireland published a chronology that set the first day of creation to the autumn equinox on October 23, 4004 BC and Christ's birth to October 4 BC on the Julian calendar.[17]

Exiguus, Ussher and others based their calendars on Christ's birth but God's timeline is based on the cross. *Anno Passionis* (or Year of the Passion) counts years from redemption at ~30 AD. That is a good ballpark estimate that Jesus Christ's Second Coming is near. Throughout the rest of the book, many Scriptures dealing with time and prophecy point to our age. Time tells us God's unsealed, fulfilled and revealed plan is quickly coming to a close.

- Exiguus: 4000 BC + 6000 + 1 = 2001 AD
- Ussher: 4004 BC + 6000 + 1 = 1997 AD
- Revised: 3971 BC + 6000 + 1 = ~2030 AD

The Roman year 2012 corresponds to the Jewish year 5772.[18] The Jewish calendar is missing ~214 years.[19] (Calendar errors are explained in a later chapter.) This gives ~5988 years from creation. There are ~1982 years from the cross and ~5982 years from creation.

God's Plan from Beginning to End

In the beginning, God told us His plan and time for redemption. The days of creation, Sabbaths, exodus out of Egypt, Jewish feasts and Passion Week point to God's seven thousand year plan. There are four thousand years from creation to the cross and two thousand years from the cross to Jesus Christ's return. The sixth day is about over.

Most Bible scholars only talk about Daniel's seventy weeks but time gives a new perspective of End Time prophecy by answering many questions of when. God's time sets up the structure to understand prophecy. When we understand God's time, we understand God's plan for our time.

Do you see creation, the Sabbaths, the exodus, Jewish feasts and redemption pointing to the end of this current age?

Chapter 10

Seven Days of God

When writing about prophecy, most authors start with Daniel 9 and the seventy weeks which deals with Christ's First and Second Comings. However, it is important to know God's time which sets the proper framework to build God's plan. Then Bible prophecies are put on this timeline.

My favorite book in the Bible is Revelation. Since the Revelation Bible study, a deacon at church affectionately calls me "Mr. Revelation." The book is the least understood and most misinterpreted book in the Bible and yet it holds a wealth of information when one digs below the surface. The last book references the Old Testament 284 times.[1] Jesus Christ reveals to John the events of the End Times, Tribulation, Second Coming and Millennium. It is the only book written especially for us about our time.

Leviticus is my least favorite book and lists the details of the Law. When reading through the Bible, I usually skip the book. God's entire prophecy timeline is dependent on one chapter. God appoints a specific place (Jerusalem) and a specific time (7 days) to fulfill His plan. This tells the sequence of key events.

Jewish Calendar

In Leviticus 23, God gave Moses seven days in which He would intervene in the lives of humanity to bring redemption and then return to set up His eternal kingdom. Four events are fulfilled with the First Coming of Jesus Christ and three events are fulfilled with the Second Coming of Jesus Christ. The Church teaches the first four holy days while the last three are rarely taught in connection with prophecy. These seven feasts are the seven days of God.

Our Roman calendar is based on the solar cycle and the Muslim calendar is based on the lunar cycle. The Jewish calendar is lunisolar based on the lunar and solar cycles.[2] God created time

Jewish Calendar[3]

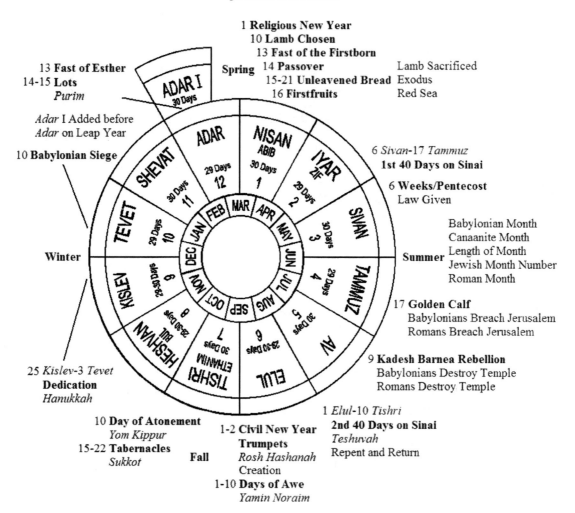

based on the Jewish calendar. The day starts at sunset and the month starts with the first observation of the crescent new moon. The religious year starts in the spring and the civil year starts in the late summer or early fall. Months are numbered in religious-year order. The Bible mentions a few Canaanite months but month names are derived from Babylonian months.

> And God called the light Day, and the darkness he called Night. And the evening and the morning were the first day (Genesis 1:5).

The Jewish lunisolar calendar stays in sequence with the moon and sun.[4] Because the lunar cycle is 29 days, 12 hours and 44 minutes, months are 29 or 30 days. The year is 353-355 days. Based on the spring barley harvest, a 30-day month is added so Passover is always after the spring equinox. Every two or three years, a leap month is added so planting and harvest seasons do not drift into the winter and summer. The Bible does not mention leap months but an agricultural society must keep the calendar and feast days aligned with the seasons.

Since God gave Moses the calendar, each month was determined by observation. By 358 AD, the Jews developed a nineteen-year perpetual calendar.[5] There are twelve regular years and seven leap years. Postponement rules were added so three fall holy days do not occur on Friday to make double Sabbath days.[6] The new year begins on Sunday, Monday, Wednesday or Friday evenings. This postponement may delay the new year by a day.

On the 1st of *Nisan* in the spring, a year is added to the reign of kings. On the 1st of *Tishri* in the fall, a year is added to the calendar. The year counts from creation using *Anno Mundi* (AM) or in the year of the world.[7] "In the beginning" is *Alpha b'Tishri* or the first of *Tishri*.[8] Jewish tradition celebrates the birth of the world and Adam. The evening of September 16, 2012 begins the Jewish year 5773 AM.

Predictions of the Messiah and of Our Time

A key part of Bible study is to know the culture. Jewish culture, history and language give a better understanding of Scripture and Bible prophecy. Every feast and fast day is a day that God intervenes in the lives of Israel and the Church.

Just as the Passover lamb reveals Jesus Christ so the Jewish calendar reveals Christ's plan of redemption and return. Jesus Christ was conceived, born, died, buried and resurrected on these Jewish holy days. You cannot understand prophecy without understanding the timing and meaning of these major and minor feast and fast days.

> We are living in the Creator's universe. The world in which we live is synchronized to His [Jewish] calendar and His time clock… Those raised within the western [Roman] paradigm have no idea what time it is. It is as if the hands have been broken from the face of the clock.[9]

Jewish Feasts

Seven Jewish holy days are found in the Law that we ignore because it is the Law and we are under grace. We are not Jewish. Why should we care about some old Jewish holidays? When God gave the Law, He revealed to humanity the days of future events, giving another glimpse of God's perfect and precise plan.

The Jews have seven feasts found in Exodus 23, Leviticus 23 and Deuteronomy 16. Since the exodus from Egypt, Israel has celebrated these days. During the Jewish temples, every Jewish man traveled to Jerusalem in the early spring, late spring and early fall.

> Three times in a year shall all your males appear before the Lord thy God in the place which he shall choose; in the feast of unleavened bread, and in the feast of weeks, and in the feast of tabernacles (Deuteronomy 16:16).

Jesus observed these feasts during His lifetime.

> Now his parents went to Jerusalem every year at the feast of the passover. And when he was twelve years old, they went up to Jerusalem after the custom of the feast (Luke 2:41-42).

> Now the Jews' feast of tabernacles was at hand. But when his brethren were gone up, then went he [Jesus Christ] also up unto the feast (John 7:2, 10).

> After two days was the feast of the passover, and of unleavened bread: and the chief priests and the scribes sought how they might take him by craft, and put him to death (Mark 14:1).

Some feast days are High Sabbath days. Work is not permitted on Trumpets, Atonement, first day of Tabernacles, day after Tabernacles, Passover, first and last day of Unleavened Bread and Weeks.[10] Cooking and carrying are permitted on holidays.

These Jewish feasts are of great importance to Christians. Four spring feasts were prophetic events fulfilled by God. Christians celebrate them as historic events and they are the foundation of the Gospel. Three fall feasts are still future events.

Jewish Holy Days and Observances[11]

Major Feasts	
Nisan 14	*Pesach*/Passover (Leviticus 23:5)
Nisan 15-21	*Hamatzot*/Unleavened Bread (Leviticus 23:6)
Nisan 16	*Bikkurim*/Firstfruits (Leviticus 23:10)
Sivan 6	*HaBikurim*/Weeks (Leviticus 23:15)
Tishri 1-2	*Rosh Hashanah*/Trumpets (Leviticus 23:24)
Tishri 10	*Yom Kippur*/Atonement (Leviticus 23:27)
Tishri 15-21	*Sukkot*/Tabernacles (Leviticus 23:34)
Minor Feasts and Observances	
Elul 1- *Tishri* 10	*Teshuvah*—Repent and Return Second Tablets Given (Exodus 34:1-27)
Tishri 1-10	*Yamin Noraim*—10 Days of Awe
Tishri 22	*Shemini Atzeret*—8th Day of the Assembly
Tishri 23	*Simchat Torah*—Rejoicing with the *Torah*
Kislev 25- *Tevet* 2 or 3	*Hanukkah*—Festival of Lights (Daniel 11:29-35)
Adar 14-15	*Purim*—Festival of Lots (Esther 9:17-21)
Fast Days	
Nisan 14	*Taanit Bkhorot*—Fast of the Firstborn
Tammuz 17	Moses Breaks First Tablets (Exodus 32) Babylon & Rome Breach Jerusalem Walls (2 King 25:2-3, Jeremiah 39:1-2, Luke 19:41-44)
Av 9	Rebellion of Israel at Kadesh Barnea Destruction of the 1st & 2nd Temples (Numbers 13-14, 2 Kings 25:8-9, Matthew 24:1-2) Various Jewish Persecutions and Wars
Tevet 10	Babylonian Siege of Jerusalem (2 Kings 25:1)
Adar 13	*Taanit* Esther—Fast of Esther (Esther 4:16)

Israeli Holidays	
Nisan 27	*Yom Hashoah Vehagevurah*—Catastrophe/Holocaust Memorial Day
Iyar 5	*Yom Haatzmaut*—Independence Day (1948)
Iyar 28	*Yom Yerushalayim*—Jerusalem Day (1967)

Seven Jewish Feasts[12]

These are the feasts of the Lord, even holy convocations, which you shall proclaim in their seasons (Leviticus 23:4).

Date	Hebrew	English	Jewish Event
Unleavened Bread—Season of Our Freedom Early Spring Harvest (March-April)			
Nisan 14	*Pesach*	Passover	Lamb Sacrificed
Nisan 15-21	*Hamatzot*	Unleavened Bread	Exodus from Egypt
Nisan 16	*Bikkurim*	Firstfruits	Red Sea
Weeks—Season of the Giving of the *Torah* Late Spring Harvest (May-June)			
Sivan 6	*Shavot*	Weeks/Pentecost	Law Given
Tabernacles—Season of Our Joy Fall Harvest (September-October)			
Tishri 1-2	*Rosh Hashanah*	Trumpets	New Year's Day
Tishri 10	*Yom Kippur*	Atonement	National Forgiveness
Tishri 15-21	*Sukkot*	Tabernacles	Live in Booths

1. Pesach (Passover)

14th of *Nisan*—Lamb Sacrificed—Christ's Crucifixion

In the fourteenth day of the first month at even is the Lord's passover (Leviticus 23:5).

God brought the ten plagues against the Egyptians so Pharaoh would release the children of Israel. Passover is the tenth plague of Egypt. Before sunset, the people of Israel killed a lamb and applied the blood on the top and sides of the doorframe in the shape of a cross. When the death angel saw the blood, he passed over the house and the firstborn children lived.

> In the tenth day of this month they shall take to them every man a lamb, according to the house of their fathers, a lamb for an house: And you shall keep it up until the fourteenth day of the same month: and the whole assembly of the congregation of Israel shall kill it in the evening. And the blood shall be to you for a token upon the houses where you are: and when I see the blood, I will pass over you, and the plague shall not be upon you to destroy you, when I smite the land of Egypt (Exodus 12:3, 6, 13).

Passover Fulfilled

The Passover is a prophecy of Jesus Christ on the cross. While Pharaoh and Moses negotiated the release of the Hebrews out of Egypt, God set His plan into action so the Passover and crucifixion are fulfilled on the same day.

> And it was the preparation of the passover, and about the sixth hour [noon]: and he [Pilate] said unto the Jews, Behold your King! But they cried out, Away with him, away with him, crucify him (John 19:14-15).

> Forasmuch as you know that you were not redeemed with corruptible things, as silver and gold, from your vain conversation received by tradition from your fathers; But with the precious blood of Christ, as of a lamb without blemish and without spot (1 Peter 1:18-19).

2. *Hamatzot* (Unleavened Bread)

15th-21st of *Nisan*—Exodus from Egypt—Christ's Burial

> And on the fifteenth day of the same month is the feast of unleavened bread unto the Lord: seven days you must eat unleavened bread (Leviticus 23:6).

The first day of Unleavened Bread is a High Sabbath. There are 430 years from God's covenant with Abraham to the exodus from Egypt. This prophecy is fulfilled to the day. The children of Israel left Egypt quickly during the night. They did not have time to allow bread to rise. Unleavened Bread is the first of three pilgrimages to Jerusalem and continues for seven days.

> And they shall eat the flesh in that night, roast with fire, and unleavened bread. And so shall you eat it; with your loins girded, your shoes on your feet, and your staff in your hand; and you shall eat it in haste: it is the Lord's passover. And it came to pass at the end of the four hundred and thirty years, even the selfsame day it came to pass, that all the hosts of the Lord went out from the land of Egypt (Exodus 12:8, 11, 41).

Unleavened Bread Fulfilled

The Feast of Unleavened Bread is fulfilled about 1550 years to the day. Jesus Christ was buried before the High Sabbath and in the tomb. Unleavened bread is a symbol of the sinless life of Jesus Christ. Because of His perfect sacrifice, we are made perfect.

> When the evening was come, there came a rich man of Arimathaea, named Joseph, who also himself was Jesus' disciple: He went to Pilate, and begged the body of Jesus. Then Pilate commanded the body to be delivered. And when Joseph had taken the body, he wrapped it in a clean linen cloth, And laid it in his own new tomb, which he had hewn out in the rock: and he rolled a great stone to the door of the sepulcher, and departed (Matthew 27:57-60).

Know not that a little leaven leavens the whole lump? Purge out therefore the old leaven, that you may be a new lump, as you are unleavened. For even Christ our passover is sacrificed for us (1 Corinthians 5:6-7).

3. *Bikkurim* (Firstfruits)

16th of *Nisan*—Crossing the Red Sea—Christ's Resurrection

When you be come into the land which I give unto you, and shall reap the harvest thereof, then you shall bring a sheaf of the firstfruits of your harvest unto the priest (Leviticus 23:10).

On the Feast of Firstfruits, God parted the Red Sea and Israel crossed on dry land at night. The Egyptians followed but God returned the waters killing Pharaoh and his army. The death of Pharaoh ended his ownership of the children of Israel. After the third day, Israel was truly free.

And the Lord brought us forth out of Egypt with a mighty hand, and with an outstretched arm, and with great terribleness, and with signs, and with wonders: And he has brought us into this place, and has given us this land, even a land that flows with milk and honey. And you shall set it before the Lord your God, and worship before the Lord your God (Deuteronomy 26:8-10).

Firstfruits Fulfilled

The firstfruits are a symbol of the resurrected Jesus Christ. On the night the children of Israel crossed the Red Sea, Christ was resurrected from the dead. As the first three feasts celebrate Jewish freedom from Egyptian bondage, Christ's redemptive work gives us freedom from the bondage of sin.

The first day of the week came Mary Magdalene early, when it was yet dark, unto the sepulcher, and saw the stone taken away from the sepulcher. Then she ran, and came to Simon Peter, and to the other disciple, whom Jesus loved, and said unto them, They have taken away the Lord out of the sepulcher, and we know not where they have laid him (John 20:1-2).

But now is Christ risen from the dead, and become the firstfruits of them that slept. For as in Adam all die, even so in Christ shall all be made alive (1 Corinthians 15:20, 22).

For I delivered unto you first of all that which I also received, how that Christ died for our sins according to the scriptures; And that he was buried, and that he rose again the third day according to the scriptures (1 Corinthians 15:3-4).

4. *Shavot* (Weeks/Pentecost)

6th of *Sivan*—Law Given—Holy Spirit Given

> Even unto the day after the seventh sabbath shall you number fifty days; and you shall offer a new meat offering unto the Lord (Leviticus 23:16).

The Feast of Weeks is fifty days from Firstfruits. It takes fifty days for the children of Israel to travel from the Red Sea to Mt. Sinai (or Mt. Horeb). The Feast of Weeks celebrates the Law and is the second of three pilgrimages to Jerusalem.

> In the third month [*Sivan*], when the children of Israel were gone forth out of the land of Egypt, the same day came they into the wilderness of Sinai (Exodus 19:1).

Weeks Fulfilled

The Feast of Weeks is fulfilled at Pentecost. This Jewish feast is for the Jewish and Gentile Church. On the day God gave the Law to Moses and Israel, God gave the Holy Spirit to the Church. Because of God's great salvation, we are no longer under the Law but rather are under grace. The Church starts at Pentecost and ends at the Rapture.

> And when the day of Pentecost was fully come, they were all with one accord in one place. And suddenly there came a sound from heaven as of a rushing mighty wind, and it filled all the house where they were sitting. And there appeared unto them cloven tongues like as of fire, and it sat upon each of them. And they were all filled with the Holy Spirit, and began to speak with other tongues, as the Spirit gave them utterance (Acts 2:1-4).

A disagreement exists over when to celebrate Pentecost.[13] The Pharisees count fifty days from the 15th of *Nisan* (High Sabbath) to the 6th of *Sivan*. Jews celebrate this day. The Sadducees count seven regular Sabbaths plus one day. The Church celebrates on Sunday.

> Three times you shall keep a feast unto me in the year. You shall keep the feast of unleavened bread: for in it you came out from Egypt: And the feast of harvest [Weeks], the firstfruits of your labors, which you have sown in the field: and the feast of ingathering [Tabernacles], which is in the end of the year, when you have gathered in your labors out of the field (Exodus 13:14-16).

Four Feasts, Four Prophecies Fulfilled

God gave Moses seven Jewish feasts. Four Jewish feasts are linked to the exodus out of Egypt. Those same feasts are prophecies fulfilled when God intervenes in the redemption of humanity. God gave Moses the days of Jesus Christ's death, burial and resurrection and the day Jesus Christ gave the Holy Spirit to the Church.

The last three feasts are not linked to a historic event or fulfilled prophecy. The fall Jewish feasts lead to the Jewish high holy days that focus on the nation of Israel's relationship with God. All seven feasts are prophecies fulfilled by God on exact days.

If four Jewish feast days were fulfilled by Jesus Christ, what do the last three days tell about the time and plan of God?

Chapter 11

The Feast of Trumpets

The first four Jewish feasts are prophetic events fulfilled by God and celebrated by Christians. The death, burial and resurrection of Jesus Christ and giving the Holy Spirit are the foundation of our Christian faith. What do the last three feasts mean to Christians and Jews? What do they mean to End Time prophecy?

The view that the Rapture occurs before the Tribulation is credited to John Darby (1827).[1] However, writings of Peter, Paul and the early Church created the basis for a Pretribulation Rapture. Although Augustine's figurative view prevailed, Ephraem of Nisibis (373) and Brother Dolcino (1307) taught a literal view of prophecy and the Rapture.[2] The Reformation caused an increase of personal Bible study. Joseph Mead (1627), Increase Mather (1669), Peter Jurieu (1687) and Morgan Edwards (1722-1795) believed the Rapture would occur before the Antichrist's rule. These interpretations are consolidated into Darby's view in 1827.[3]

> All the saints and elect of God are gathered together before the tribulation, which is to come, and are taken to the Lord, in order that they may not see at any time the confusion which overwhelms the world because of our sins.
> —Theologian Ephraem, Nisibis (Turkey), seventh century[4]

We can trace the Rapture view all the way back to about 1524 BC with Moses. God gave Moses seven days that He would intervene in the lives of humanity to bring redemption and then return. Through Jewish culture, many End Time Scriptures are understood.

> Christ was once offered to bear the sins of many; and unto them that look for him shall he appear the second time without sin unto salvation (Hebrews 9:27-28).

As part of the high holy days, look at how the Jews celebrate the Feast of Trumpets and how that applies to our time.

Fall Jewish Feasts and Observances[5]

Date	Hebrew	English	Events
Elul 1-*Tishri* 10	*Teshuvah*	Repent and Return	40 Days of Self-evaluation and Repentance
Tishri 1-2	*Yom Teruah* *Rosh Hashanah*	Trumpets Head of Year	New Year's Day
Tishri 1-10	*Yamim Noraim*	Days of Awe	Preparation for the Day of Atonement
Tishri 10	*Yom Kippur*	Atonement	Israel's National Forgiveness
Tishri 15-21	*Sukkot*	Tabernacles	Live in Booths
Tishri 22	*Shemini Atzeret*	8th Day of the Assembly	Remain an Extra Day with God
Tishri 23	*Simchat Torah*	Rejoicing with the *Torah*	Complete *Torah* Instruction and Begin Again

Teshuvah

Moses broke the first tablets after the people worship the golden calf. On the 1st of *Elul* (August/September), Moses returns to God on Mt. Sinai for a second set of Ten Commandments. The 40th day is the 10th of *Tishri*, the Day of Atonement. These forty days were a time for Israel to repent of their sin and return to God.

And the Lord said unto Moses, Cut two tables of stone like the first: and I will write upon these tables the words that were in the first tables, which you broke (Exodus 34:1).

Forty Days[6]

- During the great flood, it rained forty days (Genesis 7:4).
- Moses was with God on Mt. Sinai forty days (Exodus 24:18).
- Moses returned to God on Mt. Sinai forty days (Exodus 34:28).
- The spies explored Canaan forty days (Numbers 13:25).
- Jonah preached judgment to Nineveh forty days (Jonah 3:4).
- Jesus Christ was tested in the wilderness forty days (Matthew 4:2).
- Jesus Christ stayed after the Resurrection forty days (Acts 1:3).

Teshuvah means to repent and return. From the 1st of *Elul* to the 10th of *Tishri* (August-October), it is a spiritual preparation for the high holy days of the Feast of Trumpets and Day of Atonement. During the Hebrew month of *Elul*, at the end of the morning prayers, the *shofar* is blown.[7] The people wake up and review their lives. They repent of their sins and change their ways. On the day before *Rosh Hashanah*, no trumpet is blown.

Teshuvah (Repent and Return)[8]

1. Stop sinful behavior
2. Regret over past actions
3. Confession before God
4. Commitment to change

> If we confess our sins, he is faithful and just to forgive us our sins, and to cleanse us from all unrighteousness (1 John 1:9).

Teshuvah Prophecy

The prophecy of *Teshuvah* corresponds to the Laodicean period of the Church. While tradition says prophecies will happen during the Tribulation, specific prophecies are fulfilled during the Laodicean period. The World Wars and Iraq Wars are loud trumpet blasts. Prior to the Rapture, this is a time of alarm and awakening. As Noah had 120 years of warning before the flood so we have 120 years of warning before the Tribulation. Christians must be ready, reap the harvest and watch for the Lord's return. God is preparing the world for the last seven years. It is time for the world to repent and seek God. When the Last Trump sounds, it will be too late.

> And the Lord said, My spirit shall not always strive with man, for that he also is flesh: yet his days shall be an hundred and twenty years (Genesis 6:7).

120 Years

- 120 years of warning before the flood (Genesis 6)
- 120 years of warning before the Tribulation (Revelation 8-9)

> Blow the trumpet in Zion, and sound an alarm in my holy mountain: let all the inhabitants of the land tremble: for the day of the Lord comes, for it is nigh at hand (Joel 2:1).

5. *Rosh Hashanah* (New Year) or *Yom Teruah* (Trumpets)

1st-2nd of *Tishri*—New Year's Day

> In the seventh month, in the first day of the month, shall you have a sabbath, a memorial of blowing of trumpets, an holy convocation (Leviticus 23:24).

The Feast of Trumpets is the 1st and 2nd of *Tishri* (September/October).[9] *Tishri* means beginning and starts the High holy days. It is the anniversary of creation. Genesis 1:1 says *Aleph b'Tishri* (1st of *Tishri*).[10] The day is called *Yom Teruah* or Day of Sounding of the Trumpets, which literally means the day of shouting.

> Blow the trumpet in the new moon, in the time appointed, on our solemn feast day (Psalm 81:3).

New Year and New Moon

The Jewish culture has two major new years. The religious new year begins on the 1st of *Nisan* and the civil new year begins on the 1st of *Tishri*. *Rosh Hashanah* means the head of the year. It is the only feast that occurs on the first day of the month. Like Easter, it is a floating holiday based on the moon.

Feast of Trumpets—Names and Themes[11]

- *Yom Teruah*: Day of the Blowing the *Shofar*, Day of the Awakening Blast, Day of Shouting
- *Rosh Hashanah*: Head of the Year, Anniversary of Creation
- *Yom Harat Olam*: Creation of Humanity
- *Tishri*: 7th Month—Religious Calendar—Completion
- *Tishri*: 1st Month—Civil Calendar—Beginning
- *Beresheet (B'Tishri)*: Genesis
- *Alpha b'Tishri*: First of *Tishri* (Genesis 1:1)
- *Rosh Chodesh*: Head of the Month
- *Yom Hazikaron*: Day of Remembrance
- *Yom Hadin*: Day of Judgment
- *Yamim Arichtah*: One Long Day
- *Yom Hakeseh*: Hidden Day, The Day that No One Knows
- *Tekiah Gedolah*: Last Trump

- *Natzal*: Rapture, Resurrection of the Dead, Opening of the Gate/Door, Opening of the Books
- *Ketiva Ve-Chatima Tovah*: May You Be Written and Sealed for a Good Year
- *Nesuin*: Wedding Ceremony, Behold, the Bridegroom Comes, Blessed Is He Who Comes, Thief in the Night
- *Chevali Shel Mashiach*: Birthpangs of the Messiah
- *Yaakov Tsarah*: Jacob's Trouble
- *Yom YHWH*: Day of the Lord

Since *Elul* has twenty-nine or thirty days, *Rosh Hashanah* can occur on two days: the day after the 29th or 30th of *Elul*. That creates a problem of when the new year begins and when to keep the Feast of Trumpets.

Rosh Chodesh is the head of the month.[12] Every month was determined by observation. People witnessed the first crescent of a new moon and testified before the Sanhedrin.[13] If two reliable witnesses were found, the Sanhedrin declared the beginning of a new month. Messengers set beacon fires to signal the new month. After the new moon was declared, the new year began and the feasts of Trumpets, Atonement and Tabernacles were set.

Setting March 1 and *Tishri* 1

Roman Year	No Leap Year	February 28	March 1	March 2
	Leap Year	February 28	February 29	March 1
Jewish Year	New Moon Seen	*Elul* 29	*Tishri* 1	*Tishri* 2
	No New Moon	*Elul* 29	*Elul* 30	*Tishri* 1

The Feast of Trumpets is *Yom Hakeseh* or Hidden Day. The Jewish new year is the first day of the month and year. February has twenty-eight or twenty-nine days. March 1 is determined by knowing which years are leap years. In the Jewish calendar, *Elul* has twenty-nine or thirty days. The 1st of *Tishri* is determined by observing the moon. In the late afternoon of the 29th of *Elul*, if the first sliver of the new moon is seen and declared by the Sanhedrin, the new year starts that evening. If the moon is not seen, the 30th of *Elul* starts at evening and the new month and year are delayed one day. When Jesus Christ said it is "a day and hour that no one knows," He was using a Jewish figure of speech. The Jews knew He was referring to the Feast of Trumpets.[14]

Distant communities were not always notified by the Sanhedrin so they celebrated the holiday on both days. With David and Jonathan, the new moon festival was two days. Since the Babylonian captivity, *Rosh Hashanah* was celebrated on the 1st and 2nd of *Tishri* and was considered one long day.[15]

> And David said unto Jonathan, Behold, tomorrow is the new moon and I should not fail to sit with the king at meat: but let me go, that I may hide myself in the field unto the third day at evening (1 Samuel 20:5).

To know the time of *Rosh Hashanah* was critical because the day was a High Sabbath with no work allowed. People had to prepare in advance. Since no one knew the exact day or hour of the new moon, it kept the people in a continual state of alertness.

> Blow the trumpet in the new moon, in the time appointed, on our solemn feast day (Psalm 81:3).

Sound the Trumpets

The Feast of Trumpets is *Yom Teruah* or the Day of the Blowing of Trumpets. One requirement was hearing the *shofar* or trumpet in the synagogue.[16] The *shofar* is a horn of a ram or goat but not a bull because of the golden calf. It is not a musical instrument but more like a bugle. Blowing a *shofar* is part of new months and feast days.

Blowing the *shofar* is equivalent to the town crier, steeple bell or tornado siren. Trumpets are sounded to wake up, assemble, move and alert the people. On *Yom Teruah*, the Jewish people wake up and return to God. As part of *Teshuvah*, the *shofar* sounds the alarm, as people respond with brokenness and wailing over sin. All who sin have an opportunity to repent and request mercy before God judges.

> When I bring the sword upon a land, if the people of the land take a man of their coasts, and set him for their watchman: When he sees the sword come upon the land, he blows the trumpet, and warns the people (Ezekiel 33:2-3).

Shofar Blasts on the Feast of Trumpets[17]

- *Tekiah*: Attention—1 Long Blast
- *Shevarim*: Brokenness, Despair—3 Medium Blasts

- *Teruah*: Wailing, Urgency — 9 Short Blasts
- *Tekiah Gedolah* (Last Trump): Assemble — 1 Prolonged Blast

Hebrew tradition requires one hundred *shofar* blasts at the *Yom Teruah* service. The *shofar* is sounded in a precise order combining the *tekiah* (t-KEE-uh), *shevarim* (sh-VAW-reem) and *teruah* (t-ROO-uh).[18] The last blast of the service is a prolonged *tekiah* called the *Tekiah Gedolah* (t-KEE-uh geh-DOH-luh) which is called the Last Trump. After the morning service on *Rosh Hashanah*, the *shofar* is blown before the *Musaf* or special holy day service.[19]

- *Tekiah, Shevarim, Teruah, Tekiah* (3 times)
- *Tekiah, Shevarim, Tekiah* (3 times)
- *Tekiah, Teruah, Tekiah* (2 times)
- *Tekiah, Teruah, Tekiah Gedolah* (1 time)

Tekiah Gedolah or Last Trump is one of the Hebrew expressions for the Feast of Trumpets.

Significance of the *Shofar*[20]

1. Declare God as Sovereign King and Creator of the world.
2. Fear, respect and humility before the majesty of God.
3. Remember Abraham who offered Isaac as an act of obedience to God.
4. Remember the *shofar* at Mt. Sinai and Israel's acceptance to follow the Law.
5. Reminder of the prophets' messages to turn from sin to God.
6. Remember the destruction of the Jewish temple and prayer for its rebuilding.
7. Begin the ten days of repentance from *Rosh Hashanah* to the Day of Atonement.
8. Reminder of Israel's future return to the Promised Land.
9. Reminder of the future day of judgment of the world.
10. Reminder of the future resurrection of the dead, God's reign over the world, and a regenerated Israel.

> When they [Israel] sound the *shofar* in fulfillment of the precepts of the day, their closed hearts are opened, they regret their sins, and their thoughts turn to repentance.... Though they might originate from man's lips, they can well culminate with the coming of Mashiach ben David [Messiah son of David].
> —Jewish scholar Saadia Gaon, tenth century[21]

First Trump, Last Trump, Great Trump[22]

We always hear of the Last Trump but the Bible is clear about when the trumpet sounds. The *shofar* is blown on three Jewish feasts: Weeks, Trumpets and Atonement.

1. First Trump—Weeks

The First Trump is linked with the Feast of Weeks. When God gave Moses the Law on Mt. Sinai, the *shofar* sounded long. This day was the marriage of God and Israel.

> On the third day in the morning, that there were thunders and lightnings, and a thick cloud upon the mount, and the voice of the trumpet exceeding loud; so that all the people that was in the camp trembled (Exodus 19:16).

2. Last Trump—Trumpets

Paul used a Hebrew figure of speech "Last Trump" to refer to the Feast of Trumpets. The hundredth blast of the *shofar* is called *Tekiah Gedolah* or Last Trump. This day is the marriage of Christ and the Church.

3. Great Trump—Atonement

When Jesus Christ explains the End Times to His disciples, He says the *Shofar Hagadol* or Great Trumpet sounds after the Great Tribulation on the Day of Atonement.

> And he shall send his angels with a great sound of a trumpet, and they shall gather together his elect from the four winds, from one end of heaven to the other (Matthew 24:31).

Judgment Day

The Feast of Trumpets is *Yom Hadin* or Judgment Day.[23] The twelve tribes were given a month. Dan, which means judge, has the month *Tishri*.[24] The constellation Libra's symbol is a pair of scales which is a symbol of Jesus Christ's justice. *Tishri* is the month of His birth.

> TEKEL; You are weighed in the balances, and are found wanting (Daniel 5:27).

The Feast of Trumpets is *Yom Hazikaron* or Day of Remembrance. Like our New Year, *Yom Teruah* is a time to review the past year and make changes.[25] On *Yom Teruah*, the Jews proclaim God as King, remember His great works and repent of their sins. They remember the good and bad, make amends for mistakes and recommit to serving God. It is better to judge yourself now than to be judged by God later.

God judges people's actions in the past year according to the books.[26] The four books are the righteous (Lamb's Book of Life), wicked, intermediates and remembrance (deeds). Man is weighed in the balances compared to the righteousness of God.

With God's judgment also comes mercy and grace. The Jews read Genesis 22 when Abraham sacrificed Isaac. When a person repented from sin and turned back to God, then He forgave the sinner and provided a sacrifice. After the night's prayer service, a special greeting was used: "*Ketiva ve-chatima tovah*" (or "May you be written and sealed for a good year").[27] God opens the gates of Heaven and keeps them open until the Day of Atonement, God's final day of judgment.

> And I saw the dead, small and great, stand before God; and the books were opened: and another book was opened, which is the book of life: and the dead were judged out of those things which were written in the books, according to their works (Revelation 20:12).

Festival Celebrations

Yom Teruah is a joyous time. Families eat apples and carrots sweetened with honey. This symbolizes joy, blessings, abundance and the hope for the new year.[28] After the blessing, they say: "May it be Your will to renew for us a good and sweet year." Do not sleep during the day but study the Law or other spiritual activities.[29] Avoid anger because God judges us as we judge others.

Trumpets Prophecy

The Feast of Trumpets to Christians is the Rapture. God told Moses and us the exact days of the death, burial and resurrection of Jesus Christ and the beginning and ending of the Church Age. On *Yom Teruah*, Jesus Christ returns to take His Church home. The Jewish holy day of *Yom Teruah* teaches us about the Rapture.

1. **Day of Blowing the *Shofar***

   Since God fulfills the first four prophetic feasts, so God is about to fulfill the Feast of Trumpets on the new moon of *Rosh Hashanah* with the Rapture of the Church.

   > Speak unto the children of Israel, saying, In the seventh month, in the first day of the month, shall you have a sabbath, a memorial of blowing of trumpets, an holy convocation (Leviticus 23:24).

2. **Day of the Awakening Blast and the Day of Shouting**

   The Rapture is *Yom Teruah* or the Day of the Awakening Blast. What sound wakes the dead in Christ and the alive in Christ but not the living dead? The shout, the voice of the archangel and the trump of God do.

   > For the Lord himself shall descend from heaven with a shout, with the voice of the archangel, and with the trump of God (1 Thessalonians 4:16).

3. **Day of Judgment**

   The Rapture is *Yom Hadin* or Judgment Day. Believers in Christ are saved and live by grace but are rewarded for works.

   > For we must all appear before the judgment seat of Christ; that every one may receive the things done in his body, according to that he has done, whether it be good or bad (2 Corinthians 5:10).

   All people left behind are judged and given seven years of trials with the wrath of Satan and wrath of God during the Tribulation. Then the final judgment will come.

4. **Day of Remembrance**

   The Rapture is *Yom Hazikaron* or Day of Remembrance. We remember God as Savior and Lord. God remembers His promise of eternal life to those who believe.

   > Remember therefore how you have received and heard, and hold fast, and repent (Revelation 3:3).

And he [the thief on the cross] said unto Jesus, Lord, remember me when thou come into thy kingdom (Luke 23:42).

5. Day That Is Hidden

The Rapture is *Yom Hakeseh* or the Hidden Day. No one knew when the new year began until they saw the crescent new moon. No one saw Jesus Christ's resurrection from the dead at night so we will be resurrected and raptured in hiding.

But of that day and hour knows no man (Matthew 24:36).

6. Day of the Last Trump

The Rapture is the day of the *Tekiah Gedolah* which is the Last Trump. The *shofar* sounds one hundred times during the Jewish service. The last trump is the *Tekiah Gedolah*. Paul refers to the 100th blast of the *shofar* on *Rosh Hashanah*.

Behold, I show you a mystery; We shall not all sleep, but we shall all be changed, In a moment, in the twinkling of an eye, at the last trump: for the trumpet shall sound, and the dead shall be raised incorruptible, and we shall be changed (1 Corinthians 15:51-52).

7. Day of the Resurrection and Rapture

First, the dead in Christ will be resurrected. The alive in Christ will be raptured. Then we meet Jesus Christ in the air.

And the dead in Christ shall rise first: Then we which are alive and remain shall be caught up together with them in the clouds, to meet the Lord in the air: and so shall we ever be with the Lord (1 Thessalonians 4:16-17).

8. Day of the Opening of the Door and Gate

The Rapture is the day of the open door and open gate. All people redeemed by Christ enter into Heaven's gate.

After this I looked, and, behold, a door was opened in heaven: and the first voice which I heard was as it were of a trumpet talking with me; which said, Come up here (Revelation 4:1).

9. Day of the Open Books

The Rapture is the day of the open books. The Lamb's Book of Life and the book of remembrance are opened.

He that overcomes, the same shall be clothed in white raiment; and I will not blot out his name out of the book of life, but I will confess his name before my Father, and before his angels (Revelation 3:5).

10. Day of the Marriage Feast of the Lamb

The Rapture is the *Nesuin*, which is the wedding ceremony. On this day, Jesus Christ takes away His bride, the Church, for their great wedding in the sky and then the wedding supper. Jacob and Samson had a week-long marriage ceremony.[30] Our salvation follows the traditions of the Jewish engagement, wedding and marriage ceremonies.

In my Father's house are many [rooms]: if it were not so, I would have told you. I go to prepare a place for you. And if I go and prepare a place for you, I will come again, and receive you unto myself; that where I am, there you may be also (John 14:2-3).

11. Day of Victory Over Sin, Death and the Grave

The Rapture is a day of ultimate victory over sin, death and the grave. We will never again be separated from God because of sin. All believers will cheat death and the grave.

O death, where is your sting? O grave, where is your victory? But thanks be to God, which gives us the victory through our Lord Jesus Christ (1 Corinthians 15:55, 57).

The Feast of Trumpets to the Jews is return. God promised to gather His people back to the Promised Land. In 1948, God restored physical Israel as a nation and in 1967, reunited Jerusalem. Beginning with the Feast of Trumpets, God restores spiritual Israel so the Jews repent and return back to God.

For I will take you from among the heathen, and gather you out of all countries, and will bring you into your own land. And I will put my spirit within you, and cause you to walk in my statutes, and you shall keep my judgments, and do them (Ezekiel 36:24, 27).

The Feast of Trumpets to the world is repentance. The Rapture is followed by the Tribulation. This is a seven-year period of nuclear world wars and God's last offer of mercy and grace. Salvation in Jesus Christ is still available and a few will be saved but time runs out quickly.

I saw the souls of them that were beheaded for the witness of Jesus, and for the word of God, and which had not worshipped the beast, neither his image, neither had received his mark upon their foreheads, or in their hands (Revelation 20:4).

Rapture Day

So when is the Rapture? We can narrow when to just one day.

The rapture could happen today if ...
- today is in the late summer or early fall
- today is September or October on the Roman calendar
- today is within fifteen days of the autumn equinox
- today is set by the traditional Jewish calendar rules
- today a new moon was observed by two witnesses in Jerusalem
- today is the Jewish month of *Tishri*
- today is the 1st of *Tishri*
- today is the Jewish civil new year (*Rosh Hashanah*)
- today is the hidden day or "the day that no one knows" (*Yom Hakeseh*)
- today is the Feast of Trumpets, the sounding of the *shofar* (*Yom Teruah*)
- today is when the hundredth and last trumpet blasts sounds (*Tekiah Gedolah*)
- today is when God calls us home

Teshuvah and Trumpets

Some claim that the Rapture of the Church is a recent interpretation of Scripture but God told Moses the seven days of God. Others say that "no one knows the day or the hour" but Jesus Christ and Paul use Jewish figures of speech that refer to the Feast of Trumpets. Hebrew culture helps us understand Scripture. The Feast of Trumpets gives us the sequence of the End Times. As Trumpets happens before Atonement, so the Rapture must happen before the Second Coming.

God began His plan for the End Times. Through the season of *Teshuvah*, God wakes up the Church and calls Israel back to Himself. The Feast of Trumpets is a day that is hidden and yet it is revealed to Christians. It is a day of judgment yet Christians escape the wrath of God. It is a day of separation from the world yet it is a day of our homecoming with God and the Saints in Heaven. The Rapture can happen on any day as long as that day is the Feast of Trumpets.

It is important for Christians to know the great hope of the Feast of Trumpets. That day has a special meaning to me. My dad was the first to tell me that that the Rapture occurs on *Rosh Hashanah*. On that *Rosh Hashanah* day, I will meet my mom and dad in the air along with my Savior, Jesus Christ.

Now that we know "the day that no one knows," do you know what Trumpets means to Christians, Israel and the world?

Chapter 12

Fall Jewish Feasts

G od gave Moses seven days that He will intervene in the lives of humanity to bring
redemption and then return to set up His eternal kingdom. Four feasts were fulfilled
in the death, burial and resurrection of Jesus Christ and the giving of the Holy Spirit. The
fifth feast will be fulfilled by the Rapture of the Church. There are two more feasts. These
feasts are the seven days of God.

Yamim Noraim (Days of Awe)

The last ten days of *Teshuvah* are the *Aseret Yemei Teshuva* or the Ten Days of Repentance
that begin with the two-day Feast of Trumpets and end on the Day of Atonement.[1] This
is a time of affliction and suffering called *Yamim Noraim* or Days of Awe. The theme of
repentance intensifies. During this time, the Jews seek reconciliation with people they have
wronged during the past year. People are judged on Trumpets but actions of repentance,
prayer and charity can change God's decree.

Days of Awe Prophecy

The Days of Awe correspond to the Tribulation. Awe is a time of fear and terror described
in Revelation. For the Jews, it is called Jacob's Trouble. For the Gentiles left behind, it is a
time of great judgment and *Aph Elohim* or the wrath of God. It is the beginning of sorrow
or *Chevlai shel Mashiach*, the birth pangs of the Messiah.[2] Jeremiah describes this period
as a man going through pregnancy. It ends with *Yom YHWH* (or the Day of the Lord). These
horrible calamities can be avoided by accepting Jesus Christ as Savior now.

> Ask now, and see whether a man does travail with child? wherefore do I see every
> man with his hands on his loins, as a woman in travail, and all faces are turned into

paleness? Alas! for that day is great, so that none is like it: it is even the time of Jacob's trouble, but he shall be saved out of it (Jeremiah 30:6-7).

The Tribulation is a time of great suffering but also of mercy and grace. God could immediately send all unrepentant sinners to Hell but the world gets one last chance. Jesus Christ is still the open door. During the Tribulation, most people are deceived and follow the Antichrist but salvation is available. A remnant will repent of their sins and turn to God.

High Holy Days

Tishri	**Jewish Feast**	**Fulfillment**
1	*Yom Teruah*	Rapture
2	Feast of Trumpets	
3		
4		
5	*Yamim Noraim*	Tribulation
6	Days of Awe	
7	Days of Repentance	
8		
9		
10	*Yom Kippur* Day of Atonement	Second Coming

6. *Yom Kippur* (Atonement)

10th of *Tishri*—Israel's National Forgiveness

> Also on the tenth day of this seventh month there shall be a day of atonement: it shall be an holy convocation unto you; and you shall afflict your souls, and offer an offering made by fire unto the Lord (Leviticus 23:27).

Day of Atonement—Names and Themes[3]

- *Yom Kippur*: Day of Atonement, Sabbath of Sabbaths, The Day, The Great Day, The Fast, Face to Face
- *Yovel*: Jubilee, Day of Mercy, Day of Forgiveness, Day of Redemption, Day of Judgment
- *Shofar Hagadol*: Great Trumpet
- *Neilah*: Closing of the Gates

Yom Kippur or the Day of Atonement is on the 10th of *Tishri* (September/ October) and is the most sacred day in the Jewish calendar.[4] Three months earlier, the children of Israel worshipped the golden calf and were not ready to accept God's Law. For the forty days of *Teshuvah*, all of Israel prepared for this most holy day. Then Moses returned with the second set of the Ten Commandments. The children of Israel vowed to follow the Law and were reconciled to God.[5] This feast is all about the nation of Israel's relationship with God.

> But Aaron and his sons offered upon the altar of the burnt offering, and on the altar of incense, and were appointed for all the work of the place most holy, and to make an atonement for Israel, according to all that Moses the servant of God had commanded (1 Chronicles 6:49).

The Day of Atonement is the day of covering, canceling and pardoning sin.[6] It is a High Sabbath and the only feast day that is a national fast. It is a complete twenty-five-hour fast of food and drink. A bull and goat are sacrificed for a sin offering to forgive known sin and a ram is sacrificed for a burnt offering to forgive unknown sin and to worship God.[7] Animal sacrifices are valid when combined with a repentant heart. As the Feast of Trumpets is an opportunity to make amends for sins against other people, the Day of Atonement is about making amends with God. All unfulfilled vows to God are forgiven.

> And this shall be a statute for ever unto you: that in the seventh month, on the tenth day of the month, you shall afflict your souls, and do no work at all: For on that day shall the priest make an atonement for you, to cleanse you, that you may be clean from all your sins before the Lord (Leviticus 16:29-30).

Leviticus 16 describes the Day of Atonement. The High Priest has a ceremonial bath and changes from the traditional priestly garment to a plain white garment. He offers a bull for a sin offering and confesses his sins and the sins of his household. Then he casts lots for two goats. One goat is a sin offering and the other is the *azazel* or scapegoat.

The Day of Atonement is the only day that the High Priest enters the Jewish temple's Most Holy Place. Although face to face with God, the smoke of the incense obscures the Ark of the Covenant, so he does not die. He sprinkles the blood of the bull on the mercy seat. Back outside, the High Priest slaughters the goat as a sin offering for the people. He goes back into the temple's Most Holy Place and sprinkles the blood of the goat on the mercy seat and temple to make atonement for the people.

After leaving the temple, the High Priest sprinkles blood of the bull and goat on the altar. Then he lays his hands on the head of the scapegoat and confesses the sins of Israel. The goat is presented alive to the Lord. A man takes the scapegoat into the desert. So the scapegoat does not return, it is pushed off the edge of a cliff.[8] The High Priest bathes and changes into the traditional priestly garment. Then he sacrifices the ram as a burnt offering for himself and for the people.

> And Aaron shall lay both his hands upon the head of the live goat, and confess over him all the iniquities of the children of Israel, and all their transgressions in all their sins, putting them upon the head of the goat, and shall send him away by the hand of a fit man into the wilderness (Leviticus 16:21).

Many Jews go to the local synagogue for prayer services. *Neilah* or locked is the fifth and final prayer service on the Day of Atonement.[9] *Neilah* prayers are the last time to receive forgiveness from God. The afternoon service ends at nightfall with one single blast of the *Shofar Hagadol* or Great Trumpet.

Judgment Day

While the Day of Atonement is a day of mercy, forgiveness and redemption, it is also judgment day. On the Feast of Trumpets, the books and the gates of Heaven are opened and every person is judged. Ten days are given to repent and return to God. At the end of the Day of Atonement at the sound of the great trumpet, the books are sealed and the gates of Heaven are closed.[10] An individual's fate is sealed for the year.

Year of Jubilee

On the fiftieth year, the 10th of *Tishri* is the day of Jubilee.[11] All debts are canceled, all land is returned and all slaves are freed. The year of Jubilee is a Sabbath year.

And you shall hallow the fiftieth year, and proclaim liberty throughout all the land unto all the inhabitants thereof: it shall be a jubilee unto you; and you shall return every man unto his possession, and you shall return every man unto his family (Leviticus 25:10).

Atonement Prophecy

The Day of Atonement was partially fulfilled in Jesus Christ at Passover. He was the sacrifice who took the sins of the world. He was our substitute and our atonement. He is our High Priest, who took off His heavenly glory and put on lowly human form. When He died on the cross, He covered our sin with His blood and the veil that separated us from God was torn. Now no barrier exists between God and man. When we pray, we can come boldly into the presence of God the Father and our intercessor, Jesus Christ.

Neither by the blood of goats and calves, but by his own blood he entered in once into the holy place, having obtained eternal redemption for us (Hebrews 9:12).

Jesus Christ fulfills the Passover by His crucifixion in April. The Day of Atonement is a specific date in September/October. A future fulfillment still exists. As the Feast of Trumpets is the Rapture of the Church, the Day of Atonement is the restoration of Israel at the Second Coming of Jesus Christ.

The entire world gathers its armies at the valley of Megiddo in northern Israel. The armies begin their vicious slaughter of Israel. Over a month later on the Day of Atonement, the great *shofar* sounds. This time Jesus Christ rides on a white horse as a conquering king. He saves a remnant of Israel from immediate destruction and annihilates the armies of the Antichrist.

And he [Jesus Christ] shall send his angels with a great sound of a trumpet [*Shofar Hagadol*], and they shall gather together his elect from the four winds, from one end of heaven to the other (Matthew 24:31).

129

As High Priest, Jesus Christ steps on the Mount of Olives and walks through the eastern gate into the Jewish temple as King of Kings. The scapegoat is Satan. He is captured and exiled from humanity first bound for one thousand years and then thrown into the lake of fire for eternity.

> For I will gather all nations against Jerusalem to battle; and half of the city shall go forth into captivity, and the residue of the people shall not be cut off from the city. Then shall the Lord go forth, and fight against those nations, as when he fought in the day of battle. And his feet shall stand in that day upon the mount of Olives (Zechariah 14:2-4).

The purpose of the Day of Atonement is the redemption of Israel. They will look at their Messiah face to face whom they earlier rejected and crucified. They wail, repent and return to God. Then God forgives Israel of sin and accepts His beloved people. What a great day that will be.

> And I will pour upon the house of David, and upon the inhabitants of Jerusalem, the spirit of grace and of supplications: and they shall look upon me whom they have pierced, and they shall mourn for him, as one mourns for his only son, and shall be in bitterness for him, as one that is in bitterness for his firstborn (Zechariah 12:10).

The Day of Atonement at the Second Coming is the year of Jubilee. Israel's sins will be forgiven, all debts will be canceled, all slaves will be freed and the entire earth will be restored.

7. *Sukkot* (Tabernacles)

15th of *Tishri*—Dwell in Booths

> The fifteenth day of this seventh month shall be the feast of tabernacles for seven days unto the Lord. You shall dwell in booths seven days; all that are Israelites born shall dwell in booths (Leviticus 23:34, 42).

Feast of Tabernacles—Names and Themes[12]

- *Sukkot*: Booth or Tent
- *Zeman Simchatenu*: Season of Our Joy, The Feast, Wedding Supper
- *Hag Haasif*: Festival of Ingathering, Festival of Dedication, Festival of Lights, Feast of the Nations, Feast of the Lord
- *Hoshana Rabbah*: Great Hosannas

Sukkot (Sue-COAT) or the Feast of Tabernacles is a week-long celebration on the 15th to the 21st of *Tishri* (September/October).[13] One theme is the Wedding Supper. The Jews go from the most somber holy day to the most joyous festival. It is a feast of rest, thanksgiving and celebration. It is the last of three pilgrimages to Jerusalem.

The Feast of Tabernacles is *Hag Haasif* or the Festival of Ingathering.[14] *Sukkot* means booths. During this week-long harvest festival, the Jewish people live outside in booths made of palm, myrtle and willow branches. It reminds Israel of when God delivered them out of Egypt and provided for them in the wilderness.

God dwells with His people, first by cloud and fire and later in the tabernacle and temple. The entire Jewish culture was centered on worship at the tabernacle. It is the Feast of Dedication. The first Jewish temple was dedicated by King Solomon on this day. Besides living in booths for seven days, singing, dancing and praising God occurs. It is a season of joy and rejoicing.[15]

> And I will dwell among the children of Israel, and will be their God. And they shall know that I am the Lord their God, that brought them forth out of the land of Egypt, that I may dwell among them: I am the Lord their God (Exodus 29:45-46).

Sukkot Ceremony

Tabernacle is a feast of water and wind.[16] During the temple era, all priests participate in the *Sukkot* Ceremony. A third of priests carry twenty-five-feet long willow branches and march through the eastern gate. The willows make a sound of wind blowing through the leaves. A third of priests carry vessels of water and wine and march from the Pool of Siloam to the water gate in the south. Wind and water are symbols of the Spirit of God entering the temple and the wine is a symbol of joy. The word salvation is *Yeshua* or Jesus.

A flutist or pierced one signals the two groups to enter the temple gates as the Jews sing a song of salvation (*Yeshua* or Jesus) from Isaiah 12:3. The High Priest pours the water and wine onto the altar. Then priests with the willows circle the altar once and build a booth. The last third of priests offer sacrifices.

Therefore with joy shall you draw water out of the wells of salvation (Isaiah 12:3).

The Feast of Tabernacles is the Festival of Lights.[17] In the wilderness, the presence of God was seen as a pillar of fire at night. Four large golden candlesticks are placed on the corners of the seventy-five-foot walls of the court of women to illuminate the temple at night. The temple could be seen throughout Jerusalem.

And the Lord went before them by day in a pillar of a cloud, to lead them the way; and by night in a pillar of fire, to give them light; to go by day and night (Exodus 13:21).

Hosanna Rabbah or the Great Hosannas is on the 21st of *Tishri*, the last day of Tabernacles. During the *Sukkot* Ceremony, the priests carry the branches, circling the altar seven times while saying the Hosanna prayers.

Tabernacles Prophecy

Jesus Christ is the double fulfillment of the Feast of Tabernacles. First, Jesus Christ was born on Tabernacles. Matthew 1 says His name is Emanuel or God with us. Luke 2 describes Christ's birth as "good tidings of great joy which shall be to all people." Feast of Joy and Feast of the Nations are themes of this holy day.[18] John 1 says He is the true light who became flesh and dwells or tabernacles with us. Jesus is the light of the world, the living water, the pierced one and our salvation.

In the last day, that great day of the feast [of Tabernacles], Jesus stood and cried, saying, If any man thirst, let him come unto me, and drink. He that believes on me, as the scripture has said, out of his belly shall flow rivers of living water (John 7:37-38).

God Tabernacles with His People

- Tabernacle/Temple: God the Father dwells among His people.
- Gospels: God the Son dwells as man with His people.

- Church Age: God the Holy Spirit dwells within His people.
- Millennium: God the Son dwells as God with His people.

The second fulfillment of Tabernacles is the Millennium—the reign of Jesus Christ on earth. The Feast of Tabernacles is the week-long coronation of the King of Kings. As the presence of God was in the temple and the Holy Spirit is in us, Jesus Christ will again dwell with humanity. Our current life on earth is just temporary booths compared to the rooms in Heaven with God.

> Of the increase of his government and peace there shall be no end, upon the throne of David, and upon his kingdom, to order it, and to establish it with judgment and with justice from henceforth even for ever (Isaiah 9:7).

The Feast of Tabernacles is the seventh and final feast and points to the Sabbath rest. The day is also associated with God's future judgment of the nations. During the Millennium, all nations will go to Jerusalem to celebrate the birthday of the Messiah and anniversary of the reign of the King of Kings.

> And it shall come to pass, that every one that is left of all the nations which came against Jerusalem shall go up from year to year to worship the King, the Lord of hosts, and to keep the feast of tabernacles (Zechariah 14:16).

Shemini Atzeret & Simchat Torah

Two minor feasts occur after Tabernacles. *Shemini Atzeret* or the Eighth Day of the Assembly is on the 22nd of *Tishri* and is a High Sabbath day.[19] God tells His people to remain with Him an extra day. Jesus Christ was circumcised on *Shemini Atzeret*. God completes His seven thousand year plan for humanity then He begins again.

> On the eighth day shall be an holy convocation unto you; and you shall offer an offering made by fire unto the Lord: it is a solemn assembly; and you shall do no servile work therein (Leviticus 23:36).

Simchat Torah or Rejoicing with the *Torah* is on the 23rd of *Tishri*.[20] The annual cycle of studying the five Books of Moses concludes with Deuteronomy and begins again with Genesis. This day is fulfilled in the Word, Jesus Christ. As *Simchat Torah* begins the *Torah* study so we begin our new life with God.

God's Planned Return

The fall Jewish feasts are key prophecies to future Bible events. *Teshuvah* is the End Time period when the trumpets sound and people have an opportunity to repent of their sins and turn back to God. The hundredth and last trumpet blast of the *shofar* is when Christ raptures the Church and God focuses on the redemption of Israel. The Days of Awe are the seven years of the Tribulation but God still extends His grace and mercy to the world. The Day of Atonement is the Second Coming of Jesus Christ when Israel sees and accepts the Messiah. The Feast of Tabernacles is God with us. Unlike any other religion, God the Father, Son and Spirit choose to dwell with the children of God. We look forward to that future Feast of Tabernacles when Christ begins His eternal reign as King of Kings and Lord of Lords.

One Day
by John Wilber Chapman[21]

- Living, He loved me: *Hanukkah*/Conception, Tabernacles/Birth
- Dying, He saved me: Passover/Crucifixion
- Buried, He carried my sins far away: Unleavened Bread/Burial
- Rising He justified freely forever: Firstfruits/Resurrection
- One day He's coming: Trumpets/Rapture, Atonement/Second Coming
- Oh glorious day: Tabernacles/Coronation

Are you beginning to understand the importance of the seven Jewish feast days in God's time and plan?

Chapter 13

Minor Feasts, Major Events

S even Jewish feasts are seven days that God intervenes in the lives of humanity. The feasts of Passover, Unleavened Bread and Firstfruits were fulfilled in the death, burial and resurrection of Jesus Christ. On the Feast of Weeks, the Law was given to Israel and the Holy Spirit was given to the Church.

Three fall feasts are future. Trumpets, Atonement and Tabernacles are the Rapture of the Church, the Second Coming of Jesus Christ and the birthday and coronation of the King of Kings at the beginning of the Millennium.

Seven minor days are a part of God's time and plan. Significant historic events occur on these Jewish days. Feast and fast days reveal fulfilled prophetic events. Incredibly, Jewish holy days are directly linked to key events in American history. When we understand God's time, we understand our time.

Minor Feasts

Thus says the Lord of hosts; The fasts of the fourth month [17th of *Tammuz*], fifth month [9th of *Av*], seventh month [10th of *Tishri*] and tenth month [10th of *Tevet*] shall be to the house of Judah joy and gladness, and cheerful feasts (Zechariah 8:19).

1. 13th of *Nisan*—Fast of the Firstborn

On the 13th of *Nisan* (March/April), the firstborns remember their deliverance from the tenth plague of Egypt.[1]

2. 17th of *Tammuz*—Golden Calf

The 17th of *Tammuz* (June/July) is forty days after the feast of Weeks/Pentecost. Moses returned from Mt. Sinai, saw the children of Israel worshiping the golden calf and became so angry that he broke the stone tablets.[2]

> And it came to pass, as soon as he [Moses] came nigh unto the camp, that he saw the calf, and the dancing: and Moses' anger waxed hot, and he cast the tables out of his hands, and brake them beneath the mount (Exodus 32:19).

Babylon began their final attack against Jerusalem on the 9th of *Tammuz*. The Jewish Talmud states on the 17th of *Tammuz*, the walls were breached.[3] In 70 AD, Rome breached the walls of Jerusalem on this same day. In Jewish culture, this day begins a three-week period of mourning that ends on the 9th of *Av*.

3. 9th of *Av*—Kadesh Barnea Rebellion—Israeli Judgment Day

The first 9th of *Av* (July/August) is Israel's rebellion at Kadesh Barnea.[4] A year after God's miraculous deliverance from Egypt, twelve spies were sent into Canaan to explore the land forty days. The Hebrews had a choice to follow God's plan and take the Promised Land or believe the evil report and rebel against God. Because of a lack of faith, ten spies rebelled against God, discouraged the people and they all wander in the wilderness forty years. Observed as a fast day, it has become a day of God's judgment against Israel.[5]

> And Caleb stilled the people before Moses, and said, Let us go up at once, and possess it [the Promised Land]; for we are well able to overcome it. But the men that went up with him said, We are not able to go up against the people; for they are stronger than we (Numbers 13:30-31).

9th of *Av* in History[6]

1. Rebellion of the ten spies at Kadesh Barnea (1524 BC)
2. Destruction of the first Jewish temple by the Babylonians (587 BC)
3. Destruction of the second Jewish temple by the Romans (70 AD)
4. Roman army plowed Jerusalem with salt (71)
5. Romans defeated Simeon Bar Kochba's army (135)
6. Roman army plowed the temple mount (136)
7. Pope Urban II declared the First Crusade (1095)

8. King Edward I of England expelled the Jews (1290)
9. King Philip IV of France expelled the Jews (1306)
10. King Ferdinand II and Queen Isabella I of Spain expelled the Jews (1492)
11. More key events during the End Times

4. 25th of *Kislev*-3rd of *Tibet*—*Hanukkah*—Feast of Dedication

On the 15th of *Kislev*, 168 BC, the Greek Syrian king Antiochus IV, attacked Jerusalem.[7] His army caused the abomination of desolation by sacrificing a pig to Zeus on the altar of the Jewish temple. This starts another persecution of the Jewish people. Exactly 1150 days later on the 25th of *Kislev*, 165 BC, the Jews recaptured Jerusalem and rededicated the temple. The olive oil for the menorah in the temple miraculously lasts eight days.

Hanukkah (November/December) was fulfilled by the advent of the Messiah. While we celebrate the birth of Christ, on that day Mary conceived of the Holy Spirit and became pregnant with Jesus Christ, the light of the world.

> And, behold, you shall conceive in your womb, and bring forth a son, and shall call his name Jesus (Luke 1:31).

5. 10th of *Tevet*—Babylonian Siege of Judea

On the 10th of *Tevet* (December/January) in 588 BC, the Babylonians began their thirty-month war against Judah and Jerusalem.[8] On *Tammuz* 17, they breached the walls and on the 9th of *Av*, the Jewish temple is destroyed.

6. 13th of *Adar*—Fast of Esther

The 13th of *Adar* (February/March) is the Fast of Esther to remember God's deliverance from evil Haman.[9]

7. 14th-15th of *Adar*—*Purim*—Feast of Lots

The book of Esther is a story about God's deliverance of the Jewish people. After the exodus from Egypt, the Amalekites attacked the children of Israel in the wilderness.[10] Later, they were involved in God's judgment and King Saul's disobedience.[11]

During Ahasuerus' reign over Media-Persia, evil Haman the Amalekite plotted to kill the Jews. The lots were cast and *Adar* 14 (February/March) was chosen. However, God put Queen Esther and Mordecai in place "for such a time as this." God protected the Jews while their enemies, Haman and the Amalekites, were killed. *Purim* is a joyful day that celebrates the Jews' deliverance.

> They [Jews] should keep the fourteenth day of the month Adar, and the fifteenth day of the same, yearly, as the days when the Jews rested from their enemies, and the month which was turned from sorrow to joy (Esther 9:21-22).

Major Events

Seven Jewish feasts are seven days that God intervenes in the lives of humanity. An additional seven minor days are historic Jewish events. God gave to Moses seven days and about 1550 years later redemption through Jesus Christ was fulfilled on four days. Three days are fulfilled by His return.

In 2012, the Mayan calendar received plenty of talk about the end of the world but the Jewish calendar holds the key to recent history, prophetic events and our future. In the book *Chronology of Man*, Bill Bonnet lists Jewish historical events fulfilled on the 9th of *Av* (Kadesh Barnea).[12] These events include the destruction of the first and second temples, the First Crusade and the Holocaust. Jewish historical events occur on Jewish holy days.

Most prophecy teachers believe the United States is not in the Bible. However, there are over one hundred references to America by symbol, event, date or result of our actions. A few Scriptures tell of "all nations" but others are quite specific.

Look at history on the Jewish calendar. Amazing but true, key American and world events occur on Jewish holy days. Before the World Wars and Iraq Wars were super signs of the last days, God wrote history using Jewish feast and fast days.[13] God's time has a logical design.

1. Spanish Expulsion of Jews and the Voyage of Columbus

In 1492, King Ferdinand and Queen Isabella signed the Alhambra Decree that expelled Jews from Spain by July 31.[14] Beginning on August 2nd or the 9th of *Av* (Kadesh Barnea), Jews were forced to convert to Catholicism or die. On August 3, Christopher Columbus left Spain and reached the Bahamas on October 12, 1942 or the 21st of *Tishri* during Tabernacles.[15] Columbus was not the first person or even the first European to discover America but he started the widespread European colonization of the Americas and took the Gospel to the uttermost parts of the earth.

2. American Revolution

The United States declared independence on July 4, 1776 or the 17th of *Tammuz* which is the day of the golden calf.[16] Years later, the Babylonians and Romans breached the walls of Jerusalem. Historically, the United States has been a wall of protection for Israel but the wall has been breached and is about to fall. Since the United States was born on a Jewish holy day, what other important historic days fall on Jewish days?

The US Constitution was adopted on September 17, 1787 or the 5th of *Tishri*.[17] This is the third day of *Yamim Noraim* or the Days of Awe (Tribulation).

3. Turn of the Twentieth Century

US President William McKinley was shot by an assassin in Buffalo, New York, on September 6, 1901 or the 23rd of *Elul* during *Teshuvah* (9/11).[18] He died on September 14 or the 1st of *Tishri*. Theodore Roosevelt was president on the Feast of Trumpets marking the turn to the twentieth century. This began the Laodicean period of the Church Age and key events of the End Times.

The *Titanic* voyage began on April 10, 1912 or the 21st of *Nisan* during Unleavened Bread.[19] The *Titanic* marked the transfer of power from Europe to the United States.

4. World War I

Germany declared war on France and Russia and World War I began on August 1, 1914 which is the 9th of *Av* (Kadesh Barnea).[20] Israel's day of judgment has become a day of judgment for the world.

British General Edmund Allenby captured Jerusalem on December 9, 1918.[21] Two days later on the 25th of *Kislev* (*Hanukkah*), he walked into Jerusalem in honor of the Holy City. After World War I, the League of Nations divided the Ottoman Empire. The United Kingdom ruled Palestine on September 26, 1923 or the 16th of *Tishri* during the Feast of Tabernacles.[22]

5. World War II

The Munich Agreement was signed on September 30, 1938 or the 5th of *Tishri*. This is the third day of *Yamim Noraim* or the Days of Awe (Tribulation).[23] Germany annexed the Czech territory of the Sudetenland on October 10, 1938 or the 15th of *Tishri*, the first day of Tabernacles.

World War II began when Germany invaded Poland on September 1, 1939 or the 17th of *Elul* during *Teshuvah*.[24] The Germans implemented the "Final Solution to the Jewish Question." Severe Jewish persecution escalated into the Holocaust on July 22, 1942 or the 9th of *Av* (Kadesh Barnea). On that day, the first 6,500 Jews were transported from Warsaw, Poland to the Treblinka extermination camp.[25] World War II ended with the bombing of Nagasaki on August 9, 1945 or the 1st of *Elul* during *Teshuvah*.[26] Moses returned to Mt. Sinai for the second tablets.

Nuremberg verdicts were announced on October 1, 1946 or *Tishri* 7 during *Yamin Noraim* (Days of Awe/Tribulation).[27] Defendants were executed on October 16, 1946 or the 21st of *Tishri*, the last day of Tabernacles.

6. Israel and Jerusalem

After two thousand years, Israel became an independent nation on May 14, 1948 or the 5th of *Iyar*. Jerusalem was the undivided capital on June 7, 1967 or the 28th of *Iyar*.[28] Although not an American date, Jerusalem Day is forty days after the resurrection when Jesus Christ ascended into Heaven.

7. Cold War

During the Cold War, the Cuban Missile Crisis was the closest that the world has come to a nuclear war. The United States military collected the first photographic evidence of forty-two Soviet nuclear missiles based in Cuba on the early morning of October 14, 1962 or the 16th of *Tishri* (Tabernacles).[29]

On April 26, 1986, in the Ukrainian territory of the Soviet Union, the Chernobyl nuclear reactor exploded.[30] The nuclear fallout spread throughout Europe and Western Asia. The disaster occurred on the 17th of *Nisan* during Unleavened Bread.

8. Iraq War I

The Persian Gulf War (Iraq War I) started on August 2, 1990 with Iraq's invasion of Kuwait.[31] However, negotiations between Iraq and Kuwait failed on July 31, 1990 or the 9th of *Av* (Kadesh Barnea). Iraq War I ended on February 28, 1991 or the 14th of *Adar* (*Purim*).

9. War on Islamic Terrorism

On September 11, 2001, Al-Qaeda Islamic terrorists hijacked four large commercial passenger airplanes and crashed them into the World Trade Center in New York City, the Pentagon in Arlington, Virginia and a field near Shanksville, Pennsylvania.[32] The 9/11 attack occurred the 23rd of *Elul* during *Teshuvah*. This event marked the turn of the twenty-first century as power transferred from the United States back to Europe.

10. Afghanistan War

In response to 9/11, on October 7, 2001 or 21st of *Tishri*, the last day of Tabernacles, the United States began the Afghanistan War against Osama bin Laden, Al-Qaeda and the Taliban government.[33]

11. Quartet on the Middle East

On July, 16, 2002 or the day before the 9th of *Av* (Kadesh Barnea), the Quartet on the Middle East (European Union, Russia, United Nations, United States) announced the Roadmap for Peace, a two-state solution to resolve the Israeli-Palestinian conflict.[34]

In August 2005, the Quartet pressured Israel to evacuate the remaining twenty-one settlements from the Gaza Strip and four settlements in Judea and Samaria (West Bank).[35] On August 13, 2005 or the 9th of *Av* (Kadesh Barnea), Tropical Depression Ten formed and then dissipated. On August 23, remnants of that storm developed into Tropical Depression Twelve.[36] Hurricane Katrina crossed south Florida and then devastated the upper gulf coast of Alabama, Louisiana and Mississippi. When America cursed Israel, God judged America.

> I will gather all nations and bring them down to the Valley of Jehoshaphat [in Jerusalem]. There I will enter into judgment against them concerning my

Jewish Calendar
Fulfilled in Our Time

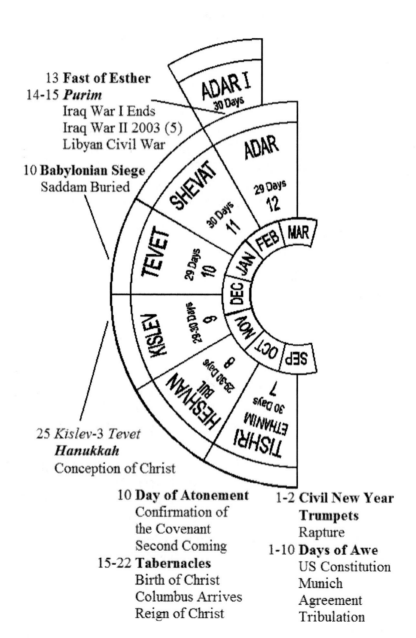

13 **Fast of Esther**
14-15 *Purim*
    Iraq War I Ends
    Iraq War II 2003 (5)
    Libyan Civil War

10 **Babylonian Siege**
    Saddam Buried

25 *Kislev-3 Tevet*
Hanukkah
Conception of Christ

10 **Day of Atonement**
    Confirmation of
    the Covenant
    Second Coming
15-22 **Tabernacles**
    Birth of Christ
    Columbus Arrives
    Reign of Christ

1-2 **Civil New Year**
    Trumpets
    Rapture
1-10 **Days of Awe**
    US Constitution
    Munich
    Agreement
    Tribulation

Jewish Calendar
Fulfilled in Our Time

1 **Religious New Year**
  10 **Lamb Chosen**   Antichrist Reigns
   13 **Fast of the Firstborn** Great Tribulation
   14 **Passover**   Crucifixion
    15-21 **Unleavened Bread** Burial
    16 **Firstfruits**   Resurrection

Chernobyl 1986 (3)
Iraq War III Ends
Russian-Islamic War

5 **Israeli Independence Day** 1948
  28 **Jerusalem Day** 1967
   Ascension
6 **Weeks/Pentecost**
  Law Given
  Holy Spirit Given
  Star of Bethlehem
   6 *Sivan*-17 *Tammuz*
   1st 40 Days on Sinai

17 **Golden Calf**
   Babylonians Breach Jerusalem
   Romans Breach Jerusalem
   United States 1776

9 **Kadesh Barnea Rebellion**
  Babylonians Destroy Temple
  Romans Destroy Temple
  Crusades 1095
  World War I 1914 (1)
  World War II Holocaust
  Iraq War I 1990 (4)
  Hurricane Katrina
  Iraq War III 20?? (6)
  Armageddon 20?? (7)

    ( ) 7 Trumpets Begin[47]

1 *Elul*-10 *Tishri*
2nd 40 Days on Sinai
Teshuvah
World War II 1939 (2)
Nagasaki
September 11, 2001
Iraq War II Ends

inheritance, my people Israel, for they scattered my people among the nations and divided up my land. (Joel 3:2 NIV).

12. Iraq War II

Exactly twelve years and one day after Iraq War I ended, Iraq War II began on March 19, 2003.[37] Both days are during the Feast of *Purim*.[38] Saddam Hussein was a type of evil Haman. Although they plotted to kill the Jews, both were hanged and their sons were killed. Saddam was executed on December 30, 2006 and buried on December 31 or the 10th of *Tevet*. On that day, ancient Babylon began the thirty-month siege of Judah and Jerusalem. The last American combat brigade left Iraq ending the war on September 19, 2010 or the 9th of *Elul* during *Teshuvah*.

13. Libya Civil War

International intervention began in the Libyan Civil War on March 19, 2011 or the 14th of *Adar* during *Purim*.[39] Muammar Gaddafi was captured and executed on October 20, 2011 or the 22nd of *Tishri* on *Shemini Atzeret* or the Eighth Day of the Assembly after Tabernacles. Eight is completion. Libya is part of the Russian-Islamic War (Gog and Magog) during the Great Tribulation which completes man's rule on earth.[40]

Unlike the Mayan calendar, the Jewish calendar is a guide for future events and the end of humanity's rule of the world.

14. Iraq War III

In the future, the Quartet will propose a treaty that transfers Judea and Samaria (West Bank) from Israel to Palestine.[41] This covenant will cause the fall of the United States and the Tribulation. Like World War I and Iraq War I, World War III/Iraq War III may begin on the 9th of *Av* (Kadesh Barnea).

15. Rapture and Tribulation

About fifty days later, the Rapture will occur on the 1st of *Tishri* (Trumpets) in September or October. This is more of a rescue mission as we are "caught up" near the start of World War III. The Tribulation will begin on the 10th of *Tishri* (Day of Atonement). The Antichrist will confirm the Israel-Palestine treaty proposed by the Quartet.[42]

Three and a half years later, the Great Tribulation begins on the 10th of *Nisan* in March or April when the Antichrist begins his reign.[43] Two Jewish witnesses will be killed on Passover and then resurrected three days later on Firstfruits.[44] Iraq War III will end during Unleavened Bread.[45] Soon afterward, the Russian-Islamic War follows when Russia, Iran, Libya and other militant Islamic nations invade Israel.[46] Those in Judea and Samaria (West Bank) must flee because they are in Palestine.

16. Armageddon, Second Coming and Millennium

Three years later, Armageddon may begin on the 9th of *Av* (Kadesh Barnea) or 1st of *Elul* (*Teshuvah*) and end on the 10th of *Tishri* (Atonement) at the Second Coming of Jesus Christ. The Millennium reign over all nations begins on the 15th of *Tishri* (Tabernacles).

Are these historic events on holy days just random coincidence or do they reveal the character and nature of a sovereign God? This is not an American centered world but a God centered universe. He fulfills His plan in His time. The Jewish feast and fast days began as historic and religious days yet became prophetic days in the life of Jesus Christ and are now being fulfilled in the major events of End Time prophecy.

Is the United States in the Bible? Like the Greeks and Romans before us and the Antichrist after us, America is described from beginning to end. As the only superpower, we help prepare the world and cause the Tribulation. The trumpets are sounding and God is warning His people and the world. Many of these dates have a Bible passage that describes fulfilled prophecies. These ancient Jewish days become super signs of the End Times.

God's Time in Our Time

The Jewish feasts and fast days have becomes the foundation of our Christian faith. Jesus Christ was conceived, born, died, buried and resurrected on key Jewish holy days. The Law and the Holy Spirit were given on the same day. The Rapture, Second Coming and coronation of the King are future Jewish days. About 3500 years ago, God gave to Moses prophetic days that correspond to United States history. Super signs such as the World Wars, Iraq Wars and End Wars occur on Jewish days. God's time is fulfilled in our time.

If key American historic events follow Jewish holy days, what else does the Bible tell us about the United States and the world during the End Times?

Chapter 14

Israel's Time Out

With any parent/child relationship, a parent must give a balance of love and discipline. God, our Father, set up boundaries to protect us as we grow in our relationship with Him. Psalm 23 says, "The Lord is my shepherd" and "thy rod and thy staff they comfort me." God uses the staff to bring us gently back and He uses the rod for a bit stronger discipline.

God's Plan for Israel

Israel reveals God's time and plan. He gave blessings when they follow and trials to test their faith. Because of sin, He gave correction. God is not waiting to zap us with a bolt of lightning but to restore us gently. When Israel refused, God gave them a time out.

1. **Egypt and Slavery**

   God chose Abraham, Isaac, Jacob and their descendants to give His Word and bring the world salvation through the promised Messiah. First, He gave Israel a time out. They were in Egypt for 215 years but slaves about 120 years.[1] Despite oppression, the people grew from 70 to 603,550 adult men.[2] God's plan was to make Israel prosper into a great nation.

   > And the children of Israel were fruitful, and increased abundantly, and multiplied, and waxed exceeding mighty; and the land was filled with them (Exodus 1:7).

2. **Exodus and the Wilderness**

   After the ten plagues of Egypt, God miraculously freed the Israelites from captivity. With the Red Sea, He destroyed the Egyptian army. Still, the children of Israel did not trust God. First, was the golden calf and a year later was Kadesh Barnea.

God had a land flowing with milk and honey ready for the taking but the Hebrews rebelled against God's plan.[3] The people believed ten fearful witnesses instead of two faithful witnesses. They did not trust God but rather feared giants. God gave them a forty-year time out. Only Joshua, Caleb and those under twenty entered the land.

> They [spies] discouraged the heart of the children of Israel, that they should not go into the land which the Lord had given them. And the Lord's anger was kindled against Israel, and he made them wander in the wilderness forty years, until all the generation, that had done evil in the sight of the Lord, was consumed (Numbers 32:9, 13).

3. Judges and Judgment

God commanded Israel to worship God and completely remove foreigners and their gods from the land. During the judges, Israel failed to obey God. He allowed Israel to be persecuted and conquered by their neighbors until they repented and turned back to God. This cycle of sin, judgment, repentance and restoration happened for another six time outs.

> They forsook the Lord God of their fathers, which brought them out of the land of Egypt, and followed other gods, of the gods of the people that were round about them, and bowed themselves unto them, and provoked the Lord to anger (Judges 2:12).

4. Kings and Captivity

When good kings followed God, they broke down altars to Baal, cut down Ashtoreth poles and led the people in worshipping God. But when evil kings ruled, they abandoned God to worship idols. After a while, God had enough. By 716 BC, the northern kingdom of Israel was conquered by King Shalmaneser V of Assyria.[4] In 587 BC, the southern kingdom of Judah was conquered by King Nebuchadnezzar of Babylon.[5] Judah was in captivity seventy years.

> Because you have not heard my words, Behold, I will send and take all the families of the north, says the Lord, and Nebuchadnezzar the king of Babylon, my servant, and will bring them against this land and against all these nations round about, and will utterly destroy them. And these nations shall serve the king of Babylon seventy years (Jeremiah 25:8-9, 11).

5. Intertestamental Period

In the four hundred years between Old and New Testaments, God worked with Judah to prepare for the Messiah. Babylon, Media-Persia, Greece and Rome rule Israel.[6] In 168 BC, Antiochus IV of Greek Syria persecuted the Jews and it escalated into revolt.[7] By 141 BC, the Maccabees won self-rule and in 110 BC, gained independence.[8] For seventy-eight years, High Priests ruled the Hasmonean Kingdom. During this time, two religious sects clashed: Pharisees and Sadducees.

> Then Jesus said unto them, Take heed and beware of the leaven of the Pharisees and of the Sadducees (Matthew 16:6).

The Pharisees educated the Jewish people in the Law at the synagogue.[9] They accepted the Hebrew Scripture. Beyond 613 rules of the Law, they added oral traditions that were burdensome to Jewish life. Focusing on works, they kept the Law to get to God. Being self-righteous, no need existed for a redeeming messiah. The Pharisees desired a political messiah to overthrow the Romans. They rejected Jesus Christ because He claimed to be God but He did not follow their interpretation of the Law.

They bribed Rome better than the Pharisees and were appointed High Priests.[10] They accepted the five books of Moses but rejected the rest of Hebrew Scripture, oral traditions, prophecies of the Messiah and resurrection of the dead. They followed the Law to get to God. Being more like deists, God was Creator and Lawgiver but not so personally involved to send a messiah. The Sadducees rejected Jesus Christ because He did not fit their religious beliefs. They feared Him because the crowds could destabilize Judea and Rome would remove their power.

The Sanhedrin was Israel's political and religious congress initiated by Moses.[11] A High Priest led the group of seventy elders. At the time of Jesus Christ, the Sadducees held the majority while the Pharisees were in the minority.

Israel's Hasmonean Kingdom failed because of conflicts over priestly succession by Pharisees and Sadducees that led to a religious civil war. Judea became a protectorate of Rome in 63 BC and the Hasmonean dynasty ended in 41 BC with the appointment of Herod the Great.[12]

> From that time forth began Jesus to show unto his disciples, how that he must go unto Jerusalem, and suffer many things of the elders [Sanhedrin] and

chief priests [Sadducees] and scribes [Pharisees], and be killed, and be raised again the third day (Matthew 16:21).

6. Messiah's Rejection

God sent His only Son, Jesus Christ, to redeem the world. The Sanhedrin, Pharisees and Sadducees rejected their promised Messiah and crucified Him. This time Israel was scattered throughout the world. God turned to the Gentiles to spread the Gospel. There are 1878 years between the destruction of the second temple in 70 AD and the creation of the nation of Israel in 1948. About 1985 years have passed since the cross.

O Jerusalem, Jerusalem, you that kill the prophets, and stone them which are sent unto you, how often would I have gathered your children together, even as a hen gathers her chickens under her wings, and you would not! Behold, your house is left unto you desolate (Matthew 23:37-38).

7. Israel's Repentance and Restoration

Despite Israel's history of disobedience, God is faithful. He keeps His promises to His people. God restored the nation and returned the Jews home. Israel is not rejected but is back in their land with no more time outs.

Behold, I will take the children of Israel from among the heathen, and will gather them on every side, and bring them into their own land: And I will make them one nation in the land upon the mountains of Israel; and one king shall be king to them all. I will save them out of all their dwelling places, wherein they have sinned, and will cleanse them: so shall they be my people, and I will be their God (Ezekiel 37:21-23).

Israel's Time Outs

- Egypt: 215 Years (Genesis 47:9, Exodus 1:6-8)
- Wilderness: 40 Years (Numbers 14:32-34)
- Mesopotamia: 8 Years (Judges 3:7-8)
- Moab: 18 Years (Judges 3:12-14)
- Canaan: 20 Years (Judges 4:1-3)
- Midian: 7 Years (Judges 6:1-6)
- Philistia & Ammon: 18 Years (Judges 10:6-8)

- Philistia: 40 Years (Judges 13:1)
- Babylon/Media-Persia: 70 Years (Jeremiah 25:6-11)
- Diaspora: 1878 Years (Matthew 23:37-39)

Prophecy Postponed

Detours have occurred because of Israel's disobedience, and delays because of God's plan. A gap occurs between Jesus Christ's First Coming and His Second Coming. Sometimes prophecy is postponed but God is still at work on His plan with His people.

1. People of Time

In God's timing, detours and delays occur. Sometimes they are a direct result of our sin and we need correction. Other times, God schedules times of trials to mature us so we can move to the next step in our relationship and ministry. Some delays are not related to our circumstances as He demonstrates His longsuffering to the world. God waits to complete His plan according to His perfect time.

God has a specific time for His people. He gave Noah and the world 120 years of warning before the flood. Abraham was seventy-five before God called him to Canaan and was one hundred before He gave his son, Isaac. Joseph was seventeen when God revealed his future but waited thirteen years to become second to Pharaoh in Egypt. Moses lived forty years in Pharaoh's palace and forty years in the wilderness before he was ready to lead the children of Israel. David is anointed king but then tested before he became king of Judah and finally Israel. Elijah waited three years to confront King Ahab and the priests of Baal. Jonah chose his detour and his time out was in a great fish. Daniel was taken captive to Babylon but God used him in the palaces of the kings.

God has a specific time for New Testament believers. It took fifty days to restore Peter before he led the Church at Pentecost. Paul was educated in Tarsus and the desert before God sent him as a missionary to the Gentiles. Even though Paul was in God's will following God's plan, he was persecuted and imprisoned, which caused many delays. John did not write the book of Revelation until he was imprisoned at Patmos. Only Mary saw God work early in her young life when she became the mother of Jesus Christ. In God's will, important delays occur.

Now all these things happened unto them for examples: and they are written for our admonition, upon whom the ends of the world are come (1 Corinthians 10:11).

2. Prophecy of Time

In prophecy, delays and detours also occur. God gave the prophets news about the present and future.[13] If it was for the future, the prophets may not understand the prophecy given. These prophecies cover the Old Testament, Church Age, End Times, Tribulation, Millennium and beyond. There is a "now and not yet" timeframe as single passages describe multiple periods. Without a thorough Bible study, it is easy to miss the timing.

But blessed are your eyes, for they see: and your ears, for they hear. For verily I say unto you, That many prophets and righteous men have desired to see those things which you see, and have not seen them; and to hear those things which you hear, and have not heard them (Matthew 13:16-17).

Mountain Peaks of Prophecy[14]

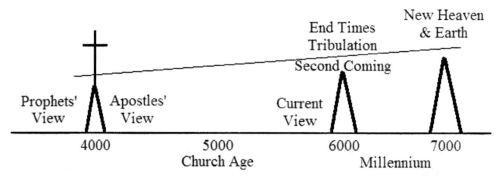

Prophecy does not tell all details of the future, only key events. The Old Testament prophets saw prophecies as mountain peaks. They did not see the valleys or understand the timing. The apostles saw the life of Christ in full view and a glimpse of the Church Age. When looking back, we have 20/20 hindsight. When we interpret Scripture correctly, we clearly see future prophecies in light of history and fulfilled prophecies.

3. Periods of Time

Although all humanity has the same salvation through Jesus Christ, a progressive reve-lation occurs. God deals with people differently in each age and He reveals His plan of salvation step-by-step. This is called dispensationalism.[15] In Genesis 3, God told Adam and Eve of a future Messiah but He required the sacrifice of lambs. In Genesis 12, God chose Abraham to be the father of a nation who brought salvation. By Exodus 20, Israel was given the Law. After the finished work of redemption, the Gentiles were included without animal sacrifices. In each successive age, God's plan is made clearer.

Bible Dispensations[16]

Scripture	Dispensation	Begins	Judgment
Genesis 2	Innocence	Adam	Curse of Sin
Genesis 3	Conscience	Fall	Flood
Genesis 8	Nations	Tower of Babel	Many Languages
Genesis 12	Promise	Abraham	Captive in Egypt
Exodus 20	Law	Exodus	Dispersion of Israel
Acts 2	Grace/Church	Pentecost	Tribulation
Revelation 20	Millennium	Reign of Christ	Final Rebellion

4. Passages of Time

Sometimes Scripture is not sequential. Genesis 12-50 tells the lives of Abraham, Isaac, Jacob and Joseph but their lives overlap. Daniel chapters 7 and 8 are before Daniel 5. In Luke 4, Jesus Christ reads Isaiah 61:1-2 and stops. Part of the passage was fulfilled at the First Coming and the rest deals with His Second Coming. In Matthew 24, Jesus referred to the End Times, Rapture, Tribulation and Second Coming but not in order. Most of Revelation is in sequence but the seals, trumpets and bowls overlap. It is important to put events in sequential order to understand the prophecy timeline.

Periods of Prophecy[17]

- Genesis 3:16: First Coming, Second Coming
- Leviticus 23: First Coming, Church Age, End Times, Second Coming, Millennium
- Isaiah 61:1-4: First Coming, Second Coming
- Isaiah 65: Millennium, New Heaven & Earth
- Ezekiel 36-39: End Times, Tribulation, Second Coming
- Daniel 2: Ancient History, End Times, Second Coming
- Daniel 7: End Times, Tribulation, Second Coming, Millennium

- Daniel 9: Ancient History, First Coming, Tribulation
- Daniel 11: Ancient History, Tribulation, Second Coming
- Matthew 24: Church Age, End Times, Tribulation, Second Coming
- John 3:16: First Coming, Second Coming
- Revelation: Church Age, End Times, Tribulation, Second Coming, Millennium, New Heaven & Earth

With a proper understanding of Scripture and timing, we can distinguish between God's plan for Israel and the Church, Rapture and Second Coming and events before or during the Tribulation.

Detours and Delays

Written into the seven thousand year plan of God are many gaps in time. Israel had detours and delays during Egypt, the wilderness, judges and Babylonian captivity. The prophets predicted the people would reject Jesus Christ. The redemption of humanity was always a part of God's original plan. The kingdom follows the Messiah's coming but because the Jews rejected their Messiah, the Church Age fills in the gap before God's kingdom on earth.

God is always at work with His people. Even through many detours and delays, God is sovereign. He knows what is going to happen and when. We have a free will but there is no "Plan B." There is only "Plan A."[18] God uses our successes and failures to prepare us for His purpose. As His people, we have the opportunity to be a part of His plan or sit in the corner for another time out until we are ready to follow Him and get to work.

Despite your detours and delays, do you turn back to God and follow Him?

Chapter 15

Daniel's Seventy Weeks

Creation, the Jewish feasts and Israel's history tell of God's timing. But no study of God's time can be complete without the seventy weeks of Daniel. God's time for the Messiah's First and Second Coming is revealed.

Daniel's Prayer

> In the first year of his [Darius] reign I Daniel understood by books the number of the years, whereof the word of the Lord came to Jeremiah the prophet, that he would accomplish seventy years in the desolations of Jerusalem. And I set my face unto the Lord God, to seek by prayer and supplications, with fasting, and sackcloth, and ashes (Daniel 9:2-3).

In 605 BC, Daniel was taken in the first round of Babylonian captivity and in 587 BC, Jerusalem fell. In 538 BC, Cyrus the Great of Media-Persia conquered Babylon.[1] Now in 515 BC, Daniel understood the end of the seventy years of Jewish captivity.[2] Although God is sovereign, we still pray, "Thy kingdom come, Thy will be done."[3]

> For thus said the Lord, That after seventy years be accomplished at Babylon I will visit you, and perform my good word toward you, in causing you to return to this place (Jeremiah 29:10).

Daniel's understanding of prophecy required action. With fasting, sackcloth and ashes, Daniel humbled himself and did some serious praying. He acknowledged his sovereign God of justice and mercy.[4] Daniel saw himself and his people as disobedient and forsaking God. Because they worshipped idols, God judged by the Law.[5] Daniel pleaded for mercy and appealed to God's honor by reminding Him of His city, Jerusalem.

At the beginning of your supplications the commandment came forth, and I [Gabriel] am come to show you; for you are greatly beloved: therefore understand the matter, and consider the vision (Daniel 9:23).

When Daniel prayed, the answer was given immediately. Gabriel, the Good News angel, appeared to him. Daniel was praying about the end of Babylon captivity and the restoration of Jerusalem but God told Daniel about His complete plan for Israel and humanity through Jesus the Messiah's redemptions and reign.

God's Plan

Seventy weeks are determined upon your people and upon your holy city, to finish the transgression, and to make an end of sins, and to make reconciliation for iniquity, and to bring in everlasting righteousness, and to seal up the vision and prophecy, and to anoint the most Holy [Place] (Daniel 9:24).

Within 490 years, God will restore Israel with His six-point plan. What begins with the redemption of humanity with the First Coming will be completed by the restoration of Israel and the establishment of the Kingdom at the Second Coming.

1. To Finish the Transgression

The root of all transgression is rebellion against God.[6] Adam broke God's law but Jesus Christ made salvation available by His sacrifice. Finishing the transgression was to restrain sin.[7] For six thousand years, sin runs rampant but at the Second Coming when Jesus Christ returns, He will stop the rebellion of humanity and restrain sin with an iron rod.

But he was wounded for our transgressions, he was bruised for our iniquities: the chastisement of our peace was upon him; and with his stripes we are healed (Isaiah 53:5).

2. To Make an End of Sins

After Israel's rebellion ends, Satan is captured. The curse of Adam's sin will be removed.[8] The world will again live in harmony with God.

The wolf and the lamb shall feed together, and the lion shall eat straw like the bull: and dust shall be the serpent's meat. They shall not hurt nor destroy in all my holy mountain, said the Lord (Isaiah 65:25).

3. To Make Reconciliation for Iniquity

Reconciliation is cover or atonement.[9] God sent Jesus Christ to reconcile the world. Israel's final reconciliation is the Day of Atonement at Jesus Christ's Second Coming.

For if, when we were enemies, we were reconciled to God by the death of his Son, much more, being reconciled, we shall be saved by his life (Romans 5:10).

4. To Bring in Everlasting Righteousness

The end of man's six thousand year reign of sin on earth is the beginning of Christ's eternal reign of righteousness. After Satan is bound, humanity can have a right relationship with God.

Behold, the days come, said the Lord, that I will raise unto David a righteous Branch, and a King shall reign and prosper, and shall execute judgment and justice in the earth (Jeremiah 23:5).

5. To Seal up the Vision and Prophecy

All prophecy dealing with Israel will be completely fulfilled. When Jesus Christ was on the earth, no need existed for an intermediary prophet. When He returns, we will receive the Word of God directly from Jesus Christ.

God, who at sundry times and in diverse manners spoke in time past unto the fathers by the prophets, Has in these last days spoken unto us by his Son, whom he has appointed heir of all things, by whom also he made the worlds (Hebrews 1:1-2).

6. To Anoint the Most Holy Place

This phrase refers to a place and not a person.[10] The Most Holy Place is the inner room of the temple that held the ark and the presence of God. During Christ's Second Coming, He will fulfill the Day of Atonement by entering the third Jewish temple's Most Holy Place.

Neither by the blood of goats and calves, but by his [Jesus Christ] own blood he entered in once into the holy place, having obtained eternal redemption for us (Hebrews 9:12).

To fulfill these six prophecies requires Jesus Christ to redeem the world, restore Israel, bind Satan, judge the world, remove the curse of sin and set up His kingdom on earth. Stopping at the cross leaves God's plan unfinished.

Seventy Weeks of Daniel

There are three periods of "sevens" that God implements in His six-point plan for Israel. Known as weeks, these are actually seventy Sabbaths of seven years.

Seventy Weeks

- 7 X 7 (49 Years): Command to Build Jerusalem to Jerusalem Built
- 62 X 7 (483 Years): Jerusalem Built to Messiah Cut Off
- 1 X 7 (7 Years): Confirm a Covenant to End of Seven Years

First Part—Seven Weeks + Sixty-Two Week

Know therefore and understand, that from the going forth of the commandment to restore and to build Jerusalem unto the Messiah the Prince shall be seven weeks, and sixty-two weeks: the street shall be built again, and the wall, even in troublesome times (Daniel 9:25).

Beginning Point—The Decrees

Time started with the command to restore and rebuild Jerusalem. Six possible decrees could begin these seventy weeks.

1. Nebuchadnezzar—Capture of Jerusalem—587 BC

And in the fifth month [*Av*], on the seventh day of the month, which is the nineteenth year of king Nebuchadnezzar king of Babylon, came Nebuzaradan, captain of the guard, unto Jerusalem. And he burnt the house of the Lord, and the king's house. (2 Kings 25:8-9).

In 587, Nebuchadnezzar of Babylon captured Jerusalem. The temple burned on the 9th of *Av* (Kadesh Barnea).[11]

2. Cyrus—Build the Temple—538 BC

Thus said Cyrus king of Persia, The Lord God of heaven has given me all the kingdoms of the earth; and he has charged me to build him a house at Jerusalem, which is in Judah (Ezra 1:2).

In 538 BC, Cyrus of Media-Persia decreed the building of the temple in Jerusalem. Ezra the prophet, Zerubbable the governor of Judea and Joshua the High Priest led a "mini exodus" of about 42,360 heads of households to Jerusalem to build the temple.[12]

3. Darius—Reauthorization to Build the Temple—519 BC

Let the work of this house of God alone; let the governor of the Jews and the elders of the Jews build this house of God in his place (Ezra 6:7).

During Cyrus, the temple was started but opposition halted construction. Now twenty years later, Darius was king and Haggai the prophet encouraged the people to finish the temple. Tattenai, governor of Trans-Euphrates, questioned their authority. After Cyrus's decree was found, Darius reauthorized the decree to build the temple. In 517 BC, the seventy years desolation of Jerusalem ended and the temple was completed in 515 BC.[13]

4. Artaxerxes—Stop Work—~463 BC

Give now commandment to cause these men to cease, and that this city be not built, until another commandment shall be given from me (Ezra 4:21).

At the beginning of Artaxerxes' reign, opposition in rebuilding Jerusalem occurred.[14] Syrians complained about a false Jewish conspiracy to rebel against Media-Persian control.[15] Artaxerxes issued a stop work order for Jerusalem.

5. Artaxerxes—Return to Israel—457 BC

> I [Artaxerxes] make a decree, that all they of the people of Israel, and of his priests and Levites, in my realm, which are minded of their own freewill to go up to Jerusalem, go with you [Ezra] (Ezra 7:13).

In 457 BC, the seventh year of his reign, Artaxerxes issued a decree that the Jewish people could return to Judea. Ezra led 1496 heads of households with their families back to Jerusalem.[16] Unlike the exodus out of Egypt, many Jews chose to stay in Babylon.

6. Artaxerxes—Rebuild Jerusalem—444 BC

> I [Nehemiah] said unto the king [Artaxerxes], If it please the king, and if your servant has found favor in your sight, that you would send me to Judah, unto the city of my fathers' sepulchers, that I may build Jerusalem. And the king granted me, according to the good hand of my God upon me (Nehemiah 2:5, 8).

In the twentieth years of Artaxerxes, Nehemiah requested permission to rebuild the city of Jerusalem. The king agreed and supplied building materials.

Ending Point—The Messiah

> And after sixty-two weeks shall Messiah be cut off, but not for himself (Daniel 9:26).

The ending point is "Messiah the Prince." The Messiah in Hebrew and Christ in Greek is the Anointed One.[17] There are five possible ending points of the decrees. After the sixty-nine weeks, the Messiah was crucified.

- Birth of Christ in Bethlehem (Luke 2:1-7)
- Baptism of Christ in the Jordan River (Matthew 3:13-17, Mark 1:9-11, Luke 3:21-22)
- Transfiguration of Christ on a Mountain (Matthew 17:1-9, Mark 9:2-9, Luke 9:28-36)
- Triumphal Entry into Jerusalem (Matthew 21:1-11, Mark 11:1-10, Luke 19:28-40, John 12:12-16)
- Destruction of the Jewish Temple in Jerusalem (Matthew 24:1-2)

Most Bible scholars point to the baptism or Triumphal Entry of Jesus Christ.[18] In the fall at His baptism, Jesus Christ is presented to His Father to minister. In the spring at the Triumphal Entry in Jerusalem, He is presented to Israel.

The Decrees to the Cross

Year	King	Decree	Rome Years 483	Babylon Years 476
587 BC	Nebuchadnezzar	Conquer Jerusalem	104 BC	111 BC
538 BC	Cyrus	Build Jewish Temple	55 BC	62 BC
519 BC	Darius	Reauthorize Cyrus's Decree	36 BC	43 BC
~463 BC	Artaxerxes	Stop Work	~21 AD	~14 AD
457 BC	Artaxerxes	Return to Judah	27 AD	20 AD
444 BC	Artaxerxes	Build Jerusalem	40 AD	33 AD

* Since no year zero, add 1 when crossing from BC to AD

Views of the Sixty-nine Weeks

When do the sixty-nine weeks begin and end? For every prophecy, at least three views exist. In this case, there are six starting points and five ending points.

1. 587 BC to 70 AD—Destruction of First and Second Temples

In 587-586 BC, Israel was taken captive by Babylon. Subtract 490 years to get 70 AD. Jewish chronology sets the time between the destruction of the first and second temples as 490 years and not 656 years.[19] This is a 173-year error in the Jewish year.

587 BC - 483 = 104 BC + 70 AD - 1 BC/AD = 173-Year Error (No year zero)

2. 457 BC to 27 AD—Artaxerxes—Return to Israel

With this decree, the answer is 27 AD. Roman and Jewish years give a similar result. However, Ezra 7 tells of a decree to return to Jerusalem but not to rebuild Jerusalem. The Roman calendar also has errors.

457 BC - 483 + 1 BC/AD = 27 AD

Daniel's Seventy Weeks Timeline

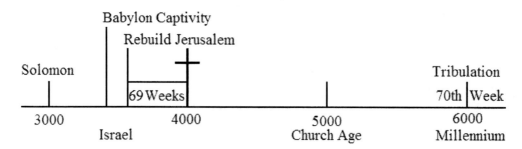

3. 444 BC to 33 AD—Artaxerxes—Rebuild Jerusalem

Nehemiah requests Artaxerxes' permission to rebuild Jerusalem. Subtract 483 years and the answer is still not close enough.

444 BC - 483 + 1 BC/AD = 40 AD

Prophecy Years: Roman, Jewish or Babylonian Calendar

Remember the culture rule of Bible study? Israel does not count the reign of kings starting on the inauguration of American presidents. Roman solar years are ~365.2425 days long and Jewish lunisolar years are ~354 days plus leap months. Solar calendars do not work.

At the time, Media-Persia ruled and used the Babylonian calendar with 30-day months and 360-day years.[20] This makes the calendar off by ~5.2425 days a year. Leap months were added erratically. Many Bible scholars talk about a prophecy calendar. The apostle John tells of 1260 days or 42 months.[21] He refers to Daniel who uses the Babylonian calendar.[22] Convert Babylonian years to Roman years for the first seven weeks of years and then sixty-nine weeks of years.

$$\begin{array}{rl} 49 \text{ Years} & \underline{17,640 \text{ Days}} = 48.2967 \text{ Years} \\ \underline{\text{X } 360 \text{ Days}} & \quad 365.2425 \quad \text{or } 48 \text{ Years, } 108.36 \text{ Days} \\ 17,640 \text{ Days} \end{array}$$

$$\begin{array}{rl} 483 \text{ Years} & \underline{173,880 \text{ Days}} = 476.06727 \text{ Years} \\ \underline{\text{X } 360 \text{ Days}} & \quad 365.2425 \quad \text{or } 476 \text{ Years } 24.22 \text{ Days} \\ 173,880 \text{ Days} \end{array}$$

The first forty-nine years is from 444 BC to 396 BC when Jerusalem was built. The next 434 years is from 396 BC to 33 AD which is the cross.[23]

444 BC - 476 + 1 BC/AD = 33 AD

Calculating Roman and Babylonian years to the various decrees and end points, the sixty-nine weeks is set. The next chapter, "The Life of Christ," reveals the exact year of the birth, death, burial and resurrection of Jesus Christ.

476-Year Prophecy

Daniel's prophecy focused on Jerusalem. On the 10th of *Nisan*, the lamb was chosen and the 14th of *Nisan* was Passover. The 9th of *Nisan* was the Triumphal Entry when Jesus Christ was publicly presented. Five days later, He was crucified.

> And some of the Pharisees from among the multitude said unto him, Master, rebuke your disciples. And he answered and said unto them, I tell you that, if these should hold their peace, the stones would immediately cry out (Luke 19:39-40).

Ending Point—Triumphal Entry[24]

- Daniel's 69th week ends at Jerusalem (Daniel 9:24).
- Zechariah's prophecy is the triumphal entry (Zechariah 9:9).
- Jesus Christ arranged the events of the day (Matthew 21:2-5).
- The first time Jesus Christ was publicly presented as the Messiah (Mark 11:8-10).
- The disciples lead the crowds in praises of Hosanna to the King (Luke 19:37).
- Jesus Christ allowed people to praise Him as the Messiah (Luke 19:39-40).
- Jesus referred to this specific hour (John 12:27).
- God the Father spoke on this day (John 12:28-30).
- Jesus Christ was crucified a few days later (Daniel 9:26).

In *Nisan* 444 BC, King Artaxerxes gave the decree to rebuild Jerusalem and in 33 AD, Jesus Christ rode into Jerusalem on a donkey. Despite the Roman calendar starting with the birth of Christ, God's calendar is synchronized to the cross. The first sixty-nine weeks are completely fulfilled.

Second Part—Prophecy Gap

God purposely delayed one part of His plan to accomplish another. The Messiah came but the Jews rejected Him. Therefore, Israel was put on hold and God took a remnant of Jews and Gentiles to build His Church and spread the Gospel. When God completes His plan for the Church, He will return for Israel. The Gospel, Church and Rapture are mysteries revealed in the New Testament.

> For I would not, brethren, that you should be ignorant of this mystery, lest you should be wise in your own conceits; that blindness in part is happened to Israel, until the fullness of the Gentiles be come in (Romans 11:25).

First Jewish-Roman War—66-73 AD

> And the people of the prince that shall come shall destroy the city and the sanctuary; and the end thereof shall be with a flood, and unto the end of the war desolations are determined (Daniel 9:26).

The pagan Romans and religious Jews had a volatile relationship. The Romans took control of Judah in 63 BC because of the conflict between the Pharisees and Sadducees.[25] They appointed governors and High Priests, collected taxes and ruled with an iron rod. Herod the Great slaughtered babies and rebels. Claudius expelled Jews from Rome.[26] In 39 AD, Caligula ordered his statue set up in the temple but later rescinded that order.[27] In 64 AD, Rome burned and Nero blamed the fire on a sect of Jews called Christians.[28] The Jews sought a political messiah and Zealots plotted to overthrow Roman control.[29] Many Jews are crucified by the Romans for various insurrections.

In 66 AD, the Jewish-Roman War began when Greeks sacrificed birds in front of a Jewish synagogue in Caesarea.[30] Eliezar ben Hanania led a successful attack on the Roman fort in Jerusalem and King Agrippa II fled to Galilee. The Jews believed since God deliver them from Greek Syria, He would deliver them from Rome. However, Christians who knew the prophecies fled the region.

Nero sent General Vespasian to crush the uprising.[31] By 68 AD, most of Judea was under Roman control except Jerusalem. After Vespasian became emperor, the army built a wall surrounding the city. In 70 AD, Rome allowed Jews to enter Jerusalem for the Passover but not leave. The population swelled to 600,000 and many people died of starvation.

Vespasian's son, Titus led the final assault.[32] On the 17th of *Tammuz*, 70 AD (Golden Calf), the army breached the walls. On the 9th of *Av* (Kadesh Barnea), the second Jewish temple was burned, then dismantled brick by brick for the gold.[33] Over a million Jews died and 95,000 were enslaved.[34] In 73 AD, Masada was the last city to fall.

> For the days shall come upon you, that your enemies shall cast a trench about you, and compass you round, and keep you in on every side, And shall lay you even with the ground, and your children within you; and they shall not leave you one stone upon another; because you knew not the time of your visitation (Luke 19:43-44).

Third Part—Seventieth Week

Confirmation of the Covenant

> And he shall confirm the covenant with many for one week (Daniel 9:26-27).

Now jump ~1950 years after 70 AD. The prince that shall come is the Antichrist.[35] He will emerge from the Roman Empire that destroys Jerusalem. He will be a great diplomat, peacemaker and political leader. On the 1st of *Tishri*, the Feast of Trumpets, Jesus Christ will rapture the Church.[36] On the 10th of *Tishri*, the Day of Atonement, the Antichrist will confirm a treaty for seven years.

After years of failure, this political leader will solve the greatest threat to world peace—the Israeli-Palestinian conflict. The peace treaty will decide the borders of Israel and Palestine and resolve the status of Jerusalem. Judea and Samaria (West Bank) are transferred to Palestine. Then Israel will rebuild the temple. God will continue His plan to restore Israel and prepare for Jesus Christ's kingdom.

Abomination of Desolation

> In the middle of the "seven," he will put an end to sacrifice and offering. And on a wing of the temple he will set up an abomination that causes desolation, until the end that is decreed is poured out on him (Daniel 9:27 NIV).

In 168 BC, Antiochus IV of Greek Syria ordered the sacrifice of a pig to the god Zeus in the Jewish temple. Antiochus was a type of the future Antichrist. In Matthew 24, Jesus Christ referred to a future "abomination of desolation." In 70 AD, Romans destroyed the temple which was an abomination but Nero died in 68 AD.[37] No one sat in the temple while it was burning.

After 3½ years on the 10th of *Nisan*, the ten-member supranational alliance will make the popular Antichrist king of the world.[38] His coronation will be a spectacular event televised live for all the world to see. Every peoples, tribes and nations will follow this charismatic leader. Full of pride, the Antichrist will enter the third Jewish temple's Most Holy Place and claim to be God. He will stop Jewish animal sacrifices which interferes in Israel's right to worship God.[39] The reign of the Antichrist will begin the Great Tribulation.

> Let no man deceive you by any means: for that day shall not come, except there come a falling away first, and that man of sin be revealed, the son of perdition; Who opposes and exalts himself above all that is called God, or that is worshipped; so that he as God sits in the temple of God, showing himself that he is God (2 Thessalonians 2:3-4).

Daniel's Tribulation Timeline

Daniel gives events during the Tribulation so applying the Jewish calendar, we see the prophetic timeline. The 10th of *Tishri* is the confirmation of the covenant. On the 10th of

Tribulation Timeline

Date	Events	
1st of Tishri, Year 1	Rapture of the Church	
10th of Tishri, Year 1	Confirmation of the Covenant Tribulation Begins	**Tribulation**
10th of Nisan, Year 3 and Month 6	Antichrist's Reign Begins Abomination of Desolation Great Tribulation Begins	
~9th of *Av*, Year 7	Armageddon Begins	
10th of Tishri, Year 8	Second Coming of Christ Antichrist's Reign Ends Tribulation Ends	
15th Tishri, Year 8	Millennium Reign Begins	

Nisan, the lamb and Jesus Christ were selected for Passover and the Antichrist begins His reign over the world. His reign of terror ends 3½ years later on the 10th of *Tishri* at the Second Coming. Despite these horrible conditions, God is still sovereign over all people. He and His people work toward implementing His plan.

The Great Disappointment Revised

> How long shall be the vision concerning the daily sacrifice, and the transgression of desolation, to give both the sanctuary and the host to be trodden under foot? And he said unto me, Unto two thousand and three hundred days; then shall the sanctuary be cleansed (Daniel 8:13-14).

Joseph Miller predicted the Rapture in 1844. Why did the prophecy not come true? Miller and the Seventh Day Adventist Church started with 457 BC and added 2300 years to come up with 1844.

Miller: 2300 - 457 BC + 1 BC/AD = 1844
Israel: 2300 - 334 BC + 1 BC/AD = 1967

Daniel 8 started with Alexander the Great's war with Media-Persia in 334 BC and not 457 BC.[40] The prophecy told of Antiochus IV's abomination of the temple that lasted for 1150 days.[41] Daniel 9 started with Artaxerxes' decrees in 444 BC.[42] These prophecies were about the Gentile's rule of Israel, Jerusalem and the temple—not the Church, Rapture or Heaven.

Views of the Seventy Weeks

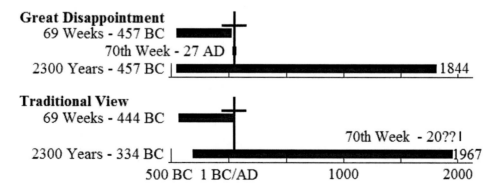

167

God has begun restoring the Jewish people.[43] In 1948, Israel became an independent nation and in 1967, Jerusalem became Israel's undivided capital. There are 2300 years from 334 BC to 1967 when Judea, Samaria and the Temple Mount returned to Israeli control.

God's Plan in God's Time

In Daniel 9, God revealed to Daniel His six-point plan for Israel. The plan is fulfilled in Jesus Christ's First and Second Comings. These six points bring complete redemption of humanity, restoration of the Jewish people, restraint of Satan, sin and the Man of Sin, removal of the curse of sin and the start of the eternal reign of Jesus Christ. Daniel's sixty-nine weeks are complete but Daniel's seventieth week is still future.

God has a specific plan for the world in His time. Satan has a plan to disrupt God's plan. The Son of God becomes sin for humanity while the Man of Sin becomes god for the world. Israel rejects their Messiah and they are exiled from the Promised Land until their recent return. During the Tribulation, Israel follows the Antichrist but returns to God. In the end, God's plan prevails.

God has a specific plan for you. Do you know God's plan for your life and are you living it out?

Chapter 16

The Life of Christ

The key to the Second Coming of Jesus Christ is found in the First Coming. Millions of sermons have been preached about Christmas and Easter but the timing is off. According to tradition, Jesus Christ was conceived on the spring equinox of March 25, 1 BC and born on the winter solstice of December 25, 1 BC. Not only is there no Santa Claus, Jesus was not born on Christ's Mass.

The dates of Jesus Christ's birth and ministry are understood with Scripture, Jewish culture, Roman history and astronomy. The cross is not only the core of redemption but also the epicenter of God's time.

Birth of Jesus Christ

Augustus Sets the Year

> And it came to pass in those days, that there went out a decree from Caesar Augustus that all the world should be taxed (Luke 2:1).

Caesar Augustus rules the Roman Empire from 27 BC to 14 AD.[1] The territory surrounds the Mediterranean Sea including Judea, Samaria and Galilee. Augustus orders three censuses: 24 BC, 8 BC and 14 AD.[2] Luke, the historian, refers to the census of 8 BC.

> Then again, with consular imperium I conducted a lustrum [census] alone when Gaius Censorinus and Gaius Asinius were consuls [8 BC], in which lustrum were counted 4,233,000 heads of Roman citizens.
> —Caesar Augustus, *The Deeds of the Divine Augustus*, 14 AD[3]

Zechariah Sets the Month

> There was in the days of Herod, the king of Judea, a certain priest named Zechariah, of the course of Abijah: and his wife was of the daughters of Aaron, and her name was Elisabeth (Luke 1:5).

Zechariah is in the temple and Luke says when. Descendant of Aaron are priests and they all work at the temple during Passover (week 2), Weeks (week 9) and Tabernacles (week 28). King David divided the year among Aaron's grandsons. Abijah's family received the eighth lot and serves at the temple on the 10th and 35th weeks from Sabbath to Sabbath.[4]

- **Priestly Order of Service**: 1) Jehoiarib, 2) Jedaiah, 3) Harim, 4) Seorim, 5) Malchijah, 6) Mijamin, 7) Hakkoz, 8) Abijah, 9) Jeshuah, 10) Shecaniah, 11) Eliashib, 12) Jakim, 13) Huppah, 14) Jeshebeab, 15) Bilgah, 16) Immer, 17) Hezir, 18) Aphses, 19) Pethahiah, 20) Jehezekel, 21) Jachin, 22) Gamul, 23) Delaiah, 24) Maaziah[5]

> These were the orderings of them [priests] in their service to come into the house of the Lord, according to their manner, under Aaron their father, as the Lord God of Israel had commanded him (1 Chronicles 24:19).

> According to the custom of the priest's office, his [Zechariah] lot was to burn incense when he went into the temple of the Lord. The angel said unto him, Fear not, Zechariah: for your prayer is heard; and your wife Elisabeth shall bear you a son, and you shall call his name John (Luke 1:9, 13).

One spring day on the tenth week in *Sivan* (May/June) of 8 BC, Zechariah had an once-in-a-lifetime opportunity to offer incense and prayer. In the temple, he met Gabriel who told him he and Elizabeth would have a son that would prepare the people for the Lord. It takes ~280 days for a woman to give birth.[6] There are 304 days between Weeks and Passover.

- **Jewish Months**: 1) *Nisan*, 2) *Iyar*, 3) *Sivan*, 4) *Tammuz*, 5) *Av*, 6) *Elul*, 7) *Tishri*, 8) *Heshvan*, 9) *Kislev*, 10) *Tevet*, 11) *Shevat*, Leap Year) *Adar* 1, 12) *Adar*

Hanukkah — Jesus Christ Incarnated

> And in the sixth month the angel Gabriel was sent from God unto a city of Galilee, named Nazareth, to a virgin espoused to a man whose name was Joseph, of the house of David; and the virgin's name was Mary (Luke 1:26-27).

Six months later in *Kislev* (December), Gabriel told Mary that she was chosen to be the mother of the Messiah. She traveled from Nazareth to the Jerusalem area to help Elizabeth for three months. Jesus Christ was not born in December but was conceived during *Hanukkah* (*Kislev* 25-*Tevet* 3). In 8 BC, the 25th of *Kislev* was December 26/27 Julian or 24/25 Gregorian.[7] After the darkest day, the Light of the World began.

Three months later in *Nisan* (April), Elizabeth gave birth to John the Baptist during Passover. The Jews kept an empty seat for Elijah.[8] John the Baptist came in the spirit and power of Elijah.[9]

Tabernacles—Jesus Christ Born

> And all went to be taxed, every one into his own city. And Joseph also went up from Galilee, out of the city of Nazareth, into Judea, unto the city of David, which is called Bethlehem; (because he was of the house and lineage of David) (Luke 2:3-4).

Six months later in *Tishri* (October), Joseph and Mary travelled from Nazareth to Bethlehem. It is a seventy-mile journey excluding the Samarian detour. All Jewish men were required to go to the Feast of Tabernacles and many women traveled for the Roman census. Jews were prohibited from traveling on Sabbaths, *Rosh Hashanah*, Atonement and the first day of Tabernacles. They lived with family but no room was available so they lived in the stable. During Tabernacles, Jews lived outside in booths. There are 287 days from *Hanukkah* to Tabernacles.

On the full moon of the 15th of *Tishri* or October 7/8 Julian or 5/6 Gregorian in 7 BC, Jesus Christ was born. In 1614, German astronomer Johannes Kepler discovered three conjunctions of the planets Jupiter and Saturn and a star in Pieces on May 27, October 6 and December 1.[10] In 8 BC, ancient Babylonian clay tablets described upcoming celestial events including these conjunctions.[11] This is not the Star of Bethlehem but a sign of the nativity for the world then and for us today.

Jesus Christ was born on the Feast of Tabernacles. Matthew, Luke and John refer to His birth with Jewish idioms. It is the Feast of Lights, Season of Our Joy and Feast of the Nations.[12] His name is Emmanuel or God with us and He tabernacles among us.[13] As the presence of God dwelt in the temple and the Holy Spirit dwells in us, Jesus Christ dwelt with humanity. The day is celebrated during the Millennium as it begins the reign of Jesus Christ.[14]

> And the angel said unto them, Fear not: for, behold, I bring you good tidings of great joy, which shall be to all people (Luke 2:10).

Εσκηνωσεν—skenoo [dwelt/tabernacled]
1) to fix one's tabernacle, have one's tabernacle, abide (or live) in a tabernacle (or tent), tabernacle
2) to dwell
   —Blue Letter Bible[15]

In him [the Word, Jesus Christ] was life; and the life was the light of men. And the light shines in darkness; and the darkness comprehended it not. And the Word was made flesh, and dwelt [tabernacled] among us (John 1:4-5, 14).

Behold, a virgin shall be with child, and shall bring forth a son, and they shall call his name Emmanuel, which being interpreted is, God with us (Matthew 1:23 from Isaiah 7:14).

And it shall come to pass, that every one that is left of all the nations which came against Jerusalem shall go up from year to year to worship the King, the Lord of hosts, and to keep the feast of tabernacles (Zechariah 14:16).

Shepherds and the Jewish Law

The Son of God was born and shepherds came to worship in Bethlehem. On the 22nd of *Tishri* (October 16), Jesus Christ was circumcised. The day was *Shemini Atzeret* or the Eighth Day of the Assembly. The 25th of *Heshvan* (November 17) was the fortieth day when Jesus Christ was dedicated at the temple. Simeon and Anna meet their promised Messiah. Then Joseph, Mary and Jesus returned to Nazareth.

When they had performed all things according to the law of the Lord, they returned into Galilee, to their own city Nazareth (Luke 2:39).

The shepherds and wise men are part of the nativity but separated by time. In Luke, Joseph, Mary and Jesus fulfilled the Law then traveled north to Nazareth. In Matthew, they fled Herod and went southwest to Egypt.

The Wise Men and the Star

Now when Jesus was born in Bethlehem of Judea in the days of Herod the king, behold, there came wise men from the east to Jerusalem, Saying, Where is he that is born King of the Jews? for we have seen his star in the east, and are come to worship him.... the star, which they saw in the east, went before them [south], till it came and stood over where the young child was (Matthew 2:1-2, 9).

The magi were wise men from the east. Judah was captive under Babylon (Iraq) and Persia (Iran). Skilled in astronomy, they searched for the Messiah of Daniel 9. They saw the triple conjunctions in 7 BC and a single conjunction in February 6 BC. Later in March/April 5 BC, they saw a comet in the eastern sky and were compelled to follow the Star of Bethlehem west to Jerusalem and south to Bethlehem. They found Joseph, Mary and Jesus in a house.

But you, Bethlehem Ephratah, though you are little among the thousands of Judah, yet out of you shall he come forth unto me that is to be ruler in Israel; whose goings forth have been from of old, from everlasting (Micah 5:2).

In the spring of 5 BC, the Chinese and Koreans recorded a tailed comet that appeared in March or April and lasted about seventy-two days (~March 9-June 16).[16] The comet started in the east and then south (Jerusalem to Bethlehem), which is contrary to stars and planets. The Star of Bethlehem sets the Magi's visit to *Sivan* (May/June) in 5 BC.

Second year of the *Chien-p'ing* reign period, second month (5 BC, March 9-April 6), a suibsing [tailed comet] appeared at *Ch'ien-niu* for over seventy days.
—Chinese Record—*Han Shu* (*History of Han Dynasty*)[17]

Year 54 of *Hyokkose Wang*, second month, (day) *Chi-yu*, a *po-hsing* appeared in *Ho-Ku*.
—Korean Record—*Samguk Sagi* (*The Chronicle of Silla*)[18]

Herod the Great's Death

Herod the Great was king at the time of Christ's birth.[19] Jesus Christ was a 1½ year-old child when the wise men visited. Herod's decree to kill boys two and under in Bethlehem was based on the first conjunction in May 7 BC. Historian Flavius Josephus wrote that Herod died after an eclipse of the moon on a Jewish fast day.[20] NASA (US National Aeronautics and Space Administration) reported a partial eclipse on March 13 in 4 BC or the Fast of Esther before *Purim*. Herod died in March or April 4 BC.[21]

The Bible is clear that Jesus Christ was born after Caesar Augustus' census decree in 8 BC and before Herod's death in the spring of 4 BC. The dates of Dionysius Exiguus and James Ussher are after Herod's death. The Christmas story points to the birth of Jesus Christ on the Feast of Tabernacles on October 7/8, 7 BC and the visit from the wise men in the spring of 5 BC. The birth sets the year of the cross.

Ministry of Jesus Christ

The birth of Jesus Christ from 1 to 7 BC pushes His ministry earlier than tradition. Follow Scripture, Jewish culture and history to find the year of the cross.

Reign of Tiberius

> In the fifteenth year of the reign of Tiberius Caesar, Pontius Pilate being governor of Judea, and Herod being tetrarch of Galilee, and his brother Philip tetrarch of Ituraea and of the region of Trachonitis [Syria], and Lysanias the tetrarch of Abilene [Syria], Annas and Caiaphas being the high priests, the word of God came unto John (Luke 3:1-2).

Caesar Augustus had a problem. When great-uncle Julius Caesar chose him to be emperor, a civil war ensued between Mark Anthony and Octavius (Augustus). Now Augustus had no heir and desired his adopted stepson, Tiberius, to be his successor. In 10 AD, he made Tiberius co-regent.[22] This forced the Roman senate to approve his choice and avoid another civil war. Later in 14 AD, Tiberius became the sole ruler. As seen in Kings and Chronicles, co-regency was counted as part of a king's reign.

> And in the fifth year of Joram the son of Ahab king of Israel, Jehoshaphat being then king of Judah, Jehoram the son of Jehoshaphat king of Judah began to reign (2 Kings 8:16).

Timing of Jesus Christ's Ministry

Luke says during the fifteenth year of Tiberius, John the Baptist and later Jesus, began their ministries at thirty. Luke, the historian, uses 10 AD for the beginning of Tiberius' reign and the 15th year is 24 AD. Since Jesus Christ was born in 7 BC and not 1 BC, the Roman calendar is off ~6 years.

> And Jesus himself began to be about thirty years of age (Luke 3:23).

Birth to Ministry: October 7 BC + 30 + 1 BC/AD = ~October 24 AD

- Exiguus: Tiberius Reign (17), Ministry Begins (30), Ministry Ends (33)
- Ussher: Tiberius Reign (14), Ministry Begins (27), Ministry Ends (30)
- Revised: Tiberius Reign (10), Ministry Begins (24), Ministry Ends (27)

Since Tiberius became co-emperor in 10 AD, then Jesus Christ started his ministry in the fall of 24 AD near His thirtieth birthday. Tradition says his ministry lasted 3½ years. The Gospel of John lists three Passovers in Jesus Christ's ministry. Some make John 5:1 a Passover but the unnamed feast could be Weeks, Tabernacles or the minor feasts of *Hanukkah* or *Purim*. With just three Passovers, Jesus Christ fulfilled every prophecy in 2½ years.

After this there was a feast of the Jews; and Jesus went up to Jerusalem (John 5:1).

Passovers in Christ's Ministry

1. 25 AD: Christ's Age—30.5, Ministry—0.5 (John 2:23)
2. 26 AD: Christ's Age—31.5, Ministry—1.5 (John 6:4)
3. 27 AD: Christ's Age—32.5, Ministry—2.5 (John 11:5)

Birth to Redemption: October 7 BC + 32.5 + 1 BC/AD = April 27 AD

Tradition says Jesus Christ was crucified on Friday but the Triumphal Entry was Friday. The year 27 AD puts the full moon Passover on Wednesday.[23] In Nisan 27 AD, Jesus was crucified Wednesday afternoon. Wednesday night/Thursday was the High Sabbath of Unleavened Bread. Thursday night/Friday was a regular day when the women bought spices. Friday night/Saturday was the regular Sabbath. Saturday night/Sunday was Firstfruits and Resurrection. This fulfilled Jesus Christ's prophecy of three complete days and nights like Jonah and matches the 3½ days of the two witnesses in Revelation 11.[24]

Passion Week—April 27 AD

1st Day	2nd Day	3rd Day	4th Day	5th Day	6th Day	7th Day	
	April/ Nisan	1　　7	2　　8	3　　9	4　　10	5　　11	
				Triumphal	Entry	Sabbath	
6　　12	7　　13	8　　14	9　　15	10　　16	11　　17	12　　18	
			Cross	Sabbath	Spices	Sabbath	
13　　19	14　　20	15　　21	16　　22	17　　23	18　　24	19　　25	
Resurrection			Sabbath			Sabbath	

The 7 BC birth of Christ sets the cross on Wednesday, April 9, 27 AD and resurrection on Sunday, April 13, 27 AD Julian.

> The Jews therefore, because it was the preparation, that the bodies should not remain upon the cross on the sabbath day, (for that sabbath day was an high day,) besought Pilate that their legs might be broken, and that they might be taken away (John 19:31).

> And when the sabbath was past, Mary Magdalene, and Mary the mother of James, and Salome, had bought sweet spices, that they might come and anoint him (Mark 16:1).

Religious Tradition

In 325 AD, the Council of Nicaea separates Easter from the Jewish Passover.[25] If Passover falls on a Tuesday, three options exist:

- Celebrate the Crucifixion on Tuesday and Resurrection on Sunday, which abandons "the third day."
- Celebrate the Crucifixion on Tuesday and Resurrection on Thursday, which abandons "the first day of the week."
- Celebrate the Crucifixion on Friday and Resurrection on Sunday, which abandons Passover. The council accepts this option.

> You shall bring a sheaf of the firstfruits of your harvest unto the priest: and he shall wave the sheaf before the Lord, to be accepted for you: on the morrow after the sabbath the priest shall wave it (Leviticus 23:10-11).

The debate over these holy days predates Christianity. Jewish tradition follows the Pharisees' interpretation that the Feast of Firstfruits is the 16th of *Nisan*, the day after the High Sabbath and Weeks is the 6th of *Sivan*. Christian tradition follows the Sadducees' interpretation that the Feast of Firstfruits is the Sunday after the regular Sabbath and Weeks is the 7th Sunday.[26]

Once the year of the cross is set, the purpose is not to move Christ's Mass and Good Friday. First and foremost, Jesus Christ died, was buried and rose again for our sin. Second, the cross is the key to God's timeline and Bible prophecy. With Christ's birth at 7 BC and the cross at 27 AD, we get a rough estimate of the dates of creation and the end of our age.

Jesus Christ's Life Reveals God's Time

The Bible is proven in different ways. Jesus Christ's birth, the visit from the wise men, Christ's ministry and His work of redemption are confirmed by history, Jewish culture and astronomy. After placing the cross on the timeline, everything else falls in place. Even after ~1985 years, debate still continues over the timing and events of the First Coming of Jesus Christ. Much more debate exists over the timing and events of the Second Coming.

God's plan of redemption reveals God's time. Creation, the exodus, the Jewish Feasts, Israel's detours and delays, Daniel's seventy weeks and the life of Christ tell God's time. The cross moves the Roman calendar, Rapture and Second Coming thirty-three years later and then six years earlier. After knowing various parts of God's time, now it is time to put God's plan in a seven thousand year timeline.

Since the timing and events of the First Coming of Jesus Christ literally happened then should the timing and events of the Second Coming of Jesus Christ literally happen?

Chapter 17

Basic Bible Chronology

When? That is the question that Daniel asks the angel and disciples ask Jesus. That is the question we still ask today. When is the end of this present age? Scripture answers that question through Bible chronology.

Prophecy is about God and God's time. Our sovereign God designed this present age to last seven thousand years. The timeline is given throughout the historical accounts of the Old Testament and the Gospels. The begot verses are difficult to read but reveal God's time. Chronology confirms we are at the end of man's six thousand years and near the beginning of Jesus Christ's one thousand years.

> And on the seventh day God ended his work which he had made; and he rested on the seventh day from all his work which he had made (Genesis 2:2).

Just like End Time prophecy, chronology has many different views. The book, *21st Century Revelation*, gives a view that keeps true to the Word of God, aligns to the cross and totals seven thousand years. Many detours occur but Scripture safeguards time. The intertestamental time is silent so history fills in 143 years. There is a good reason as to why so much prophecy is happening in our time.

Time from Genesis to Revelation

1. Adam to Abraham

Genesis 5 tells the genealogy from Adam to Noah and the flood is 1656 years. Genesis 11 tells the genealogy from Noah to Abraham. There are 292 years. Two chapters give a total of 1948 years from creation.

And Adam lived an hundred and thirty years, and begat a son in his own likeness, and after his image; and called his name Seth: And the days of Adam after he had begotten Seth were eight hundred years: and he begat sons and daughters: And all the days that Adam lived were nine hundred and thirty years: and he died (Genesis 5:3-5).

When Abraham was seventy-five, God made a covenant with him.

And I [God] will make of you a great nation, and I will bless you, and make your name great; and you shall be a blessing: And I will bless them that bless you, and curse him that curses you: and in you shall all families of the earth be blessed. Abram was seventy-five years old when he departed out of Haran (Genesis 12:1-4).

2. Abraham to the Exodus

The years of Abraham, Isaac, Jacob and Joseph are given but the years of slavery in Egypt are missing. Exodus 13 and Galatians 3 tell the years from Abraham's covenant to the Exodus. The total years are 430 or 2453 years after creation.

Now the sojourning of the children of Israel, who dwelt in [Canaan and] Egypt, was four hundred and thirty years. And it came to pass at the end of the four hundred and thirty years, even the very day it came to pass, that all the hosts of the Lord went out from the land of Egypt (Exodus 12:40-41).

The exact day that God gave the covenant to Abraham was the day the children of Israel left Egypt. This first day of Unleavened Bread is the day Jesus Christ completed His work of redemption.

And this I say, that the covenant, that was confirmed before of God in Christ, the law, which was four hundred and thirty years after, cannot disannul, that it should make the promise of none effect (Galatians 3:17).

They left Egypt in the month *Xanthicus*, on the fifteenth day of the lunar month; four hundred and thirty years after our forefather Abraham came into Canaan, but two hundred and fifteen years only after Jacob removed into Egypt.
—Flavius Josephus, *The Antiquities of the Jew*, 94 AD[1]

Abraham to Moses

Year	Age	Son	Death	430 Years
2023	*25	Abraham	175	215 Covenant to Jacob in Canaan
2048	60	Isaac	180	
2108	87	Jacob	147	
2195	~60	Levi	137	
~2255	~60	Koath (1)	133	~95 Jacob in Egypt to Death of Levi
~2315	~55	Aram (2)	137	~120 Death of Levi to Exodus
~2370	83	Aaron (3)	120	
2453		Eleazar (4) Ithamar		
	430	Total		Exodus

* Isaac was born 25 years after the Covenant.

1-4 The generations of Levi.

~ The Bible does not give the ages of Levi, Koath, Aram and Aaron when they had children. Those years are averages.

The children of Jacob were not slaves in Egypt 430 years. They lived in Canaan 215 years and Egypt 215 years. In Egypt, they were free 95 years and slaves ~120 years.

> But in the fourth generation they shall come again: for the iniquity of the Amorites is not yet full (Genesis 15:16).

> And Joseph died, and all his brethren, and all that generation. And the children of Israel were fruitful, and increased abundantly, and multiplied, and waxed exceeding mighty; and the land was filled with them. Now there arose up a new king over Egypt, which knew not Joseph. Therefore they did set over them taskmasters to afflict them with their burdens (Exodus 1:6-8, 11).

Genesis 15 says the fourth generation returns from Egypt. Levi left Canaan for Egypt. Exodus 6 lists his heirs: Koath, Aram and Aaron. Eleazar and Ithamar entered the Promised Land.

3. The Exodus to Solomon

The children of Israel wandered in the wilderness forty years. They conquered most of the Promised Land in five years. The time of the judges (Joshua to Samuel) was 436 years. Israel was conquered by foreign powers six times. King David ruled forty years. The 521 years gives 2974 years from creation.

> And now, behold, the Lord has kept me [Caleb] alive, as he said, these forty-five years, even since the Lord spoke this word unto Moses, while the children of Israel wandered in the wilderness: and now, I am this day eighty-five years old. And the land had rest from war (Joshua 14:10, 15).

In Acts 13, Paul gave years that included Isaac to the exodus, wilderness and conquering the land. The 455 years was with this period and not the judges.

Isaac to the Promised Land

- Chose Our Fathers (195 Years)
- Stay in Egypt (215 Years)
- In the Desert (40 Years)
- Overthrew Seven Nations (5 Years)

> The God of the people of Israel chose our fathers; he made the people prosper during their stay in Egypt, with mighty power he led them out of that country, he endured their conduct for about forty years in the desert, he overthrew seven nations in Canaan and gave their land to his people as their inheritance. All this took about 450 years (Acts 13:17-20 NIV).

The judges are described in Joshua, Judges and 1 Samuel. The judges and captivities happened sequentially from Joshua to Abdon. Then judges Samson, Eli and Samuel overlapped with the forty years of Philistine captivity. Samuel as prophet/judge overlapped with King Saul. Acts 13 says forty years, which is Samuel's rule as judge because Saul reigned less than twelve years.[2]

> And after that he gave unto them judges until Samuel the prophet. And afterward they desired a king: and God gave unto them Saul the son of Cis, a man of the tribe of Benjamin, by the space of forty years (Acts 13:20-21).

182

Judges to Solomon

Year	Event	Scripture
376	Joshua—Abdon	Joshua—Judges
7	Philistines—40 Samson—20	Judges 13:1 Judges 15:20
40	Philistines Samson Eli—40 Samuel—40	1 Samuel 4:18 1 Samuel 3:1, 20
7/12	Philistines Take Ark	1 Samuel 2:17
12.5	Ark Returned Kirjath Jearim Samuel < 12.5 Saul < 12.5	1 Samuel 6:21-7:2 1 Samuel 7:1-13 1 Samuel 10:20-24
436	Total Judges	
7.5	David—Judah	2 Samuel 5:4-5
33	David—Israel Ark Moved to Jerusalem	2 Samuel 6:1-2
4	Solomon	
480	Judges to Temple	

The Ark of the Covenant confirms a short reign of Saul. During the battle of Shiloh, the ark was taken by the Philistines the day Eli died. Seven months later, the Philistines sent the ark back and it stayed in Kirjath Jearim twenty years. David was king over Judah seven years and all Israel before the ark was moved.[3]

> And it came to pass, while the ark abode in Kirjath Jearim, that the time was long; for it was twenty years: and all the house of Israel lamented after the Lord (1 Samuel 7:2).

> So David gathered all Israel together, from Shihor of Egypt even unto the entering of Hemath, to bring the ark of God from Kirjath Jearim (1 Chronicles 13:5).

As a check, 1 Kings 6 counts 480 years. This includes the judges, King David to the fourth year of King Solomon's reign.

> And it came to pass in the four hundred and eightieth year after the children of Israel were come out of the land of Egypt, in the fourth year of Solomon's reign over Israel, in the month Zif [*Iyar*], which is the second month, that he began to build the house of the Lord (1 Kings 6:1).

4. Solomon to Babylon Captivity

Solomon reigned forty years. Through many wives, His heart turned to idolatry and God divided the kingdom. The northern kingdom of Israel rejected Rehoboam because of oppressive taxes. The ten tribes built their capital in Samaria. The southern kingdom of Judah, Benjamin and Levi stayed with David's family line.

> And [God] had commanded him [Solomon] concerning this thing, that he should not go after other gods: but he kept not that which the Lord commanded. Wherefore the Lord said unto Solomon, Forasmuch as this is done of you, and you have not kept my covenant and my statutes, which I have commanded you, I will surely rend the kingdom from you, and will give it to your servant (1 Kings 11:10-11).

The chronology through the divided kingdoms is complicated. Most kings rule alone but some rule as co-regents with their fathers or sons so reigns overlap. Kings and Chronicles provide the length of the kings of Israel and Judah.

The northern kingdom of Israel was ruled by wicked kings. A good king could not be found among them. The nation immediately turned from God to idolatry and never repented. They worshipped Baal and offered their children as human sacrifices to Asteroth. Israel lasted 287 years through eleven dynasties and three civil wars. After years of ignoring God's warnings through the prophets, Assyria conquered Israel in 716 BC.[4]

The southern kingdom of Judah was ruled by good kings who worshipped God and wicked kings and a queen who worshipped Baal and Asteroth. David's house was the only dynasty which made the kingdom more stable. After 376 years, Judah followed Israel's lead. In 587 BC, the Jewish temple was destroyed. The 40 years of Solomon and 376 years of Judah give 3390 years after creation.[5] For this chronology, 587 BC plus 3390 years gives 3977 BC for Adam.

And this whole land shall be a desolation, and an astonishment; and these nations shall serve the king of Babylon seventy years (Jeremiah 25:11).

5. Babylon Captivity to the Cross

Captivity under Babylon lasted forty-nine years. In 539 BC, Cyrus the Great of Media-Persia, conquered Babylon and allowed Judah to rebuild the temple.[6] The desolation of Jerusalem lasted seventy years.[7] It ended in 517 BC after Darius reauthorized Cyrus's decree to build the temple. Scripture omits years but history tells us there are ninety-four years from Darius's second year to Artaxerxes' twentieth year. The 143 years gives 3533 years from creation.

> Behold, there shall stand up yet three kings in Persia; and the fourth shall be far richer than they all: and by his strength through his riches he shall stir up all against the realm of Greece (Daniel 11:2).

- **Kings of Media-Persia**: Cyrus II the Great, Cambyses II, Smerdis, Darius I the Great, Ahasuerus (Xerxes), Artaxerxes ... [8]

During the four hundred year intertestamental time, the Bible gives an incomplete history of Media-Persia, Greece, Israel's independence and Rome. Just as credible, Daniel 7-12 foretells key events between rebuilding Jerusalem and the cross. This includes Alexander the Great's conquest of Media-Persia, the wars between Greek Egypt and Greek Syria, the Maccabeus revolt and Judea's independence. The prophecy of Daniel's seventy weeks bridges the gap. The first 69 weeks of years are 483 Babylon years or 476 Roman years which gives 4009 years since creation.

> Know therefore and understand, that from the going forth of the commandment to restore and to build Jerusalem unto the Messiah the Prince shall be seven weeks, and sixty-two weeks: the street shall be built again, and the wall, even in troublous times. And after sixty-two weeks shall Messiah be cut off, but not for himself (Daniel 9:25-26).

Gentile Rule over Judea[9]

- Babylon: 587 BC (49 Years)
- Media-Persia: 538 BC (206 Years)
- United Greece: 332 BC (27 Years)

Bible Chronology[10]

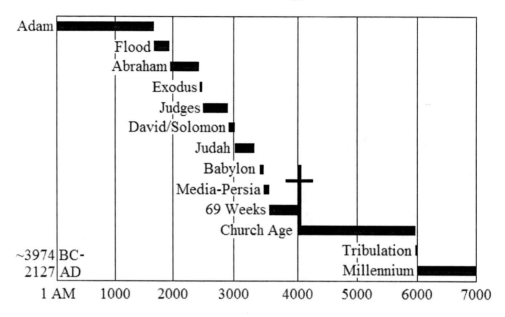

- Ptolemy (Greek Egypt): 305 BC (108 Years)
- Seleucus (Greek Syria): 197 BC (56 Years)
- Hasmonean (Independence): 141 BC (78 Years)
- United Rome: 63 BC (457 Years)

There are 4009 years after creation yet the cross is 4001 AM. Because of Dionysius Exiguus, move the birth from 1 BC to 7 BC and cross from 33 AD to 27 AD. The chronology year adjusts to 4003 AM. This chronology says redemption is 4003 years from creation.[11] Subtract two years to 4001 AM. The Word reveals God's perfect time — four thousand years past and three thousand years future.

6. The Church Age to the Second Coming

After the Resurrection of Jesus Christ, there are fifty days to Pentecost. Now the plan of God includes Jews and Gentiles in the Church. Between the cross and Second Coming is the Church Age and Tribulation period for ~2000 years. There are six thousand years from creation. Over 1985 years have passed since the cross with the end in sight.

How that by revelation he made known unto me [Paul] the mystery; that the Gentiles should be fellow heirs, and of the same body, and partakers of his promise in Christ by the gospel (Ephesians 3:3, 6).

7. Millennium Reign of Jesus Christ

Finally, the reign of Jesus Christ on earth lasts one millennium or one thousand years. This is the Sabbath of rest. The total from beginning to end is seven thousand years.

And they [martyred Saints] lived and reigned with Christ a thousand years (Revelation 20:4).

Bible chronology in this book is based on the work of Bill Bonnett, author of *The Chronology of Man* and the website Abdicate.net.[12] The chronology goes verse-by-verse through the people and events of time. Helpful notes are included to explain complex timing.

The Fullness of Time

But when the fullness of the time was come, God sent forth his Son, made of a woman, made under the law, to redeem them that were under the law, that we might receive the adoption of sons (Galatians 4:4-5).

God sent Jesus Christ to earth in the fullness of His perfect time. Within four thousand years, God prepared the world's political, cultural and religious systems so people could hear the Gospel, accept the Messiah as Savior and spread the message throughout the world.

1. Roman Government

Rome controlled the Mediterranean region and starting with Caesar Augustus, enjoyed a *Pax Romana*, a peace that lasted two centuries.[13] A peaceful succession of strong emperors and expanding territory occurred. War was limited to regional conflicts. The Roman army kept peace and spread ideas throughout the empire.[14] Judah was the cross-roads of trade routes between Africa, Asia, and Europe. Roads greatly enhanced travel. Those conquered by Rome reevaluated their relationship with their failed gods. After losing independence in 63 BC, the Jews tried but failed to overthrow local Roman control in 70 AD, 115 AD and 132 AD.[15]

Then he [Jesus Christ] says unto them, Render therefore unto Caesar the things which are Caesar's; and unto God the things that are God's (Matthew 22:21).

2. Greek Culture

In 331 BC, Alexander the Great controlled the eastern Mediterranean region.[16] When the Romans conquered the Greeks, they kept the Greek culture and language which united the empire. The Romans adopted Greek gods but Greek philosophers promoted a monotheistic view.[17] Plato made a distinction between the current temporal world and future unseen world. Stoicism taught God as father, doing good to other people and a higher standard of moral conduct. Jesus Christ lived out these messages.

And a superscription also was written over him in letters of Greek, and Latin, and Hebrew [Aramaic]. THIS IS THE KING OF THE JEWS (Luke 23:38).

3. Jewish Religion

During the time of the judges and kings, the Hebrews followed many gods. This resulted in Babylonian captivity for both Israel and Judah. Afterward, the Jews recommitted to follow the one true God. The Hebrew Bible was available at the synagogues and translated into Greek.[18] The temple was the center of worship and the Pharisees and Sadducees focused on keeping the Law. The Sadducees were the majority in the Sanhedrin and bribed the Romans to be High Priest.[19] The people sought to keep the Law but additional rules made life unbearable and they needed a new covenant.

For I [Jesus Christ] say unto you, That except your righteousness shall exceed the righteousness of the scribes and Pharisees, you shall not enter into the kingdom of heaven (Matthew 5:20).

4. Messianic Fulfillment

God promised Adam, Abraham, Moses, David and the prophets a Messiah. Those that understood the prophecies looked for His coming. In contrast to the world, Jesus Christ brought true peace with God. During the Babylonian captivity, synagogues began local worship.[20] Early Christians went to synagogues to preach the Gospel of Jesus Christ. Missionaries helped establish local churches for the Christian community.

By the name of Jesus Christ of Nazareth, whom you crucified, whom God raised from the dead, even by him does this man stand here before you whole (Acts 4:10).

The Roman government, Greek culture and Jewish religion set up the fullness of time for Jesus Christ. With the example of Christ's life, the message of redemption, the miracle of the resurrection and the power of the Holy Spirit, this new Church grew and thrived. Persecution from Jews and Gentiles dispersed Christians and spread the Gospel throughout the world. In the fullness of time today, political, religious and economic systems are preparing the world for the Tribulation.[21]

The Beginning to the End

Bible chronology gives the big picture and a better understanding of God's plan throughout time. The Word confirms four thousand years before the cross and two thousand years to the Second Coming. Bible chronology and current events point to the end of man's six thousand year rule. A future one thousand year reign of Jesus Christ on earth is coming.

The end of man's rule will be less than one thousand years, less than one hundred years and less than fifty years. Two World Wars and three Iraq Wars tell us that. The point is not to pick a year for the Rapture because of discrepancies. However, creation, the chronology of the Bible and the cross point to our time. Look at God's time from creation until now and see a clear picture of God's purpose and plan for humanity. The purpose of prophecy is to know God, to grow in our personal relationships with God and to work with Him in His Church until He comes.

Since Bible chronology tells us we are near the end of the End Times, what does that mean to you and your relationship with God?

Chapter 18

Spring Forward or Fall Back?

I n March in most of the United States, clocks spring forward giving an extra hour of daylight in the evening. During daylight savings time, clocks are off by one hour. Add that hour to about twenty-seven years that our calendar is off from God's time.

For every calendar, there is a big asterisk caused by a multitude of errors. In the study of God's time and Bible chronology, plenty of discrepancies exist. Roman and Jewish calendars are off days and years moving End Time events forward or backward.

> He has made every thing beautiful in his time: also he has set the world in their heart, so that no man can find out the work that God makes from the beginning to the end (Ecclesiastes 3:11).

Roman Calendar

The Roman calendar is a collection of political and religious rules and errors. The calendar began as a lunar calendar with inconsistent leap months. In 46 BC, ninety days were added to "the year of confusion." Then Rome implemented the Julian solar calendar.[1] Leap days were added every third year so from 8 BC to 4 AD, leap years were omitted.[2] When setting the birth of Jesus Christ, dates do not match the erroneous but actual Roman day.

Years began to drift. The earth takes ~365.24275 days to orbit the sun.[3] The Julian calendar moved Easter toward summer and spring equinox toward winter. This error was 11.23 minutes a year or one day every ~128 years.[4] In 1582, the Gregorian calendar was adopted. It removed ten days and limited century leap years. The pope set the day back to the First Council of Nicaea in 325 AD. It should be twelve days but it moved Christ's Mass from the pagan winter solstice.[5] In 1752, the British and their colonies adopted the new system. The date is off two days then adds 25.9 seconds a year or one day every ~3336 years.[6]

Additionally, the Roman year is incorrect. Herod the Great was living at the time of Christ's birth. Historian Flavius Josephus said Herod died after an eclipse on a fast day.[7] NASA lists a partial lunar eclipse on March 13, 4 BC or the 13th of *Adar* (Fast of Esther).[8] Herod's successors minted coins in 4 BC. Dionysius Exiguus set Christ's birth to December 25, 1 BC.[9] James Ussher set Christ's birth to October 4 BC.[10] Both dates are after Herod's death.

> Now it happened that during the time of the high priesthood of this Matthias, there was another person made high priest for a single day, that very day which the Jews observed as a fast.... And that very night there was an eclipse of the moon.
> —Flavius Josephus, *The Antiquities of the Jews*, 94 AD[11]

In 532, Dionysius Exiguus used 27 BC as the start of the reign of Caesar Augustus. However, in 31 BC at the Battle of Actium, Octavius defeated Anthony and became emperor without the title. The Roman Senate balked because of their trouble with Julius Caesar. In 27 BC after a political compromise, the senate made Octavius emperor as Augustus.[12]

Dates of Creation and Christ

- Exiguus: Creation (4000 BC), Birth of Christ (1 BC), Cross (33 AD)
- Ussher: Creation (4004 BC), Birth of Christ (4 BC), Cross (30 AD)
- Revised: Creation (3974 BC), Birth of Christ (7 BC), Cross (27 AD)

In 10 AD, Caesar Augustus made Tiberius co-regent and by 14 AD, Tiberius was sole ruler.[13] This made the Roman senate approve of his successor. It also made a calendar error because kings counted their co-regent years. Luke says John began his ministry during Tiberius's fifteenth year. Jesus Christ began His ministry in October 24 AD and 2½ years later completed His work of redemption in April 27 AD.

Jewish Calendar

The Jews have a lunisolar calendar. Since the time of Moses, Jews have set the calendar by observation. When two witnesses viewed the new moon, the Sanhedrin declared the beginning of the month. About sixteen hours occurs between the astronomical new moon (no moon) and crescent new moon.[14] A solar year was over eleven days longer then twelve lunar months so a leap month was added.[15] Without this adjustment, the first day of spring would drift to the first day of winter in nine years.

By 358 AD, Hillel II, leader of the Jewish Sanhedrin, implemented a perpetual calendar with a nineteen-year cycle.[16] To avoid a high Sabbath next to the Sabbath, the calendar may postpone a new month and year by a day. Using the perpetual calendar, the year is longer by about one day every 224 years or 8 days late.[17] Dates before 358 AD are estimated because of the difference between the perpetual and observed calendars.

In addition, the Jewish year is incorrect. January 1, 2012 correlates to the Jewish year 5772 AM.[18] Since the Jewish calendar counts from creation, the year is off by over two hundred years. The Jewish chronology is based on Rabbi Yose ben Halafta's work *Seder Olam Rabbah*.[19] It follows Bible chronology except for three critical omissions of years.[20]

1. Abraham was seventy-five not seventy years old when he received God's covenant (5 years).
2. The 480 years starts at Joshua as judge to Solomon's temple. Forty years in the wilderness and five years conquering the Promised Land are not included (45 years).
3. During the intertestamental period, there were 656 years from the destruction of the first and second temples not 490 years.[21] For 207 years, Media-Persia ruled Judea.[22] The Jewish chronology gave fifty-two years based on Daniel 11:1-2. This passage does not list all the kings of Media-Persia. Nehemiah indicates a longer time (166 years).[23]

Some suggested Jewish chronology purposely avoided Jesus Christ while Jews say Christians make time match.[24] In the second century, Yose ben Halafta's chronology, *Seder Olam Rabbah*, points to a messiah, Bar Kokhba and his failed rebellion in 132 AD.[25] The Jewish chronology gives 3830 years to 70 AD. Bill Bonnett's chronology gives 4046 years to 70 AD.[26] Since the cross is 2003 years from creation, subtract two years. There is a difference of ~214 years.

Passion Calendar

There was talk about the Rapture happening on January 1, 2000. To imagine going home was good but the date was off. First, the Rapture will occur in the fall on the Feast of Trumpets. Second, the Roman calendar has a six-year error. The two thousand anniversary of the birth of Jesus Christ was 1994. Third, the Rapture would occur seven years before the Second Coming or 1987. Fourth, years are aligned to the cross.

Jewish Calendar Discrepancies[27]

Revised		Jewish		Change	Event
AM	Length	AM	Length		
1	1656	1	1656		Creation & Adam
1656	292	1656	292		Flood
1948	75	1948	70	5	Abraham
2023	430	2018	430		Covenant
2453	40		0	40	Exodus & Wilderness
2493	5		0	5	Conquer Land
2498	480	2448	480		Judges to Solomon's 4th
2078	2	2928	2		Temple Complete
2980	410	2930	410		Solomon 6th & Judah
3390	656	3338	490	166	1st Temple (587 BC) to 2nd Temple (70 AD)
4046	1942	3830	1942		September 16, 2012 *Tishri* 1, 5773 (~5985 AM)
5988	-2	5772	-2	216	Chronology Error
5986	-1			214	Year Begins at 1
5985		5772			January 1, 2012 Jewish Year 5772

We began a new millennium on the Roman calendar. But on God's calendar, we are at the end of the sixth millennium. Jesus Christ has not started His reign. The Second Coming is a few more years and then the seven years of Tribulation.

The Roman Gregorian calendar counts from the birth of Jesus Christ. It is called *Anno Domini* or the Year of our Lord.[28] *Anno Passionis Christi* or Year of the Passion of Christ counts from the cross. In God's calendar, there are 4000 years before the cross and 3000 years after the cross. April 2012 is ~1985 years from the cross of 27 AD or ~5985 years from creation.

Timing Issues

After tracking Bible chronologies from creation to the Millennium, known errors adjust the year. However, unanswered questions move the date forward or backward.

1. Life of Jesus Christ

Events of the life of Christ change the timeline. Jesus Christ was born between 7 BC-1 AD. His ministry lasted 2½ to 3½ years. The year of the cross was 27-33 AD.

2. Year Starts at Birth or the Cross

The year starts at the birth of Jesus Christ or the cross. In Daniel 9, the sixty-nine weeks ends at the cross. Since we are still here after 1999, add thirty-three years to the countdown clock then subtract years in the twenty-first century.

3. Spring to Fall

If Jesus Christ was born in October 7 BC and redeemed the world in April 27 AD, six months are between Passover and Trumpets. The Feast of Trumpets can occur from September 4 to October 6.[29] This moves the Rapture and Second Coming forward or backward six months.

4. Rapture and Tribulation

The view of the Rapture and Tribulation impacts the timeline. The Rapture will happen zero to seven years before the Second Coming. The Tribulation period is zero to seven years.

5. Gap between Rapture and Tribulation

A gap exists between the Rapture and the beginning of the Tribulation. The time could be a few days or a few years.

6. Time Between Advents

The Bible does not tell the years between Christ's First Coming and Second Coming. If the Church Age is 2000 years and the Tribulation is seven years, the answer is 2007.

If the Church Age is 1993 years and the Tribulation is seven years, the answer is 2000. That is another plus or minus seven years.

7. Calendar Errors

The Roman calendar has a six-year error for the birth of Jesus Christ. The Jewish calendar is off ~214 years. More errors may exist in the Roman and Jewish calendars.

8. Predictions of the Rapture

If a minister predicts an early Rapture, it discredits the person and his ministry but if the prediction is late, we will be in Heaven so it will not matter.

> Don't ever prophesy; for if you prophesy wrong, nobody will forget it; and if you prophesy right, nobody will remember it.
> —American Humorist Josh Billings, 19th Century[30]

If a minister predicts God could come back any day in the next one hundred years, he ignores the signs of the times, fails as a watchman for the Church and leaves the Saints unaware of the time and plan of God.

> If the watchman see the sword come, and blow not the trumpet, and the people be not warned; if the sword come, and take any person from among them, his blood will I require at the watchman's hand (Ezekiel 33:6).

9. Live and Watch for Christ's Return

If a person lives as if Christ will never return, remember a judgment day is coming. If a person believes Jesus Christ will return soon, it will change his heart and life to impact the Church.

> Blessed is that servant, whom his lord when he comes shall find so doing. Verily I say unto you, That he shall make him ruler over all his goods (Matthew 24:46-47).

10. Personal Bias

The final issue is my personal bias. Although clear evidence exists that the Rapture happens sooner rather than later, there is a personal relevance to this study. I want to go home but I must help wake up the Church and encourage Christians. The more I study End Time prophecy, the more urgent the message becomes. It is about time but it will not happen until God completes His plan for the Church Age through the Church.

Some Answers and More Questions

Prophecy is about time. After a deeper understanding of creation, Jewish holy days and history, Daniel's seventy weeks, the life of Christ and Bible chronology, we have a better understanding of God's time. Studying the Roman and Jewish calendars correct a few errors while leaving a few unresolved issues. These corrections move the Rapture and Second Coming forward or backward.

Radio preacher Harold Camping predicted the Rapture would occur on May 21, 2011 and then October 21, 2011 but nothing happened.[31] Previously, he predicted May 21, 1988 and September 6, 1994. The Rapture can be a great hope for Christians but his predictions discouraged his followers and encouraged his critics. Two things are true. Jesus Christ is going to Rapture his Church and we are twenty-five years closer than his first prediction.

Despite various interpretations of time and prophecy, we are living within the margin of error. Scripture points to the Jewish feasts of Trumpets and Atonement but we still do not know the year of the Rapture and Second Coming. Many people talk about an endless future with better opportunities for our children and grandchildren. That is just not true. God's time tells us we are the people living in the End Times when Jesus Christ will return. We see the final preparations for the Tribulation. We will witness our unsaved family, friends and neighbors left behind. In ten years, we will be on the edge of the apocalypse or the world will be inside the Tribulation.

Now that the time of prophecy is better understood, the events of prophecy are examined and placed on the timeline. The seven churches, seven world powers, seven seals and seven trumpets are God's plan for our time. We are further into the book of Revelation than most scholars say. Knowing the fulfilled American prophecies through the World Wars and Iraq Wars gives a complete picture of God's time and God's plan. Fulfilled prophecy tells us exactly where and when we are and what war is next.

Do you see where we are in God's plan for our time?

Section 4

God's Plan for Our Time

Chapter 19

Church Age & End Times

After setting the foundation of prophecy with God, God's Word and God's time, the rest of this study continues sequentially through the prophetic events of the Church Age, End Times, Rapture, Tribulation, Millennium and beyond. God's Plan for Our Time explains a current view of events during the Church Age and End Times before the Rapture.

The Revelation of Jesus Christ was written for seven churches in the province of Asia Minor in present-day Turkey. God is personally involved in the lives of His people so He evaluates the spiritual condition of His churches. Through the Bible, prayer, a local church and trials, the Holy Spirit helps us improve our relationships with God and empowers us as a part of the body of Christ.[1]

While seven messages were given to seven churches in the first century, we can evaluate the scriptural health of contemporary Christian churches. Additionally, the churches are seven prophetic sequential periods of the Church Age.[2]

Seven Churches[3]

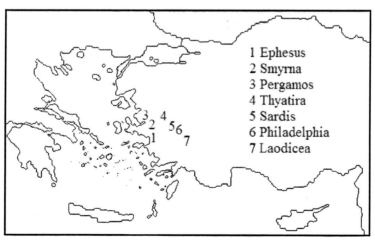

1 Ephesus
2 Smyrna
3 Pergamos
4 Thyatira
5 Sardis
6 Philadelphia
7 Laodicea

Seven Churches of Revelation

1. Ephesus — Revelation 2:1-7 (Years 27-100 AD)

Ephesus is the apostolic church and the name means desirable.[4] It was the port capital of Western Asia Minor along the Aegean Sea. Under Roman control, it became the religious, cultural and economic center of the region. In the city was the temple for the Greek goddess Diana, one of the seven wonders of the ancient world. Paul founded the church on his second missionary journey and returned on his third journey. He worked with the community three years. Later, Timothy and John pastored the church. During the early Church Age, the Church grew quickly and kept true to the apostles' doctrine.

> Nevertheless I have somewhat against you, because you have left your first love. Remember therefore from where you have fallen, and repent, and do the first works; or else I will come unto you quickly, and will remove your candlestick out of his place, except you repent. To him that overcomes will I give to eat of the tree of life, which is in the midst of the paradise of God (Revelation 2:4-5, 7).

Jesus Christ describes Himself holding the seven stars (pastors) in the middle of the seven golden lampstands (churches). The church at Ephesus is praised for its hard work, endurance and discernment of genuine apostles. Yet, despite their great apostolic heritage and true doctrine, they left their first love. They were zealous for God, eager to grow but now are stale in their relationship. If they remember where they have been, repent and do the first works, they will eat from the Tree of Life.

2. Smyrna — Revelation 2:8-11 (Years 100-313)

Smyrna is the persecuted church and the name means myrrh.[5] The city was a port along the Aegean Sea — an economic and cultural center and home to the first temple for Caesar Tiberius, Roman emperor during Christ's life. This period was the worst persecution in Church history. Polycarp was a convert of John and pastor of the church until he was martyred in 153 AD. The Romans martyred many Christians for their faith by crucifixion, feeding them to lions and burning them at the stake. In 303, Diocletian reign of ten years was the last and greatest persecution of Christians. Despite severe persecution, the Church endured, prospered and the Gospel spread throughout the empire.

> Fear none of those things which you shall suffer: behold, the devil shall cast some of you into prison, that you may be tried; and you shall have tribulation ten days: be faithful unto death, and I will give you a crown of life. He that overcomes shall not be hurt of the second death (Revelation 2:10-11).

Jesus Christ describes Himself as the First and Last, who was dead and came to life. This is a reminder of His martyrdom but also His eternal nature, salvation and power over death. The church is praised for their good works and being spiritually rich despite their poverty and great trials. Opposition comes from Jews who have not accepted Christ. Trials refine believers and advance God's purpose. The Church will suffer and some believers will be imprisoned and die. Those who are faithful to death will not only obtain eternal life but also will be rewarded with the martyr's crown.

3. Pergamos—Revelation 2:12-17 (Years 313-606)

Pergamos is the compromising church and the name means elevation of power.[6] The city was a Greek capital after Alexander the Great's empire was divided. It had the first temple to Caesar Augustus in Asia Minor, the great altar for Zeus and the temple of Esculapius, the serpent idol, is Satan's throne. John ordained Antipas as pastor who was martyred during the reign of Domitian in 92 AD. In 313, Constantine and Licinius issued the Edict of Milan, which proclaimed religious toleration.[7] By 391, Theodosius made Christianity the official religion of the Roman Empire.[8] The end of persecution was the beginning of compromise as the Christian Church and pagan Roman state merged.

> But I have a few things against you, because you have there those that hold the doctrine of Balaam, who taught Balac to cast a stumbling block before the children of Israel, to eat things sacrificed unto idols, and to commit fornication. To him that overcomes will I give to eat of the hidden manna, and will give him a white stone, and in the stone a new name written, which no man knows saving he that receives it (Revelation 2:14, 17).

Jesus Christ describes himself holding a sharp double-edge sword (the Word). The church is praised for their loyalty to God, even though they live where Satan has his throne and Antipas and others are martyred. However, as Balaam brings idolatry to Israel, the Roman Empire brings paganism to the Church.[9] Nicolaitan means to conquer the people. God designed Christ as the head and Church as the body. Instead, the Nicolaitans made a priestly order (religious) rule the laity (secular). The church must repent or God will cleanse them with His sword of truth. If they obey, they will receive heavenly manna that fulfills spiritual hunger, a white stone which is a clean slate and a new name, the child of *Yahweh* God.

4. Thyatira—Revelation 2:18-29 (Years 606-1517)

Thyatira is the corrupt church and the name means sacrifice of labor.[10] The city was a thriving marketplace with many trade unions, each with a different pagan god. In Acts 16, Lydia of Thyatira was a trader of purple fabric. During this period, many false doctrines and pagan practices were brought into the Church. Among these traditions were holy images, worship services in Latin, priestly celibacy, purgatory and sale of indulgences to forgive sin.[11]

> Notwithstanding I have a few things against you, because you allow that woman Jezebel, which calls herself a prophetess, to teach and to seduce my servants to commit fornication, and to eat things sacrificed unto idols. And he that overcomes, and keeps my works unto the end, to him will I give power over the nations (Revelation 2:20, 26).

Jesus Christ describes Himself as eyes like a flame of fire and His feet like brass. He knows the human heart, is steadfast and judges fairly. The church has love, faith, perseverance and good works yet tolerates the false prophetess Jezebel. The most godless king of Israel was Ahab. He married a Phoenician woman, Jezebel, who brought idolatry to Israel in the form of Baal.[12] This Jezebel in Thyatira brings false doctrines and idolatry into the church all in the name of God. He will punish her with sickness and give trials to people who sin with her. Those who hold to good doctrine will rule the nations during the Millennium and will be given the morning star which is Jesus Christ.

5. Sardis—Revelation 3:1-6 (Years 1517-1750)

Sardis is the reformation church and the name means prince of joy.[13] The city was the former capital of the kingdom of Lydia. It was home to the goddess, Cybele, the Earth Mother. The city was wealthy and immoral. In 17 AD, an earthquake occurred but the city was rebuilt. The church was once great but has declined far from its former glory. This period of the Church Age rejected one centralized church and corrected doctrine through the Protestant Reformation.

> I know your works, that you have a name that you live, and are dead. Remember therefore how you have received and heard, and hold fast, and

repent. He that overcomes, the same shall be clothed in white raiment; and I will not blot out his name out of the book of life, but I will confess his name before my Father, and before his angels (Revelation 3:1, 3, 5).

Jesus Christ describes Himself having the sevenfold Spirit of God and seven stars (pastors). The church thinks it is alive but is spiritually dead. The people have a form of godliness but are powerless. They are told to wake up, remember what they have heard, obey and repent. Christ will come as a thief to judge and they will be caught off-guard. Even this dead church has a few Christians who still live uprightly and walk with God. They will be dressed in God's righteousness, be kept in the Book of Life and Jesus Christ will confess their names before God the Father.

6. Philadelphia—Revelation 3:7-13 (Years 1750-1900)

Philadelphia is the faithful church and the name means brotherly love.[14] King Eumenes II of Pergamon names the city for the love of his brother. Founded in 198 BC, it is the youngest of the seven but became prosperous. The city was built to spread the Greek way of life. During this period, the Church grew spiritually. It was a time of great evangelism and missionary outreach throughout the world. The Gospel spread the Christian way of life—not out of persecution but out of love. Philadelphia is our example of a spiritual church.

> Behold, I have set before you an open door, and no man can shut it: for you have a little strength, and have kept my word, and have not denied my name. I will keep you from the hour of temptation, which shall come upon all the world, to try them that dwell upon the earth. I will write upon him the name of my God, and the name of the city of my God, which is new Jerusalem, and I will write upon him my new name (Revelation 3:8, 10, 12).

Jesus Christ describes Himself as holy and true and as the keeper of the keys and the door . The church is given an open door of evangelism. They are weak but receive their strength from God. They are praised for keeping the Word and being faithful. Although there is conflict from the Jews, the church will be proven right by their accusers. Since they are steadfast, they will be kept from the Tribulation. They are encouraged to hold on to their spiritual gains so no one takes their victor's crown. He who overcomes will be a strong, stable pillar in God's temple and one that withstands earthquakes. Because of his close relationship, he will know the names of God the Father and Jesus Christ.

Seven Churches[15]

Church/ Period	Meaning	Strength	Weakness	Character
Ephesus 27-100	Desirable	Labor Patience Discernment	Left Your First Love	Apostolic
Smyrna 100-313	Myrrh	Spiritually Rich Martyrs Faithful until Death	Poverty Tribulation Testing	Persecution
Pergamos 313-606	Elevation of Power	Hold Fast Faithful	False Doctrine Balaam Nicolaitans	Compromise
Thyatira 606-1517	Sacrifice of Labor	Love Service Faith Patience	False Prophetess Jezebel	Corrupt
Sardis 1517-1750	Prince of Joy	A Few Walk with God	Dead	Reformation
Philadelphia 1750-1900	Brotherly Love	Kept My Word Not Denied My Name	Little Strength	Faithful
Laodicea 1900-20??	Lay People		Lukewarm	Mediocre

7. Laodicea — Revelation 3:14-22 (Years 1900-20??)

Laodicea is the mediocre church and the name means lay people.[16] Antiochus II of Greek Syria names the city after his wife, Laodice. It is a Roman free city and the regional capital. Because of its location on the trade route, the city prospered. Cold and hot springs were located near the city. In 62 AD, the city was destroyed by an earthquake but was rebuilt by the wealth of its own citizens. Paul wrote the book of Colossians to Colosse and the neighboring churches of Hierapolis and Laodicia to confront legalistic Judaism and Gnostic knowledge apart from Christ. In history, this period covers the end of the Church Age, which is the End Times.

I know your works, that you are neither cold nor hot: I would you were cold or hot. So then because you are lukewarm, and neither cold nor hot, I will spew you out of my mouth. To him that overcomes will I grant to sit with me in my throne, even as I also overcame, and am set down with my Father in his throne (Revelation 3:15-16, 21).

Jesus Christ describes Himself as the Faithful and True Witness. He has ruled with God the Father since the beginning of creation. The church's spiritual works are neither hot nor cold but rather lukewarm which makes God sick. Instead of depending on God, the church is content with physical wealth. They are unaware of their spiritual health and others in need. Without God's holiness, they are wretched, miserable, poor, blind and naked. They are commanded to buy gold refined by fire and white garments to cover themselves then apply eye salve to see. The church avoids trials that would purify them. They must repent and be passionate about their relationship with God. While Philadelphia is the open door, Laodicea is the closed door with Christ outside. Christians who open the door will have perfect fellowship with Him. Those who overcome will sit with Jesus Christ on His throne during the Millennium.

Christian Churches Today

These seven churches are used to evaluate the spiritual health of contemporary Christian churches. The mediocre church of Laodicea is the dominant characteristic of today's local churches which are filled with a form of godliness but are weak. In the United States, the church is physically rich but spiritually poor. Christians attend church but people are not living out their faith in a radical self-sacrificing way that shines a bright light to a dying world. The persecuted church of Smyrna is in China and Islamic nations where Christians are faithful despite great persecution. The dead or dying churches of Sardis and Thyatira are found throughout Europe as shadows of their former glory. The faithful church of Philadelphia is evident in India where despite great poverty there is growing faith.

Let your light so shine before men, that they may see your good works and glorify your Father which is in heaven (Matthew 5:16).

Which church would we be? How much time and effort do we put into building our relationships with God? How do we balance truth and love? Are we living what we believe and encouraging other Christians to do the same? How are we using our gifts and talents in our local churches? Revival starts with one person wholeheartedly obeying God.

Laodicean Period and the End Times

The seven churches of Revelation 2-3 are prophetic and follow seven sequential periods of the Church Age. The Laodicean period is the last period. It is a time when the church is lukewarm and trusts in wealth instead of God. The church gets a feel-good message and watered-down Gospel. The sermons are of God's love, grace and mercy, health and wealth but rarely about God's holiness, righteousness and justice or man's sin and need for repentance. People complain when the pastor preaches too long. If someone experiences conviction, they may be offended and go to another church. The focus is on personalities and entertainment in order that people do not become bored with that old, old story of Jesus.

> This know also, that in the last days perilous times shall come. For men shall be lovers of their own selves, having a form of godliness, but denying the power thereof: from such turn away (2 Timothy 3:1-2, 5).

The average church is a top-down Sunday morning service in which the preacher hand-feeds the people their weekly meal. In most churches, eighty percent of the people warm the pews and do not use their spiritual gifts. The twenty percent suffer burnout because they fail to make disciples. Strong verse-by-verse Bible studies, fervent prayer, communion and commitment to one another is lacking in church. We need to stop running by the world's system like a mouse on a wheel—running faster and faster but not getting anywhere.

The Laodicean church is contrasted with the growing, healthy church of Acts 2. They eagerly studied God's Word together and lived their faith. When growing together in the church, we prepare for difficult days ahead and minister together as we spread the Gospel to the world.

> And they continued steadfastly in the apostles' doctrine and fellowship, and in breaking of bread, and in prayers. And fear came upon every soul: and many wonders and signs were done by the apostles. And all that believed were together, and had all things common; And sold their possessions and goods, and divided them to all men, as every man had need. And they, continuing daily with one accord in the temple, and breaking bread from house to house, did eat their meat with gladness and singleness of heart, Praising God, and having favor with all the people. And the Lord added to the church daily such as should be saved (Acts 2:42-47).

Scholars who believe in seven sequential periods of the Church Age begin the Laodicean period at ~1900. The Laodicean period is the End Times. Some include the Tribulation and

Millennium as part of the End Times. However for Christians, the end of the Church Age is the Rapture. Everything beyond Trumpets begins our new and glorious life.

The 1st of *Elul* is God's second chance for Israel. It is the day Moses returns for a second forty days with God to replace the broken tablets. The Jews have forty days of repentance called *Teshuvah*. This is preparation of the high holy days that include the Feast of Trumpets and Day of Atonement.

For Christians, the first thirty days correlates to the Laodicean period. The Tribulation is the last seven days. God sounds the trumpets to wake people up so they first turn to God for salvation. Then Christians are used by God in local churches. The End Times reconfigure the world's political, religious and economic systems in preparation for the Tribulation.

Seven Churches and the End Times

In Revelation 2-3, Jesus Christ evaluates seven local first-century churches. These churches are used to appraise our modern churches and our own lives. Do our spiritual lives measure up to God's standards? Although we are out of Egypt, are we stuck wandering in the wilderness because we do not follow God or are we fulfilling our personal ministry by entering the Promised Land and conquering new territory for the Kingdom of God?

The seven churches are seven sequential periods of the Church Age. The Laodicean church is the last period characterized by lukewarm Christianity and fulfilled prophecy. The end of the Church Age is the Rapture.

Since we are one hundred years into the Laodicean period, do you clearly see the signs of the times?

Chapter 20

Players in the Game

Before getting into prophecy, who are the present End Time powers? Some scholars say you cannot take Scripture and compare events in the news. Others believe current events are important yet neglect recent history.

> You know how to discern the face of the sky, but you cannot discern the signs of the times (Matthew 16:3).

Commentaries written twenty-five years ago are out-of-date because three Iraq Wars change everything. If you want to know the End Times, look at a map. China, the European Union, India, Iran, Iraq, Israel, Libya, Russia and the United States are described in Bible prophecy. In God's plan, it is all about regime change. He tells us which countries rise and fall and in what order. By the Second Coming, all nations fall so Jesus Christ reigns on earth.

> The Lord said unto my Lord, Sit thou at my right hand, until I make thine enemies thy footstool (Psalm 110:1).

> To the skeptic who says that Christ is not coming soon, I would ask him to put the book of Revelation in one hand, and the daily newspaper in the other, and then sincerely ask God to show him where we are on His prophetic time-clock.
> —Hal Lindsey, *There's a New World Coming*[1]

King of the Hill

As a child, I played the game "King of the Hill."[2] The object of the game is to become king by teaming up with others to remove the king off the hill and take his place. As king, you defend your position while others attempt to topple you. Another game I played was Risk.

The object of Risk is to remove every player and conquer the world.[3] With many players, it helps to form alliances and work together to conquer your enemies and later your allies.

Although war is no mere game, leaders such as Ramses, Nebuchadnezzar, Cyrus, Alexander, Julius Caesar, Charlemagne, Napoleon, Stalin, Hitler, Mao, Churchill and Roosevelt conquered their world and briefly became "king of the hill." Since the beginning of nations, dominant regional powers have existed. Currently, the United States is the lone superpower. Other nations desire to topple us and "win."

> Uh, it's like in chess. First, you strategically position your pieces and when the timing is right you strike.... Checkmate!
> —*Independence Day*, 1996[4]

Countries use people and natural resources, form alliances and compete against other countries to gain power. "He who has the gold, rules." English historian John Acton said, "All power corrupts and absolute power corrupts absolutely."[5] Because of man's fallen nature, flawed people govern flawed nations.

God is sovereign over all peoples and keeps nations in check. Look at the world from God's perspective. He makes nations rise and fall and uses both good and evil to advance His purpose. His plan is not driven by pride, greed or power but rather by love, mercy and grace. The real conflict is a war for the hearts and minds of humanity.

> Blessed be the name of God for ever and ever: for wisdom and might are his: And he changes the times and the seasons: he removes kings, and sets up kings: he gives wisdom unto the wise, and knowledge to them that know understanding (Daniel 2:20-21).

The purpose of God since creation has been the redemption of humanity through Jesus Christ. God has stirred up nations and reached out to individuals so that people repent from their sins and turn to God. During the benevolent reign of Jesus Christ, people will truly live in peace and harmony.

Bible Prophecy

> There is a way to connect the dots, to anticipate future headlines.
> —Joel Rosenberg, *Epicenter*[6]

A simple algebraic formula is: A + B = C. A is the current snapshot of nations: America reigns. C is fulfilled Bible prophecy: Christ reigns. B is the unknown of how to get from point A to C or from America to Christ. The unknown is known by understanding history, current events and prophecy. Before exploring prophecy, look at the End Time map. Seven End Time powers are ready for the Tribulation. Later chapters will examine the prophecies of these nations.

> From one man [Adam] he [God] made every nation of men, that they should inhabit the whole earth; and he determined the times set for them and the exact places where they should live (Acts 17:26 NIV).

End Time Nations

1. United States

The United States is the undisputed superpower. It is the leading economy, military, government, agriculture, innovator and culture in the world. It sends more missionaries and humanitarian aid to foreign countries. It is a member of the United Nations Security Council, G-8 (Group of Eight) and G-20 (Group of Twenty) economic leaders, NATO, the nuclear club and the Quartet on the Middle East. It uses its economic and military resources to spread democracy, improve human rights and increase wealth.

- Economic Powers: North America Union (NAFTA)* (23.72), European Union* (20.42), United States (19.73), Organization of Islamic Cooperation* (13.65), China (13.58), Japan (5.80), Union of South American Nations* (5.47), India (5.46), Germany (3.95), Russia (2.99), United Kingdom (2.92), Brazil (2.92), France (2.88), Italy (2.38) Mexico (2.11), South Korea (1.96)
  GDP – Percent of Gross Domestic Product[7] * Alliance
- United Nations Security Council: China, France, Russia, United Kingdom, United States[8]
- G-8: Canada, France, Germany, Italy, Japan, Russia, United Kingdom, United States[9]
- G-20: Argentina, Australia, Brazil, Canada, China, European Union, France, Germany, India, Indonesia, Italy, Japan, Mexico, Russia, Saudi Arabia, South Africa, South Korea, Turkey, United Kingdom, United States[10]
- NATO: Albania, Belgium, Bulgaria, Canada, Croatia, Czech Republic, Denmark, Estonia, France, Germany, Greece, Hungary, Iceland, Italy, Latvia, Lithuania, Luxembourg, Netherlands, Norway, Poland, Portugal, Romania, Slovakia, Slovenia, Spain, Turkey, United Kingdom, United States[11]

After the Soviet Union fell, America became the only superpower. The United States is coasting on its past greatness as a shadow of its former glory. It is undermined by government spending and trade deficits. Since 2000, these huge spending sprees have spiraled out of control. Taxes and interest payments rise as the value of the dollar falls. As a result, Americans lose more liberty and the federal government gains more power over our lives. Dependence on foreign oil leaves our economy vulnerable. Oil makes Middle East peace and fighting radical Islamic terrorism a national security priority. Losing good manufacturing jobs to Asia worsens economic problems.

> Estimates indicate over the next twenty years, U.S. oil consumption will increase 33 percent... Yet we produce 39 percent less oil today than we did in 1970, leaving us ever more reliant on foreign suppliers.
> —2001 National Energy Policy[12]

Democrats and Republicans attempt to solve capitalistic problems with socialistic answers. Congress refuses immediate spending cuts and tax reforms to avoid the next depression. Washington and banks set bad lending policies and cause the mortgage crisis yet no one goes to jail. Bailouts help bank corporate executives while Washington gains more power. Our foreign creditors, most importantly China, are buying up our assets.[13] America's days are numbered.

> The rich rule over the poor, and the borrower is servant to the lender (Proverbs 22:7).

- Foreign Holding of US Treasury Securities: China (22.65), Japan (21.28), OPEC* (5.19), Caribbean* (4.54), Brazil (4.47), Taiwan (3.60), Switzerland (2.84), Russia (2.83), Belgium (2.45), United Kingdom (2.27)[14]
  * Alliance

[Jenny] Can you say why America is the greatest country in the world?

[Will] It's NOT the greatest country in the world.... Sure used to be. We stood up for what was right. We fought for moral reasons. We passed laws, struck down laws, for moral reasons.... We built great big things, made ungodly technological advances, explored the universe, cured diseases, and we cultivated the world's greatest artists and the world's greatest economy. We reached for the stars.... First step in solving any problem is recognizing there is one. America is not the greatest country in the world anymore.
—*The Newsroom*, 2012[15]

Our actions result in global consequences. History tells us all superpowers rise and fall. The United States is missing as a leader during the Tribulation. Since the Cold War ended in 1991, we have seen a sharp decline of the United States. Nature abhors a vacuum. China, the European Union, India, Islam and Russia exploit our weaknesses and plot to replace us as king of the hill.[16]

> America, for some years, has been broke and getting in more financial trouble all the time with an incredible, mind-boggling federal deficit. A financial judgment day is going to come to the United States before the end of this century unless the budget can be balanced and we start paying back what we owe.
> —Billy Graham, *Approaching Hoofbeats*[17]

By the mercy of God, America's judgment day is delayed but certain. Our financial problems reveal how difficult it is to keep superpower status. By the 2020's, our economic depression will make us choose between entitlements, discretionary spending, interest on the debt or the next world war. It will be a disaster one hundred times greater than Greece with no one to bail us out.

> We have been the recipient of the choicest bounties of Heaven. We have been preserved, these many years, in peace and prosperity. We have grown in number, wealth and power, as no other nation has ever grown. But we have forgotten God.
> —US President Abraham Lincoln, Proclamation Appointing a National Fast Day, 1863[18]

Just changing political parties, economic policy or society's morality will not fix the problem. America's economic crisis is a direct result of our rejection of God. That results in broken families, powerless churches, moral weakness and judgment from God. Only faithful Christians working together in strong churches have the Holy Spirit's power to change communities and our nation.

> If my people, which are called by my name, shall humble themselves, and pray, and seek my face, and turn from their wicked ways; then will I hear from heaven, and will forgive their sin, and will heal their land (2 Chronicles 7:14).

Through the World Wars, Iraq Wars and End Wars, the Bible describes in many dramatic details the great rise and even greater fall of the United States and rise of the next world superpower.

2. Russia

Russia, as part of the Soviet Union, was a superpower. After the Berlin Wall fell, the bear went into hibernation. It is still a political, economic and nuclear power with a large stockpile of nuclear missiles and top supplier of weapons to about eighty countries.[19] It is the largest country by area and is first in oil exports with Saudi Arabia a close second. As part of the United Nations Security Council, G-8, BRIC, the nuclear club, Quartet on the Middle East and since 1997, has a partnership with the European Union, it still has a great influence as a world power.

- Quartet on the Middle East: European Union, Russia, United Nations, United States[20]
- BRIC Emerging Economies: Brazil, Russia, India, China[21]
- Leading Oil Producers: Russia, Saudi Arabia, United States, Iran, China, Canada, Mexico, United Arab Emirates, Brazil, Kuwait[22]
- Leading Oil Consumers: United States, China, Japan, India, Russia, Germany, Brazil, Saudi Arabia, Canada, South Korea[23]

Since 2000, President Vladimir Putin has awakened Russia and reverted to those old Soviet ways. He increased centralized power, bypassed the democratic process, reversed human rights, strengthened Islamic alliances, interfered with Ukraine and invaded Georgia. When beneficial, Russia joins with China, Europe and other countries. The Russian-Islamic alliance is described in a future prophecy war.[24]

3. China

China is the most populated country in the world. It is a member of the United Nations Security Council, G-20, BRIC and the nuclear club. The economy is third to the European Union and United States but is on track to pass the US by 2016.[25] Financial success results in a better standard of living for some citizens but not greater personal liberty. Problems exist with overpopulation and aging because of the one-child policy.[26]

A growing Chinese economy significantly increases its military. China's defense spending is 4.3 percent of its GDP.[27] In 2007, the reported budget was 45 billion but the US Pentagon estimated the amount was between 97 and 139 billion dollars.[28] China is preparing the military to use that power.

- Top Population: Organization of Islamic Conference* (23.07), China (19.32), India (17.45), European Union* (7.24), North American Union (NAFTA)* (6.59), Union

of South America Nations* (5.59), United States (4.50), Indonesia (3.43), Brazil (2.75), Pakistan (2.55), Nigeria (2.28), Bangladesh (2.18), Russia (2.06), Japan (1.85), Mexico (1.62), Philippines (1.36)[29]
* Alliance

The question that the American people have to ask is why it is that corporate America—with the active support of the president of the United States and the congressional leadership—is selling out the American people and making China the economic superpower of the 21st century.
—US Senator Bernie Sanders of Vermont, 2005[30]

Both China and the United States compete for limited natural resources such as oil and iron. America is at a growing disadvantage because our shortsighted politicians, federal deficits, imports and greedy corporations seek cheap labor overseas. China is a much bigger threat to the United States than Islamic terrorism. When their economy passes ours then Red China challenges the United States for world leader. In the last one thousand years, war always preceded a change of superpower.

4. India

India is the second most populated country in the world with over a billion people and is a member of the G-20, BRIC and the nuclear club.[31] On its current path, its population will pass that of China by 2025.

In 1947, India gained independence from the United Kingdom. With the help of its democracy, global trade and a large English-speaking population, it is an emerging global power with a fast-growing economy. India is a founding member of the Non-Aligned Nations and has joined with Brazil, Germany and Japan to request membership of the United Nations Security Council.

• Nuclear Nations: China, France, India, Iran, Israel, North Korea, Pakistan, Russia, United Kingdom, United States[32]

India faces major problems with overpopulation, poverty, corruption and ethnic strife. It has border disputes with Pakistan and China. After four wars with Pakistan and both obtaining nuclear weapons, its relationship with its Islamic neighbor is a fragile coexistence. India's location, population and economy make a good counterbalance to China. Its workforce and growing economy make India an influential world player.

5. Israel

Israel is a small country of about eight million people and is about the size of New Jersey.[33] It has a good economy and stable democracy in the Middle East. A close ally with the United States, Israel has a strong military and membership in the nuclear club. Since 2000, Israel has been an associate member of the European Union through the Union for the Mediterranean.[34] It is working to become a full member. Israel has little influence in the world.

In sixty years, Israel has been in eight wars with its Arab neighbors and constantly deals with Islamic terrorism. Only Egypt and Jordan recognize Israel's right to exist. One of many roadblocks to Middle East peace is border disputes with the Palestine territory and Syria. The Quartet on the Middle East is working with Israel and Palestine on the peace process.[35] In 1994, Israel built a barrier along Judea and Samaria (West Bank) to curb terrorism.

Of all the nations and alliances, Israel is the least likely to conquer the world. After their last minute conversion, Israel will be the only nation standing after Jesus Christ returns at His Second Coming.

End Time Alliances

Besides individual nations, there is an unprecedented rush toward regional alliances based on the European model.[36] Nations form a government that sets trade policy and includes a central bank and court system. These unions control defense, security, foreign policy and currency. The biggest challenge is to integrate multiple peoples, cultures, languages, nations and governments.

Sixteen major regional political and economic unions cover about ninety-five percent of the world. Africa, Europe and South America grew from smaller alliances to cover most of their continent. That is a good strategy in the game of Risk. When united with other nations, alliances lead by consensus and provide weak countries more influence in the world. However, top-down centralized government diminishes national sovereignty and drastically weakens democracies and individual liberty.

Regional Alliances[37]

Alliance	Year/ Members	Population Percent	GDP Percent
Association of Southeast Asian Nations (ASEAN) Plus Three (APT)	1999 13	30.54	25.50
North American Free Trade Agreement (NAFTA), Security and Prosperity Partnership of North America (SPPNA)	1994 3 2005	6.95	23.72
Union for the Mediterranean (EuroMed)	1995 43	11.45	23.61
European Union (EU)	1951 27	7.24	20.42
Shanghai Cooperation Organization[38]	2001 6	22.22	18.94
Organization of Islamic Cooperation (OIC)[39]	1971 57	23.07	13.65
Union of South American Nations (USAN)	2008 12	5.47	5.59
South Asian Association for Regional Cooperation (SAARC)	1984 8	23.07	5.09
Association of Southeast Asian Nations (ASEAN)	1967 10	8.66	4.15
African Union (AU)	2002 54	13.95	3.83
Arab League (AL)	1945 21	5.19	3.72
Eurasian Union (EAU)	1996 5	2.59	3.47
Cooperation Council for the Arab States of the Gulf (CCASGC)	1981 6	.56	1.39
Pacific Island Forum (PIF) Pacific Union	1971 16	.46	1.25
Central American Integration System (CAIS)	1960 7	.74	.43
Caribbean Community (CARICOM)	1973 15	.23	.12

End Time Alliances[40]

The Lord said, Behold, the people is one, and they have all one language; and this they begin to do: and now nothing will be restrained from them, which they have imagined to do (Genesis 11:6).

God set up nations to limit dictators and protect people. Instead of 190+ individual nations that limit bad governments, these regional alliances remove national borders and prepare for world government. Without any opposition, one charismatic leader will become an all-powerful, all-controlling king of the world.

1. European Union

The European Union is the most advanced supranational alliance with twenty-seven member states, twenty associates and twenty-three official languages.[41] Since the Roman Empire divided in 476, various leaders from Charlemagne to Hitler attempted to reunite the region by war. Finally in 1950, six countries of the former Holy Roman Empire unite based on economic resources. The EU has grown to be the largest economy in the world. It promotes tolerance and multiculturalism. The EU has the Euro currency and with the Union for the Mediterranean, a land mass greater than the original Roman Empire.

What is this sovereign remedy? It is to re-create the European family, or as much of it as we can, and to provide it with a structure under which it can dwell in peace, in safety and in freedom. We must build a kind of United States of Europe.
—Prime Minister Winston Churchill, United Kingdom, 1946[42]

The EU is a complete government with executive, legislative and judicial branches. It deals with the economy, trade, agriculture, energy, environment, transportation, defense, foreign policy and security. France, Germany and the United Kingdom are about half the economy. France and the United Kingdom are permanent members of the United Nations Security Council and have nuclear weapons. France, Germany, Italy and the United Kingdom are members of the G-8. Twenty-one nations are part of NATO (North Atlantic Treaty Organization). The EU is part of the G-8, G-20 and Quartet on the Middle East. The European Defense Agency supplies troops for the military.[43] The EU sees itself as a counterbalance to the United States. This was evident during the Iraq War when France and Germany played the game.

This is not about Saddam Hussein, and this is not even about regime change in Iraq or … missiles or chemical weapons. It's about whether the United States is allowed to run world affairs.
—Pierre Lellouche, foreign-policy adviser to French President Jacques Chirac, 2003[44]

History of the European Union[45]
*   European Coal and Steel Community (1952)
*   European Economic Community (1958)
*   European Union (1993)

Besides twenty-seven members, the European Union influence is growing. The EU is working with the Balkans and since 1997, has been partners with Russia.[46] The Union for the Mediterranean (UM) extends its reach into Africa and Asia to develop economic cooperation and prepares for future EU expansion.[47]

The European Union is starting to develop an enormous sphere of influence, extending way beyond its borders, that could be called the "Eurosphere." This belt of eighty countries covering the former Soviet Union, the Middle East, and North Africa accounts for 20 per cent of the world's population.
—Mark Leonard, *Why Europe Will Run the 21st Century*[48]

European Union Eurosphere

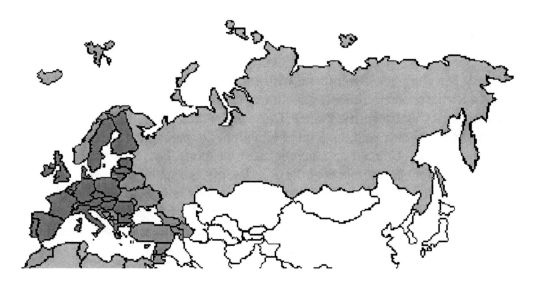

European Union Members and Associates[49]

- 10 Original Members: Belgium, France, Germany, Greece, Luxembourg, Italy, Netherlands, Portugal, Spain, United Kingdom
- 17 Additional Members: Austria, Bulgaria, Cyprus, Czech Republic, Denmark, Estonia, Finland, Hungary, Ireland, Latvia, Lithuania, Malta, Poland, Romania, Slovakia, Slovenia, Sweden
- 16 Associates (UM): Albania*, Algeria, Bosnia and Herzegovina, Croatia*, Egypt, Israel, Jordan, Lebanon, Mauritania, Monaco, Montenegro*, Morocco, Palestine†, Syria, Tunisia, Turkey*
- 4 Other: Iceland*, Kosovo, Macedonia*, Serbia*
- 1 Partnership: Russia
  *Candidate, †Territory

The EU has many issues to solve before it is king of the hill. The socialist policies of Portugal, Ireland, Italy, Greece and Spain (PIIGS) created an Euro crisis and exposed weaknesses in the EU.[50] After the United States falls, the European Union will fill the void as the next superpower. Lacking a spiritual foundation, moral character and political will, it is doomed to fall more quickly than it rises.

2. North American Union

In 1994, Canada, Mexico and the United States ratified the North American Free Trade Agreement (NAFTA).[51] In 2005, they approved the Security and Prosperity Partnership (SPPNA) to provide greater cooperation on economic and security issues.[52] Mexican President Fox supported a common currency and a free flow of people across the borders. Canada and Mexico are major US oil importers.[53] Our demand for oil sets immigration policy. This alliance trails other regions but follows the same path of economic then political merger toward a North American Union.

> So our proposal is to move to a second phase of NAFTA where in five to ten years that border will be open to free flow of people, workers, transiting in the border between our two countries....
> —Mexican President Vicente Fox, 2000[54]

End Time Religions

After considering individual nations and political/economic alliances, two major religious alliances exist. Islam and Catholicism have many worshipers and religious structures that influence the world during the End Times.

1. Islam

Islam has over a billion members in its religion. The Organization of Islamic Cooperation has fifty-seven members that have authority over twenty-three percent of the world's population.[55] Despite the conflict between Sunni and Shiite Muslims, secular and theocratic nations, Islam exerts a growing influence on the world.

Islamic nations are united by a political and religious system. Oil is a powerful economic and political asset of Iran, Iraq, Libya, the Persian Gulf states and Saudi Arabia. Pakistan has nuclear weapons and Iran is working to develop them.[56] Peace between Israel and Palestine is a critical foreign-policy issue.[57] Islam is a key player in the End Times.

2. Catholicism

For the last 1700 years, the Roman Catholic Church has been an influential world power. The Church was instrumental in leading the Crusades and controlled many nations. Today, Catholicism has a worldwide structure with over a billion members.[58] According to prophecy, the closer we get to the end of the age, the worse apostasy becomes. Many Christians in name only from Catholics and Protestant churches will abandon their faith. In a world absent of Christians during the Tribulation, the apostate church will merge with false religions them unite with a political world power.

End Time Government

1. United Nations

The United Nations is a multinational alliance of 193 countries.[59] From the start, it has failed in its mission to stop war. However, it has transformed into a powerful economic and political force controlling the World Bank, World Trade Organization, World Court, World Health Organization, International Monetary Fund and global environmental policy. These global initiatives become the policy of member states. The United Nations will be part of world government during the Tribulation.

End Time Powers

The United States is the current world superpower. Brazil, China, the European Union, India, Islam and Russia can rise to become a superpower within the twenty-first century and take our place.[60] Our government "kicks the can down the road" expecting our children or grandchildren to pay but we will pay with our lives. The Bible describes events that explain why America falls, who pushes us off the hill and who takes our place as superpower. In this life-and-death game for the control of the world, there can be only one winner. God uses the nations of the world to accomplish His plan.

Take a good look at the current End Time map. Instead of focusing on national borders, look at the game. What are the powers that rule the world? What are their philosophies and goals? What are their strength and weaknesses? Who are their allies and enemies? Look at the world from God's perspective. Through prophecy, the Bible describes seven End Time powers: Capitalism, Catholicism, Communism, the European Union, Islam, Israel and the United Nations. All of these powers fall before Jesus Christ reigns.

How do we get from America to the reign of Jesus Christ?

Chapter 21

Four Horses on the Run

2 1 *st Century Revelation: World Wars, Iraq Wars & End Wars* starts with a premise that we are living in the End Times right before the Rapture and Tribulation. The seals and trumpets explain why this is true. In one hundred years, over twenty super signs have occurred and are linked to specific Bible passages and Jewish dates. When God gave prophecy, He gave enough information for the people living in the End Times to identify not only whose they are but where and when they are. We must be ready to meet our Savior and Lord Jesus Christ and minister together as the Church until He comes.

Have your knife and fork ready because this is meat and not milk. It will require cutting away of the fat of tradition and gristle of denominational teachings. Major chewing is required to receive this message. Do not take my word but examine this message in the light of Scripture. Beyond the symbols and traditions, prophecy becomes quite simple. Why? Because God's unsealed and fulfilled Word is revealed. Prophecy is given so those who seek truth will find it. After knowing the End Time powers, then history and current events reveal four horses on the run.

> At that time Jesus answered and said, I thank thee, O Father, Lord of heaven and earth, because thou has hid these things from the wise and prudent, and has revealed them unto babes (Matthew 11:25).

The Seven Sealed Scroll

> I saw in the right hand of him that sat on the throne a book written within and on the backside, sealed with seven seals. And I saw a strong angel proclaiming with a loud voice, Who is worthy to open the book, and to loose the seals? And no man in heaven, nor in earth, neither under the earth, was able to open the book, neither to

look on. And I wept much, because no man was found worthy to open and to read the book, neither to look thereon (Revelation 5:1-4).

In Revelation 4-5, John views the throne of God. He witnesses God the Father seated on the throne as sovereign of the universe. Scripture reveals the character and nature of God. In His right hand is a scroll with seven seals. During the Roman Empire, a will was sealed with seven seals.[1] The scroll is God the Father's will which contains the title deed of earth.

The question is "Who is worthy to open the scroll?" No human is able because of sin. No angel is able because they are created beings. Neither is able because they are not God and did not earn the right to open the scroll. John cries because no one was worthy.

Jesus Christ is worthy to open the scroll. He is the Lion from the tribe of Judah and the Root of David. He willingly gave Himself as the perfect sacrifice on the cross. He is worthy because He is God, man and Savior. Because of His selfless action, He is worthy to inherit the earth.

> And all that dwell upon the earth shall worship him, whose names are not written in the book of life of the Lamb slain from the foundation of the world (Revelation 13:8).

Before the creation of the world, God knew Adam would fall. But His plan all along was to send Jesus Christ as Savior for humanity. Jesus Christ is worthy of love, worthy to judge and worthy to reign as King of Kings.

> Worthy is the Lamb that was slain to receive power, and riches, and wisdom, and strength, and honor, and glory, and blessing (Revelation 5:12).

The remainder of Revelation 5 focuses on praise and worship to God. Everyone in the presence of the throne falls down and worships God the Father and Jesus Christ, the Lamb of God who was slain. Worthy is the Lamb!

Four Horses of the Apocalypse

Jesus Christ takes the scroll and begins to break the seals and open the scroll. The seven sealed scroll is God's plan to judge the world and transition from Gentile rule to the reign of Jesus Christ.

Revelation 6 describes the Four Horses of the Apocalypse or four horses revealed. These horses are first referenced in Zechariah chapters 1 and 6. The horses and chariots have been roaming the earth for about 2500 years before the Tribulation.

> I saw by night, and behold a man riding upon a red horse, and he stood among the myrtle trees that were in the bottom; and behind him were there red horses, speckled, and white. Then said I, O my lord, what are these? These are they whom the LORD has sent to walk to and fro through the earth.... all the earth sits, and is at rest (Zechariah 1:8-11).

Zechariah described red, black, white, speckled and dappled horses with chariots that are loose on the earth. These were God's angels that brought judgment to Israel's neighbors during the Media-Persian era.

Traditional View

The Four Horses of the Apocalypse are four of the seven seals judgments. The Rapture, Tribulation and Millennium Reign of Christ are still future. Futurists believe all seal, trumpet and bowl judgments of Revelation happen in sequence in the seven-year Tribulation period.[2]

The first horse is white and the rider has a bow and a crown. He went out to conquer. The rider is the Antichrist who is given authority during the Tribulation. He conquers all who oppose him. Others say the rider is Christ because He returns on a white horse at the Second Coming. The second horse is red and the rider has a great sword. He takes peace from the earth which describes a great war. The third horse is black and the rider has a pair of scales. A days wage buys a quart of wheat or three quarts of barley. This describes a great famine because of the war. Food is scarce but luxuries are still available. The fourth horse is pale and the rider's name is Death and Hades follows him. He kills a fourth of the earth's population with the sword, hunger, death and beasts. As a result of the Antichrist, war and famine, many people die.

Key Words of the Four Horses

- White Horse: Conqueror—Bow, Crown, Conquer
- Red Horse: War—Take Peace, Sword, Kill
- Black Horse: Famine—Pair of Scales, Wheat, Barley
- Pale Horse: Death & Hell—Sword, Famine, Plague, Beasts

Prophecy is interpreted literally or figuratively. Through the Church Age, scholars interpreted passages with current world events when they were not fulfilled. Some believed Nero was the Antichrist. During the Reformation, Protestants taught that the pope was the Antichrist and Catholics taught that Protestants were the Antichrist. Futurists teach a literal view but fall back to a figurative view of the seals and trumpets. What happens when the future becomes the present?

Present View of the Seven Seals[3]

In Revelation 11, the sixth trumpet ends when the two witnesses are resurrected from the dead. This occurs at the middle of the Tribulation. In Revelation 16, the seventh bowl is the final judgment that occurs at the Second Coming. Scripture does not specifically tell when the other judgments begin or end.

Revelation 13 describes an unholy trinity. The Antichrist leads a world political government, the false prophet leads a world religion and they control people through the world economy. Revelation 6 describes those political, religious and economic systems before they unite.

Since we are at the end of the End Times, we can interpret prophecy with current events because they are unsealed, fulfilled and revealed. What is the current interpretation of the seals? Would we see the four horses if they ran right in front of our noses? Instead of getting lost in the symbolism, a more current interpretation makes prophecy relevant for our lives. Look at these horses from the perspective of color. Who has been on the run these past one hundred years? Of the seven End Time powers, four powers are four horses.

To make it easier, start with the red horse.

1. Red Horse of War—Communism/Socialism—Politics

> And when he had opened the second seal, I heard the second beast say, Come and see. And there went out another horse that was red: and power was given to him to take peace from the earth, and that they should kill one another: and there was given to him a great sword (Revelation 6:3-4).

One definition of red is Communism and Socialism. In 1848, Karl Marx wrote a book *Communist Manifesto* and launched the communist philosophy.[4] The term "Red

Communist" was frequently used during the Cold War to describe the Soviet Union and other Communist nations.

> Red (Adjective)
> 4 a: inciting or endorsing radical social or political change especially by force
>   b: often capitalized: Communist
>   c: often capitalized: of or relating to a communist country and especially to the Union of Soviet Socialist Republics
>   —*Merriam-Webster's Online Dictionary*[5]

Since 1919, we have seen the rider of the red horse loose on the world. The Red Communist armies of the Soviet Union, China and their allies make war. At the end of World War I, the Soviet Union emerged as the first communist country and after World War II became a superpower. At the time, Communists ruled a third of the world. During the leadership of Lenin, Stalin and Mao, millions of people were killed due to internal purges and external wars. World War I, World War II and the Cold War took peace from the earth.

> The red horse (vs. 4) produces wars and rumors of wars. Perhaps Russia (red) might have a part here.
> —Jack Van Impe, *Dictionary of Prophecy Terms*[6]

Today, the red army rules a quarter of the world. Socialism permeates many democracies. Like the days of Robin Hood, government steals from the people and gives to the bureaucracy. James says it is the responsibility of the church to help widows and orphans but the government has taken over these tasks.[7]

When the iron curtain fell in 1989, the Russian bear went into hibernation for a little while. Russia took steps to embrace capitalism but with Vladimir Putin, they are back to their old communist ways. Russia and China are End Time nations that still desire to control the world and become superpowers. The red horse leads two End Wars.[8]

The second seal is the red horse of Communism and Socialism.

2. Black Horse of Trade—Capitalism/Materialism—Economics

> And when he had opened the third seal, I heard the third beast say, Come and see. And I beheld, and lo a black horse; and he that sat on him had a pair of

balances in his hand. And I heard a voice in the midst of the four beasts say, A measure of wheat for a penny [denarius], and three measures of barley for a penny [denarius]; and see you hurt not the oil and the wine (Revelation 6:5-6).

In the color spectrum, red is the opposite of green. In accounting, when a company is in the red, they have a loss but when they are in the black, they have a profit. The black horse is Capitalism and Materialism.

Black (Noun)
7: the condition of making a profit—usually used with the <operating in the black>—compare red.
—*Merriam-Webster's Online Dictionary*[9]

Black days exist in American history. Black Monday, October 28, 1929, was the beginning of the Great Depression.[10] The day after Thanksgiving is referred to as Black Friday in the United States.[11] It is one of the largest sales days of the entire year. It is the beginning of the month-long capitalist holiday known as Christmas. Crowds of people stand outside in the cold in the early morning and wait for stores to open so they can spend money. Many retailers have their biggest sales and profits in the last quarter of the year. The season of Jesus Christ's birth has become a month-long pagan holiday of materialism, greed, gluttony and drunkenness.

Famine or Free Trade?

The rider of the black horse is holding a pair of balancing scales. On the front of United States paper currency is the Treasury Department seal with a pair of scales, a symbol of just trade.[12] The prophecy is a picture of a marketplace where people buy and sell. The current price for a quart of wheat or three quarts of barley is a denarius or a day's wage. That is enough bread for one or three days. Additionally, olive oil and wine are for sale at the marketplace.

Contrast this to 2 Kings 6. During a severe famine in Samaria, a donkey's head cost about sixteen months of pay.[13] Famines exist in Africa and Asia but this is not famine. In Matthew 20:1-16, the workers in the vineyard receive a *denarius* or day's wage based on the supply of workers and demands of the vineyard owner. People work paycheck-to-paycheck—some get envious or greedy and resources are limited but food is available.

Since 1588, the United Kingdom and later the United States have led the capitalistic nations.[14] The black horse is one of more than one hundred prophecies of the United States in the Bible. America was founded on the principles of religious and economic liberty. By the end of World War II, the economy made America a superpower. During the Cold War, the red and black horses fought to rule the world. While Red Communists took steps toward capitalism, democracies took steps toward socialism. Capitalism without morality becomes materialism and greed, which are prevalent in America.

The United States is an End Time power, the richest country in the world and builds the global economy. Revelation describes America in one End War against the red horse of Communism.

The third seal is the black horse of Capitalism and Materialism.

3. Green Horse of Death—Islam—False Religion

> And when he had opened the fourth seal, I heard the voice of the fourth beast say, Come and see. And I looked, and behold a [*chloros*] horse: and his name that sat on him was Death, and Hell followed with him. And power was given unto them over the fourth part of the earth, to kill with sword, and with hunger, and with death, and with the beasts of the earth (Revelation 6:7-8).

Translators have difficulty with "*chloros*". The word is used four times in the New Testament. In three verses, it is translated green in the context of grass or plants.[15] In botany, chlorophyll gives plants their green color.

> And he [Jesus Christ] commanded them to make all sit down by companies upon the [*chloros*] green grass (Mark 6:39).

> The first angel sounded, and there followed hail and fire mingled with blood, and they were cast upon the earth: and the third part of trees was burnt up, and all [*chloros*] green grass was burnt up (Revelation 8:7).

> And it was commanded them that they should not hurt the grass of the earth, neither any [*chloros*] green thing, neither any tree; but only those men which have not the seal of God in their foreheads (Revelation 9:4).

Chloros Translations[16]

Bible Translation	English
21st Century King James	Pale
American Standard Version	Pale
Amplified Bible	Ashy Pale
Contemporary English Version	Pale Green
Darby Translation	Pale
English Standard Version	Pale
Holman Christian Standard	Pale Green
King James Version	Pale
The Message	Colorless, Sickly Pale
New American Standard	Pale
New Century Version	Pale
New International Version	Pale
New King James Version	Pale
New Life Version	Light Colored
New Living Translation	Pale Green
Worldwide English	Ashes
Wycliffe New Testament	Pale
Young's Literal Translation	Pale

Χλωρος *(Chloros)* — Green

The Greek word "*chloros*" is translated green. It is a horse of a different color. Has anyone ever seen a green horse? This is not a literal green horse but like communism and capitalism, it is a symbol for a philosophy that is a world power during the End Times and is determined to rule the world.[17]

Islam is the green horse. Its color is green from Mohammed's tribal banner. The Quran says the people in paradise wear green garments of fine silk. Many Islamic flags, Quran covers and mosques are green.[18] Crusaders did not wear green so that they would not be mistaken for Muslims during battle. The estimated population of Muslims is over 1.6 billion people or about twenty-five percent of the world's population.[19] The Bible does not say they kill a fourth of the earth. Rather, the green horse is given authority to rule a fourth of the earth and has the power to kill by sword, famine, plagues and beasts.

We have heard that Islam is a religion of peace but Islam means submission.[20] People are required to convert to Islam or die. They use suicide bombers, terrorism and holy wars to fight jihad against infidels and other Islamic sects. Shiites kill Sunnis, Iraqis kill Kurds and Kuwaitis, Iranians kill Iraqis and Muslims kill Christians. Civil wars in Ethiopia and Sudan caused severe famines and pestilence. The rider of the green horse is Death.

In 622, Mohammed founded Islam in the Arabian Peninsula and by 711, the religion spread to Spain before the Crusades.[21] For over thirty years, the green horse has been in the news.[22] In 1979, the Iran Hostage Crisis began. During the 1980's, Iran and Iraq fought eight years of war. In 1983, Iran assisted Hezbollah in the Beirut barracks attack. In 1990, Saddam Hussein invaded Kuwait (Iraq War I). Since 1988, Islamic terrorists organized by Al-Qaeda, Iran and Libya have attacked American targets outside our borders. These events led to the 1993 World Trade Center bombing and attacks in New York City and Washington in 2001. The black horse retaliated against Osama bin Laden's Afghanistan in 2001 and Saddam Hussein's Iraq in 2003.[23] In 2011, Egypt, Libya, Syria and other Islamic nations had an Arab Spring that led to civil wars.[24] Then add many Arab-Israel wars. Islam will not stop until they control the world.

Iran President Mahmoud Ahmadinejad became the loudest voice of the Muslim people. He called for the destruction of Israel, dismissed the Holocaust as a myth and developed nuclear weapons.[25] Iran and Syria supports terrorists Hamas in Palestine and Hezbollah in Lebanon who attack Israel.[26] As a Shia Muslim, Ahmadinejad believed he could create a catastrophe so the twelfth imam and their End Time messiah would establish Islam throughout the world.[27] Iran, Libya and other Islamic countries will invade Israel during the Tribulation.[28] God uses Islam to bring Israel back to God.

The fourth seal is the green horse of Islam which is false religion.

4. White Horse of Conquest — Catholicism & Protestantism — Apostate Religion

> And I saw when the Lamb opened one of the seals, and I heard, as it were the noise of thunder, one of the four living creatures saying, Come and see.

And I saw, and behold a white horse: and he that sat on him had a bow; and a crown was given unto him: and he went forth conquering, and to conquer (Revelation 6:1-2).

Who is the rider of the white horse? Some say Jesus Christ since later he rides a white horse. However, Christ is not on earth from the Ascension in Acts 1 until the Second Coming in Revelation 19. Another choice is the Antichrist but his reign starts at the middle of the Tribulation. He becomes emperor of the world by peace and not conquest. The white horse is apostate Catholicism and Protestantism. Cardinals wear red and bishops wear purple but the pope wears white. The pope has a white popemobile and white airplane. White in the dictionary is a symbol of purity.

White (Noun)
3: free from spot or blemish: as
    a (1): free from moral impurity: innocent (2): marked by the wearing of white by the woman as a symbol of purity <a white wedding> —Merriam-Webster's Online Dictionary[29]

In 313 AD, Constantine the Great proclaimed religious toleration in the Roman Empire.[30] By 380, Christianity was made the official religion. Church and state merged for the next 1481 years.[31] The rider was given a *stephanos* or victors crown and not a *diadema* or royal crown. He had a bow and went out to conquer. A sword was a weapon in the battle but a bow and arrow was a weapon shot from a distance.

The green horse represents false religion outside the church and the white horse represents apostasy within the Catholic and Protestant churches. Apostasy adds or subtracts from the finished work of Jesus Christ.

Every spirit that confesses that Jesus Christ is come in the flesh is of God: And every spirit that confesses not that Jesus Christ is come in the flesh is not of God: and this is that spirit of antichrist, whereof ye have heard that it should come; and even now already is it in the world (1 John 4:2-3).

Since 711, the white horse of Catholicism and green horse of Islam have been at war.[32] In 1095, the white horse invaded the Holy Land of Israel during a series of Crusades. Many Christians, Jews and Muslims were killed in the name of God. More people were

End Time Powers[33]

killed during the Reformation and various inquisitions because of not following the church's teachings.

Currently, the Catholic Church has a worldwide organization and works to unite all religions in an ecumenical movement. It is not the Antichrist. After all Christians are raptured, the False Prophet will seize the organization of the Catholic Church and merge apostate and false religions into the worship of the Antichrist. Catholics believe "Peter the Roman" will be pope during the Tribulation.[34]

The first seal is the white horse of apostasy within Christian churches.

Take a look at the world map from God's perspective. Find the four major philosophies that rule the world. Communism controls China, Russia and Southeast Asia. Capitalism controls Australia, Eastern Asia, India and the United States. Islam controls North Africa, Indonesia and Southwest Asia. Catholicism controls Canada, Central Africa and Latin America. The European Union is a different kind of beast. As nations prepare the way for the Tribulation, see the sovereign plan of God fulfilled.

Four Horses of the Apocalypse

Horse	Key Words	Power	Philosophy
White	Bow, Crown, Conquer	Apostate Religion	Catholicism/ Protestantism
Red	Take Peace, Sword, Kill	Politics	Communism/ Socialism
Black	Pair of Scales, Wheat, Barley	Economics	Capitalism/ Materialism
Green	Sword, Famine, Plague, Beasts	False Religion	Islam

The Four Horses of the Apocalypse were unsealed early in the Church Age and are active during the End Times. The red horse of Communism builds the political system, the white horse of the apostate church with the green horse of Islam builds the religious system and the black horse of Capitalism builds the economic system. By Revelation 13, the Antichrist controls the political, religious and economic systems and rules the world.

5. Martyrs

> And when he had opened the fifth seal, I saw under the altar the souls of them that were slain for the word of God, and for the testimony which they held: And they cried with a loud voice, saying, How long, O Lord, holy and true, do you not judge and avenge our blood on them that dwell on the earth? And white robes were given unto every one of them; and it was said unto them, that they should rest yet for a little season, until their fellow servants also and their brethren, that should be killed as they were, should be fulfilled (Revelation 6:9-11).

Martyrs faithful to God who have paid with their lives have been around since Abel was murdered by Cain. They wait impatiently for God to bring justice. Persecution of the Saints continues throughout the Old Testament, Church Age and Tribulation.

> Blessed are they which are persecuted for righteousness' sake: for theirs is the kingdom of heaven. Blessed are you, when men shall revile you, and

persecute you, and shall say all manner of evil against you falsely, for my sake (Matthew 5:10-11).

The martyrs in Revelation 6 are the Saints from the Tribulation. They are given white robes which is a picture of God's righteousness. They are told to rest for a while since they have not been resurrected. God's primary goal is to redeem the world but a secondary goal is to bring judgment against those who reject His Son and persecute His people.

6. Armageddon and Second Coming

And I beheld when he had opened the sixth seal, and there was a great earthquake; and the sun became black as sackcloth of hair, and the moon became as blood; For the great day of his wrath is come; and who shall be able to stand? (Revelation 6:12, 17).

The sixth seal is Armageddon. This will be examined in a later chapter.

7. Silence in Heaven

And when he had opened the seventh seal, there was silence in heaven about the space of half an hour (Revelation 8:1).

At this point Heaven is silent. During Armageddon, Jesus Christ will gather the Saints from Heaven and they all descend upon the earth. All angels in Heaven are silent as they watch in awe as events unfold on earth.

The Seven Seals in Matthew

The seven seals repeat Matthew 24 as Jesus Christ describes the end of the age.

The four horses are described in Revelation 6. They are almost an exact repeat of the first four signs of the end of the age that Jesus gave in Matthew 24:4-9, 30.
—Evangelist Billy Graham, *Approaching Hoofbeats*[35]

• White Horse of Apostate Religion: Jesus answered and said unto them, Take heed that no man deceive you. For many shall come in my name, saying, I am Christ; and shall deceive many.

- Red Horse of Politics: And you shall hear of wars and rumors of wars: see that you be not troubled: for all these things must come to pass, but the end is not yet.
- Black Horse of Economics: For nation shall rise against nation, and kingdom against kingdom.
- Green Horse of False Religion: And there shall be famines, and pestilences, and earthquakes, in diverse places. All these are the beginning of sorrows.
- Martyrs: Then shall they deliver you up to be afflicted, and shall kill you: and you shall be hated of all nations for my name's sake.
- Armageddon and Second Coming: And then shall appear the sign of the Son of man in heaven: and then shall all the tribes of the earth mourn, and they shall see the Son of man coming in the clouds of heaven with power and great glory (Matthew 24:4-9, 30).

Four Horses, Four Freedoms

In his 1941 State of the Union address to Congress, US President Franklin Roosevelt spoke of Four Freedoms.[36] For the last one hundred years, we have been fighting with the same four horses of the Apocalypse.

1. Politics: Freedom of Speech
2. Religion: Freedom of Worship
3. Economics: Freedom from Want
4. Terrorism: Freedom from Fear
—US President Franklin Roosevelt, 1941[37]

For years, we have seen the conflicts between the white horse of Catholicism, the red horse of Communism, the black horse of Capitalism and the green horse of Islam. War and fear unite the world into a political, religious and economic world system described by Revelation 13.

God uses the natural supernaturally. The seals are principalities and powers that are at work during the End Times. Next, the seven trumpets describe specific details of seven wars. These Bible prophecies tell us exactly where we are.

Do you see the four horses on the run today?

Chapter 22

Keys to the Trumpets

W hen do the seals occur? The traditional view says they happen during the Tribulation but the horses have been on the run for years. What does the Bible say about the trumpet judgments? Plenty! During God's Time, there was an explanation of Bible chronology from creation to the Millennium. Seven trumpets reveal a shorter timeline beginning with the Laodicean period of the Church Age and ending with Armageddon.

When I was growing up, a key was hidden outside the house. If I got home from school first, I would find the key and open the door. Before getting to specific details of prophecy, we have to find the keys to unlock the trumpets.

God put two keys in prophecy to unlock the trumpet judgments: Wormwood and Destroyer. They are not symbols but proper nouns. These two words reveal specific events that align the seven trumpets and change the traditional future view to a present view of prophecy. They can only be found by people living in the End Times. Only those who know God's Word and correctly interpret signs and symbols are able to open the prophecy. God wants us to know His plan.

> Surely the Sovereign Lord does nothing without revealing his plan to his servants the prophets (Amos 3:7 NIV).

1. Wormwood

> And the third angel sounded, and there fell a great star from heaven, burning as it were a lamp, and it fell upon the third part of the rivers, and upon the fountains of waters; and the name of the star is called Wormwood: and the third part of the waters became wormwood; and many men died of the waters, because they were made bitter (Revelation 8:10-11).

Revelation 8 says a star named Wormwood will strike the earth and one-third of the fresh water will be contaminated. Wormwood means bitterness.

English—Greek[1]—Latin[2]
Star—αστερος *(Aster)—Stellae*
Wormwood—αψινθος *(Apsinthos)—Absinthius*

Wormwood is a plant from the sunflower or aster (star) family.[3] The entire family is identified by the extreme bitterness of the plant. Although poisonous in large quantities, it is used as medication for stomach ailments.

Wormwood
1: artemisia; especially: a European plant (*Artemisia absinthium*) that has silvery silky-haired leaves and drooping yellow flower heads and yields a bitter dark green oil used in absinthe
2: something bitter or grievous: bitterness
    —Merriam-Webster's Online Dictionary[4]

Scientific Classification[5]
Kingdom: Plantae (plant)
Division: Magnoliophyta (flowering plant)
Class: Magnoliopsida (dicots—two embryonic leaves)
Order: Asterales (sunflowers, daisies, thistles)
Family: Asteraceae (aster family)
Genus: Artemisia (herbs and shrubs)
Species: Wormwood—Artemisia Absinthium—Grand Wormwood
Species: Mugwort—Artemisia Vulgaris—Common Wormwood

Wormwood is a plant and Revelation tells us it is a proper noun. In the Russian language, mugwort or common wormwood is a specific place: Chernobyl, Ukraine. Chernobyl is *chornyi* (black) and *byllia* (grass blades or stalks), literally black grass. It is named after the plant mugwort.[6] *Polyn* is used in the Ukrainian Bible which is the genus Artemisia. The English-Ukrainian dictionary translates the word as *Chornobyl*.

The name of the star is called Wormwood [*Chernobyl* or *Chornobyl*] (Revelation 8:11).

English: Wormwood
Ukrainian: *полин, чорнобиль; гіркота, прикрість*
Transliteration: *polyn, chornobyl; hirkota, prykrist'*
——English-Ukrainian Dictionary[7]

On Saturday, April 26, 1986 or the 17th of *Nisan* during Unleavened Bread in the former Soviet Union territory of Ukraine, the Chernobyl nuclear facility became the world's worst nuclear disaster. After a severe nuclear meltdown, the reactor explodes uranium and plutonium into the sky. It rains down radioactive nuclear waste into the waters of Europe and Western Asia.

> Strange, is it not, that wormwood in the Ukrainian language and Bible is "Chernobyl."
> —Jack Van Impe, *Dictionary of Prophecy Terms*[8]

A debate exists whether Chernobyl is the third trumpet.[9] The New York Times published "Chernobyl Fallout" that connected Chernobyl to Wormwood then quickly retracted the story.[10] Both mugwort and grand wormwood are from the genus Artemisia. The apostle John was not a botanist and the biological classification system was not developed until the 1500's.[11] However, prophecy reveals the seven trumpet wars. Beyond coincidence, these events are connected to a specific plan from our sovereign God.

Wormwood or Chernobyl is the first key.

2. Destroyer

> And they had a king over them, which is the angel of the bottomless pit, whose name in the Hebrew tongue is *Abaddon*, but in the Greek tongue has his name *Apollyon* (Revelation 9:11).

- English: Destroyer
- Greek: *Apollyon*
- Hebrew: *Abaddon*

The fifth trumpet is the longest description of the trumpets. On one side of the war was a king named Apollyon or Destroyer. Apollo was the Greek god of light and sun, truth and prophecy.[12] He was the god of medicine and healing and could cure sickness or bring deadly plagues. The Greeks link Apollo's name with *apollyon* or destroyer.

Destroyer is the name of Saddam Hussein, the former dictator of Iraq. He was the leader during the Iran-Iraq War and Iraq Wars I and II. His name means he who confronts or crushes obstacles or destroyer.[13]

> "Saddam Hussein" is best translated as Hussein-Who-Crushes-Obstacles or Hussein-the-Destroyer.
> —Bruce Gottlieb, *What's the name of Saddam Hussein?*[14]

Unlike western naming conventions, Middle East names do not have last names. Saddam is his name followed by his father's name, family and tribe.

> Saddam Hussein Abd al-Majid al-Tikriti
> Saddam son of Hussein of al-Majid family and al-Tikriti tribe
> صــدام حســين عبــد المجيــد التكريــتي (right to left)
> ytyrktla dygmla dbc nysh mads (transliteration)
> ص د ا م = mads = sdam or Saddam[15]

Dr. Wheeler M. Thackston, Jr. is a professor of the Practice of Persian and Other Near Eastern Languages at Harvard University.

> [Dr. Thackston] explained that the actual form of the word saddam is "an intensive noun." … Confrontation in this sense of the word is how one derives the meaning of Saddam's name as Hussein-Who-Crushes-Obstacles or Hussein-the-Destroyer. "He confronts you in the way a locomotive would confront you on impact. It would crush or destroy you."
> —*Endtime Magazine*, "The Saddam Destroyer Debate: Is His Name Really in the Bible?"[16]

The Jerusalem Post tells how Saddam Hussein was given his name.

> When Saddam's mother encountered difficulties in her pregnancy, doctors recommended aborting the baby. Instead, she traveled to Baghdad for medical care, staying with Jewish friends. Eventually, a healthy boy was delivered, whom she named Saddam, or "destroyer," for the pain the pregnancy had caused.
> —*Jerusalem Post, Under Saddam's Eye*, 1997[17]

Independent secular sources verify the Destroyer. Tariq Aziz, former Iraqi Deputy Prime Minister under Saddam, named his son Saddam. In 2003, Saddam was overthrown and the name became despised. Tariq Aziz changed his son's name to Zuhair.

> The change puts a somewhat gentler moniker on Aziz's second son. Saddam means "crusher" or "destroyer," while Zuhair was the name of a 6th century Arab poet, considered the greatest of pre-Islamic times.
> —CBS News, *A Saddam by Any Other Name?*, 2003[18]

In 2007, Muqtada al-Sadr, the exiled Iraqi Shiite Muslim, gave a speech which said the coalition forces "removed the Destroyer."[19] This is a clear reference to Saddam.

Saddam Hussein was the Destroyer in name and in life.[20] He started the Iran-Iraq War and Iraq War I. Like his namesake Apollo, he was a controlling tyrant over his people and sent plagues of mustard and Sarin chemical weapons against the Kurds and Iranians. During the al-Anfal Campaign, he committed genocide against 180,000 Kurdish Iraqis. He supported terrorist groups to undermine Israel. Found in a literal pit, Saddam was the king, the messenger of Satan.

Apollyon or Saddam the Destroyer is the second key.

Wormwood is Chernobyl and Saddam is the Destroyer. Is prophecy that simple? Yes. Prophecy is unsealed, fulfilled and revealed. As we complicate God's simple plan of salvation, we complicate prophecy.

Prophecy Views: Past, Present or Future?[21]

Before placing the trumpet judgments on a timeline, it is important to view Bible prophecy correctly. When is Revelation fulfilled? When is the Tribulation and Millennium? When are the seals, trumpets and bowls? What is the sequence? Who is the Antichrist?

1. Preterist (Past)

Most or all events of Revelation 1-22 were fulfilled in the past during the first century after Christ. The Tribulation happens by 70 AD with the persecution of the Church. The Antichrist was Nero. The Preterist follows the Amillennium or no literal millennium reign of Jesus Christ on earth.

2. Historicism

Most events of Revelation 1-18 are fulfilled throughout the last two thousand years. The Church Age and the Tribulation occur in the same period. The Antichrist is the Pope, the head of the Roman Catholic Church. Some believe in a future Millennium reign of Jesus Christ. This view was popular during the Reformation.

3. Idealism

Idealists hold to a figurative interpretation of prophecy and no literal Tribulation or Millennium. The timing of most events is undetermined. The Antichrist and Tribulation represent the Christian fight between good and evil.

4. Futurist

Events in Revelation 4-22 are still future. All seals, trumpets and bowls are fulfilled sequentially within a seven-year period. Futurists believe the Tribulation occurs before the millennial reign of Jesus Christ. The Antichrist will be the leader of the revived Roman Empire. Most futurists believe America is not mentioned in the Bible. The majority of Protestants accept the futurist view.

5. Presentist

Most events of Revelation 4-6 and 8-9 are being fulfilled in the present 120-year period before the Second Coming.[22] The seals, trumpets and bowls are fulfilled in parallel timelines of different lengths and all end with Armageddon. There is a future seven year Tribulation described in Revelation 6-7 and 9-19 that occurs before the millennial reign of Jesus Christ. America prepares the global economy which the Antichrist will use to rule the revived Roman Empire (European Union) and the world. The book, *21st Century Revelation*, accepts this view.

Timing of the Trumpets

In Revelation 1, Jesus Christ tells John to record the events revealed of the past, present and future. This gives the outline for the book of Revelation.

Write the things which you have seen, and the things which are, and the things which shall be hereafter (Revelation 1:19).

Revelation Outline

1. Past: Things which you have seen (Revelation 1)
2. Present: Things which are (Revelation 2-3)
3. Future: Things which shall be (Revelation 4-22)

Futurist View[23]

Church Age	Rapture	Tribulation	Second Coming	Millennium Reign
Rev 2-3	4-5	6-18	19	20
	Seals ——>	Trumpets——>	Bowls——>	

With the keys of Chernobyl as Wormwood and Saddam the Destroyer, the question is when do the Trumpets begin?

> As was true of all futurists, of course, Darby maintained that none of the events foretold in the Revelation had yet occurred nor could they be expected until after the secret rapture of the church. Christ might come at any moment.
> —Ernest Sandeen, *The Roots of Fundamentalism*[24]

My neighbor, Marylyn Ward and I had plenty of discussions on the Bible and current events to encourage one another. She suggested that I listen to Pentecostal minister, Dr. Irvin Baxter through radio broadcast *Politics and Religion*. He explains the seals and trumpets are happening before the Tribulation and America's critical role in prophesy.[25]

Being a student of the Word, I take what Dr. Baxter says about the End Times and compare it against Scripture. I disagree with some of his doctrines, prophecy timing and Post-Tribulation view. However, his teachings of Daniel's quartet, four horses and seven trumpets agree with Scripture. Four seals and six trumpets begin before the Rapture.

> Futurists (future) usually believe that almost no prophetic events are occurring in the Church Age, but will take place in the following future episodes: the Tribulation, the Second Coming, the Millennium, and the eternal state.
> —Thomas Ice, *Four Approaches to Prophetic Fulfillment*[26]

Do the seals and trumpets fit inside the Tribulation period? No! Four seals and five trumpets are fulfilled so the futurist view does not accurately follow Scripture or recent history. We are not waiting for the Rapture in Revelation 4 but waiting in Iraq by the Euphrates River in Revelation 9.

Because of the futurist view, the Church misses events in the End Times that occur before the Rapture. If they are just "wars and rumors of wars" then we turn off God's alarm clock and go back to sleep. If Wormwood is Chernobyl and Saddam is the Destroyer, then God is telling us to wake up now before the Rapture.

Revised Timeline

Most of the Premillennium, Pretribulation view is correct. The Rapture, Tribulation, Second Coming and Millennium are still future. Instead of cramming seven seals and seven trumpets into seven years some seals and trumpets are out of the box. The trumpet judgments start at the beginning of the Laodicean period. We are so far into the End Times that we see seals and trumpets unsealed, fulfilled and revealed today.

Sometimes God speaks in a still small voice but today He speaks loud and clear. As we watch the news, major historic events are fulfilled on Jewish holy days. God desires the Church to see the signs of the times. The four horses are on the run. God wants the Church to hear the sound of the trumpets. Five trumpets have sounded. Since World War I in 1914, a 120-year plan for Israel to turn back to God has been in place. There is a different 120-year plan for the Church to experience revival and the Rapture. It is time for the Church to wake up, to be ready and to minister through the Church until Jesus Christ comes.

In contrast to the futurist view, seals, trumpets and bowls are not consecutive but are parallel within three different time periods. Seals begin near the start of the Church Age, trumpets begin in the Laodicean period while bowls begin in the Great Tribulation. The 6th and 7th seals, 7th trumpet and 7th bowl describe the battle of Armageddon and the Second Coming of Jesus Christ.

> Blow the trumpet in Zion, and sound an alarm in my holy mountain: let all the inhabitants of the land tremble: for the day of the Lord comes, for it is nigh at hand (Joel 2:1).

Many events of Revelation 4-6 and 8-9 are being fulfilled at the end of the Church Age before the Tribulation. Four seals and six trumpets prepare Christians for the Rapture and the world for the Tribulation.

Presentist View[27]

Church Age End Times	Rapture	Tribulation	Second Coming	Millennium
Revelation 1-6, 8-9	None	6-7, 9-18	19	20
Seals————————————————————————————>				
Trumpets—————————————————————————>				
Bowls————————————>				

Revelation Outline

1. Past: Things which you have seen (Revelation 1)
2. Present: Things which are (Revelation 2-3)
3. Future: Things which will take place (Revelation 4-22)
   A. Church Age (Revelation 4-6:8, 8-9)
   B. Tribulation (Revelation 6:9-7:17, 9-11)
   C. Israel's History, Satan's Fall (Revelation 12)
   D. Great Tribulation (Revelation 13-18)
   E. Second Coming (Revelation 19)
   F. Millennium (Revelation 20)
   G. New Heaven and Earth (Revelation 21-22)

Wake Up! Look Up!

Christians live in exciting times. Wormwood is Chernobyl and Saddam is the Destroyer. These are the keys that unlock the trumpets. The Bible is relevant for our time because we see Revelation fulfilled. Can you discern the signs of the times? The horses are on the run and the trumpets are sounding. Do you see God at work during the End Times? God is giving the world 120 years of warning. Wake up, Church! Look up!

If Wormwood and Destroyer are the keys to the trumpets, what do these keys unlock and reveal about the seven trumpet judgments?

Chapter 23

World Wars, Cold War

While many Protestant scholars say seven trumpet judgments happen during the Tribulation, God gives specific details of prophecy fulfilled during our time. Chernobyl and Saddam unlock the trumpet judgments, the United States in prophecy and God's plan for our time.

It is easier to interpret a passage that is fulfilled. The chapter *Prophecy Fulfilled* is an example of knowing history to interpret Daniel 11. Here are examples of knowing history to interpret Revelation 8. Do not worry about symbols because in the vision of the trumpets, John describes our recent world history. God's Word is alive, amazing and relevant for today! A better interpretation of Scripture gives a clear view of God actively involved in the middle of world events. It is time to see God and join Him at work.

The United States in Bible Prophecy

> One of the hardest things for American prophecy students to accept is that the United States is not clearly mentioned in Bible prophecy, yet our nation is the only superpower in the world today.
> —Tim LaHaye, *Is the United States in Bible Prophecy?*[1]

The United States is the most powerful country in the world. It is strange this End Time power is not mentioned in Bible prophecy or is it? If you misinterpret Scripture, you miss seeing God's plan for our time. Why is the United States a superpower during the End Times but not the Tribulation? It is not because of the Rapture. Seven trumpets describe seven wars and America actively participates in all seven. If you ignore America in the End Times, you do not see how the world gets into the Tribulation. Starting with Moses, the Bible tells the story of the rise and fall of the United States.

**The Bible refers to the United States over one hundred times
by symbol, event, date or result of our actions.**

In the chapter, *Minor Feasts, Major Events*, over twenty-five American historical events are fulfilled on Jewish holy days. Now add fulfilled prophecies. Daniel 2 and 7 are two key chapters about the Tribulation that are examined later. One verse needs to be examined now. In Daniel 7, the prophet Daniel has a vision. He sees four beasts that describe four End Time nations. Here are two beasts.

> The first was like a lion, and had eagle's wings: I beheld till the wings thereof were plucked, and it was lifted up from the earth, and made stand upon the feet as a man, and a man's heart was given to it (Daniel 7:4).

Dollar Symbols

Look at a United States one dollar bill.[2] On the front of the dollar is the Treasury seal with a pair of scales.[3] The rider of the black horse has a pair of scales. The black horse is capitalism. On the back of the dollar is the Great Seal with an eagle, the national symbol.[4]

The lion is the national symbol of the United Kingdom.[5] In 1588, the British defeated the Spanish Armada.[6] Then from colonization to World War II, the British Empire was the military and economic superpower with control over a quarter of the world's land and population.[7] The lion had vast territories on seven continents around the globe so the sun never set on its empire.

Symbols in the Bible mean something specific. The United States (eagle) was a colony of the United Kingdom (lion). In 1776 during the war for independence, the eagle's wings were torn from the lion.[8] The economy makes the black horse rise to superpower. This is seven of over one hundred details in the Bible describing symbols, events and dates that directly involve or affect the United States or consequences of our actions.

United States in the Bible[9]

1. The United States' national symbol is the eagle.
2. The United Kingdom's national symbol is the lion.
3. The United States was a colony of the United Kingdom.
4. The United States (eagle) was torn from the United Kingdom (lion) by the American Revolutionary War.
5. The Declaration of Independence was adopted on July 4, 1776 or the 17th of *Tammuz* (Golden Calf).
6. The United States Treasury seal has a pair of scales.
7. The United States is part of the black horse of capitalism and leads the world in building the global economy for the Tribulation.

Now there are two keys. Chernobyl is Wormwood and Saddam is Destroyer. There are two End Time powers. The United Kingdom is the lion and the United States is the eagle. Within a 120-year period, these two countries are in five trumpet prophecies, describe recent history and prepare Israel and the world for the Tribulation.

Present View of the Seven Trumpets

> And I saw the seven angels which stood before God; and to them were given seven trumpets. And the seven angels which had the seven trumpets prepared themselves to sound (Revelation 8:2, 6).

> The trumpets of heaven sound an alarm throughout the world announcing the public judgments of God. Each blast ushers in an added judgment.
> —Jack Van Impe, *Dictionary of Prophetic Terms*[10]

In Revelation, Jesus Christ gives John visions that he records. He is seeing twentieth and twenty-first century wars that he describes in first-century terms.

1. First Trumpet—Earth

> The first angel sounded, and there followed hail and fire mingled with blood, and they were cast upon the earth: and the third part of trees was burnt up, and all green grass was burnt up (Revelation 8:7).

History

The first trumpet was World War I and judgment was against the earth. In 1914, after military buildups and the assassination of Archduke Franz Ferdinand of Austria-Hungary, foreign alliances escalate Europe into war.[11] On August 1 or the 9th of *Av* (Kadesh Barnea), Germany declared war on Russia. The conflict was between the Central Powers led by Austria-Hungary, Germany and Ottoman versus the Allies led by France, Russia and the United Kingdom. Later, Russia left but Italy and the United States joined the Allies. The war was fought in Europe with battles in Africa and Asia.

Prophecy

There is a scene of hail, fire and blood. Advances in artillery, especially machine guns, shoot a hail of bullets. There are many firsts: tanks, airplanes and anti-aircraft guns. Weapons of mass destruction were used by both sides in the form of chlorine, mustard and tear gasses. Battleships, submarines and aircraft make it a modern war of land, sea and air.

A defining characteristic of World War I was trench warfare. These trenches with a "no man's land" stretched 475 miles along the French and German borders devastating the earth. John described the war as a third of the trees and grasses burned up. Both sides used scorched-earth tactics to destroy fields and military assets when retreating.[12] About twenty million people died.

Results

The war ended powerful monarchies with vast colonies. Austria-Hungary, Germany, Ottoman and Russia ended the reign of kings. Strong monarchs were replaced by weak democracies or strong dictators. The British and French were severely weakened. About forty years later, most colonies became independent. The American black horse of capitalism and the Soviet red horse of communism started their rise. World War I led to World War II.

The war was the beginning of world government. The League of Nations had fifty-eight members.[13] Despite US President Woodrow Wilson's effort, the United States did not join. The League failed to stop World War II but was the predecessor to the current United Nations.

The first trumpet impacted the Jewish people. In 1917, the British issued the Balfour Declaration favoring a homeland for the Jews.[14] On December 9, 1917, the British captured Jerusalem from the Ottomans. Two days later on the 25th of *Kislev* or *Hanukkah*,

British Marshal Edmund Allenby honored the Holy City by dismounting from his horse and walking into the city. The League of Nations gave the United Kingdom the Palestine territory on September 26, 1923 or the 16th of *Tishri* during Tabernacles.

Beginning of the End Times

> World War I did not signal that we should look for the immediate coming of Christ or "the end of the age." It signaled that we should look for more birth pains.
> —Tim LaHaye, *Are We Living in the End Times?*[15]

The End Times is divided into the Church Age, Tribulation and Millennium. The Church began at Pentecost and will end at the Rapture. Bible scholars give 27 to 33 AD as the beginning of the Church. Then add two thousand years. Most Bible scholars start the Laodicean period at 1900. US President William McKinley died and Theodore Roosevelt became president on the Feast of Trumpets in 1901.[16] The first trumpet of World War I was from 1914 to 1918.[17] Noah's world had 120 years of warning before the flood.[18] Adjust for the seven years of Tribulation.

Church Age and End Times

	Early Years	**Later Years**
Church Age	27 + 2000 - 7 = 2020	33 + 2000 - 7 = 2026
Laodicean Period	1900 + 120 = 2020	1914 + 120 = 2034
Second Coming	27 + 2000 = 2027	33 + 2000 = 2033

Despite calendar errors, 2020-2034 gives a ballpark estimate. The seven trumpets time-line proves how close we are to the Tribulation. If you still doubt, five of seven trumpets are complete.

2. Second Trumpet—Sea

> And the second angel sounded, and as it were a great mountain burning with fire was cast into the sea: and the third part of the sea became blood; and the third part of the creatures which were in the sea, and had life, died; and the third part of the ships were destroyed (Revelation 8:8-9).

History

The second trumpet was World War II and judgment was against the sea. In an effort to appease German leader Adolph Hitler and avoid war, France, Germany, Italy and the United Kingdom signed the Munich Agreement on September 30, 1938 or the 5th of *Tishri*, the third day of *Yamin Noraim* (Days of Awe/Tribulation).[19] Then on October 10, 1938 or the 15th of *Tishri* (Tabernacles), Germany annexed the Czech territory of the Sudetenland.

World War II began on September 1, 1939 or the 17th of *Elul* during *Teshuvah* with Germany's invasion of Poland.[20] This conflict was between the Axis of Germany, Italy, Japan and the Soviet Union versus the Allies of France and the United Kingdom. Later the Soviet Union and United States joined the Allies. History repeated itself, except this time the Axis conquered most of Europe for a time. The war was fought on two fronts: Europe with North Africa and Eastern Asia. About sixty million people died.

Prophecy

A major part of the war was fought on the sea. In the Battle of the Atlantic, U-boats sank merchant ships and naval convoys transporting armies, supplies and equipment to the war.[21] In the Pacific War, battles were fought island-to-island and were dependent on naval power.[22] Of the 105,127 ships in the war, 36,387 were destroyed.[23]

> Some have suggested the mountain falling into the ocean represents a mushroom cloud from an atomic explosion that pollutes the waters.
> —Tim LaHaye, *The Popular Encyclopedia of Bible Prophecy*[24]

A nuclear explosion looks like a mushroom cloud but John describes it as a mountain on fire tossed into the sea. The first atomic bomb was dropped on Hiroshima, the city of water.[25] The second atomic bomb was dropped on Nagasaki on August 9, 1945 or 1st of *Elul* during *Teshuvah*.[26] In Jewish history, the 1st of *Elul* is the day Moses returned to Mt. Sinai for a second forty days with God which ended on the Day of Atonement.

Holocaust

In 1933, Hitler became chancellor of Germany and he removed liberty, then lives of political opponents, Jews, gypsies, mentally disabled and others who he considered "life unworthy of life."[27] Germany conquered Poland in 1939 and segregated Jews into

Polish cities. The Warsaw Ghetto had about 440,000 Jews crammed into 4.5 percent of the city.[28] Many Jews died of starvation. In 1942, Heinrich Himmler, architect of the Nazi genocide, ordered Jewish deportations. On July 23 or the 9th of *Av* (Kadesh Barnea), the first trains departed to the Treblinka extermination camp.[29] Of the ~11 million people who died in the Holocaust or *Shoah* (catastrophe), 6 million were Jews.

> Then shall they deliver you up to be afflicted, and shall kill you: and you shall be hated of all nations for my name's sake (Matthew 24:9).

Nuremberg trial verdicts were announced on October 1, 1946 or 7th of *Tishri* during *Yamin Noraim* (Days of Awe/Tribulation).[30] Defendants were executed on October 16, 1946 or the 21st of *Tishri* (Tabernacles).[31]

Results

The United States and the Soviet Union became superpowers. They divided Germany and the rest of Europe, Korea and Vietnam. The Cold War began with the red and black horses fighting proxy wars. The League of Nations was replaced by the United Nations which expanded world government. In 1951, Belgium, France, Germany, Italy, Luxembourg and the Netherlands began an economic alliance of coal and steel which developed into the European Union. As France, Germany, Italy and the United Kingdom signed the Munich Agreement on the third day of *Yamin Noraim* with Adolph Hitler, they will surrender power on the third year of the Tribulation to the Antichrist.

> And there was given unto him a mouth speaking great things and blasphemies; and power was given unto him to continue forty and two months (Revelation 13:5).

Since 63 BC, the Holy Land was ruled by Gentile nations. The United Kingdom became the only nation in history to voluntarily surrender control of Israel. The United Nations divided the territory between Israel and Palestine and the nation of Israel was born on May 14, 1948.[32] Since then, Israel has fought eight wars with their Arabic neighbors. During the Six Day War, Israel captured Judea and Samara (West Bank), Gaza, Golan Heights and the Sinai Peninsula. Israel reunited east and west Jerusalem on June 7, 1967. Jerusalem Day is the 28th of *Iyar*, forty days after the resurrection when Jesus Christ ascended into Heaven.

Thus says the Lord of hosts; Behold, I will save my people from the east country, and from the west country; And I will bring them, and they shall dwell in the midst of Jerusalem: and they shall be my people, and I will be their God, in truth and in righteousness (Zechariah 8:7-8).

3. Third Trumpet—Rivers & Springs

And the third angel sounded, and there fell a great star from heaven, burning as it were a lamp, and it fell upon the third part of the rivers, and upon the fountains of waters; and the name of the star is called Wormwood: and the third part of the waters became wormwood; and many men died of the waters, because they were made bitter (Revelation 8:10-11).

History

The third trumpet was the Chernobyl nuclear accident in the Ukraine region of the Soviet Union.[33] Judgment was against the rivers and fountains. The event was the least significant of the seven trumpets and yet Chernobyl is mentioned by name—Wormwood.

On April 26, 1986 or the 17th of *Nisan* during Unleavened Bread, the three-year-old Reactor 4 was powered down to test the backup generator. The output decreased making the reactor extremely unstable. When the shutdown occurred, the reactor reached 3600 degrees Fahrenheit and electricity increased to 30 gigawatts or ten times safe output.[34] The reactor overheated, first causing a steam explosion that blew the 1000-ton lid off the reactor. A second explosion caused a graphite inferno which started the nuclear meltdown and released uranium and plutonium about a mile up into the atmosphere. The radioactive fallout was three hundred times Hiroshima.[35] It spread throughout Europe and Western Asia. Some radiation was detected in North America and Japan. It rained in Europe for a week, poisoning the fresh waters.

After thirty-six hours, the Soviets evacuated 3.5 million people from Belarus and Ukraine. It took a week to transport the citizens. The Reactor 4 fire burned sixteen days.[36] For the next eight months, the Soviets used about 600,000 liquidators to clean up the reactor.[37] A twenty miles exclusion zone still exists and the area will not be safe for about three hundred years.[38]

Soviet President Mikhail Gorbachev was silent. However, on April 27, workers at the Forsmark Nuclear Power Plant in Sweden detected unusually high radiation.[39] After checking their plant, the radiation was tracked back to the Soviet Union and the Chernobyl disaster 684 miles away. From 2,500 to 250,000 people died as a result of the accident. Because of the secrecy of the Soviets, no one will ever know how many people died or how many lives were shortened because of the disaster.

Prophecy

Revelation 8 says the name of the star is Wormwood, a bitter plant in the sunflower or aster (star) family. The entire family is known for the bitterness. "'*Hirke yak polyn*' — Bitter as wormwood. That's the phrase uttered by Ukrainians if something is really bitter. *Polyn*/ wormwood (*Artemisia*) really is as bitter as it comes."[40]

> The city [Chornobyl] name is the same as a local Ukrainian name for *Artemisia vulgaris* (mugwort or common wormwood), which is also ... "chornobyl."[41]

A nuclear reactor creates energy like a star. John sees an asteroid or star-like object falling from the heavens. The reactor lid and the fiery rubble from the explosions fell back to earth. A third of fresh water was poisoned by the nuclear fallout. Europe and Western Asia were directly affected by the radiation.

Results

In the context of the Cold War, the Soviet Union with its failing economy could not keep up with the military buildup of the United States. The Chernobyl nuclear accident was another step toward its collapse. By 1991, Gorbachev decided it was better for the bear to hibernate. Since 2000, the leadership of Vladimir Putin confirmed the bear's resurgence. Russia will return with their Islamic allies.

> You shall come from your place out of the north parts, you, and many people with you, all of them riding upon horses, a great company, and a mighty army: And you shall come up against my people of Israel, as a cloud to cover the land; it shall be in the latter days, and I will bring you against my land, that the heathen may know me, when I shall be sanctified in you, O Gog, before their eyes (Ezekiel 38:15-16).

At the end of the Cold War, the Berlin Wall fell. East and West Germany were reunited. The wounded head (or nation) was healed and Germany became the strongest nation in the European Union. Most of the former Communist states in Eastern Europe became democracies and joined the European Union. Most of the Asian states became Islamic nations. Since 1997, Russia has been a partner with the EU.[42] The Russian bear began its merger with Germany and the United Kingdom.[43]

> And the beast [European Union] which I saw was like unto a leopard [Germany], and his feet were as the feet of a bear [Russia], and his mouth as the mouth of a lion [United Kingdom]. And I saw one of his [seven] heads [or nations—Germany] as it were wounded to death; and his deadly wound was healed: and all the world wondered after the beast (Revelation 13:2-3).

The fall of the Soviet Union allowed many Jews to immigrate from Russia and Eastern Europe to Israel. Former Soviet countries opened borders to missionaries. By 2000, Israel became an associate member of the EU.[44]

Revelation History

> The first angel sounded [World War I], and there followed hail and fire mingled with blood, and they were cast upon the earth: and [because of trench warfare] the third part of trees was burnt up, and all green grass was burnt up (Revelation 8:7).

> And the second angel sounded [World War II], and as it were a great mountain burning with fire [or mushroom cloud from an atomic bomb] was cast into the sea [at Hiroshima and Nagasaki]: and the third part of the sea became blood; And the third part of the creatures which were in the sea, and had life, died; and [because of the Atlantic and Pacific battles] the third part of the ships were destroyed (Revelation 8:8-9).

> And the third angel sounded [the Cold War], and there fell a great star from heaven [nuclear reactor debris], burning as it were a lamp, and it [nuclear radiation] fell upon the third part of the rivers, and upon the fountains of waters; And the name of the star is called [Chernobyl, Mugwort or Common] Wormwood: and the third part of the waters became wormwood; and many men [citizens and liquidators] died of the waters, because they were made bitter (Revelation 8:10-11).

Three Trumpets Sound

Humanity is lulled to sleep by times of peace. God's plan for the End Times is to wake up His people and the world with trumpet judgments of war. During this time, Christians need to proclaim the Good News of the Gospel to those who live in fear and who seek true peace.

The seven trumpets have already started. World War I burned up a third of the battlefield. World War II sank a third of the ships and the atomic bomb was like a burning mountain. The Cold War poisoned a third of the fresh water in a place called Chernobyl (Wormwood).

During this time, God had a plan for His people. Israel was brought from occupation to an independent nation. America's independence from the United Kingdom, our rise to power through capitalism and our involvement in World War I, World War II and the Cold War was described in precise details in the Bible. Meanwhile, the powerful elite of the world have a plan to unite all nations under a political, religious and economic system. Even in humanity's open rebellion, God will be glorified as He provides redemption and prepares for the Millennium.

If the first three trumpets are the World Wars and Cold War, what do the next four trumpets tell us?

Chapter 24

Between Iraq and a Hard Place

W hen I was growing up, I heard sermons about the End Times. I wanted to be living at the Rapture to leave this life without dying. There were all those horrible events during the Tribulation. However, I was a little disappointed that I would not get to see events unfold. After watching cable television, I wondered how the Tribulation would look on the news channels. Although we will not endure the Tribulation, I wanted to see prophecy fulfilled.

Whether we should have fought Iraq or not is a topic for another book. How God uses three Iraq Wars in prophecy is a topic for this book. Why is the Iraq Wars important to End Time prophecy? Know symbols, history and current events to interpret Revelation 8-9. These fulfilled events are not on one twenty-four-hour news channel but on all news programs. They are not generic wars and rumors of wars but specific events with amazing details that reveal God's plan for our time.

4. Fourth Trumpet—Sun, Moon and Stars

> And the fourth angel sounded, and the third part of the sun was smitten, and the third part of the moon, and the third part of the stars; so as the third part of them was darkened, and the day shined not for a third part of it, and the night likewise (Revelation 8:12).

History

The fourth trumpet was the Persian Gulf War (Iraq War I) and judgment was against the heavens. Iraq accumulated a large debt with Saudi Arabia and Kuwait from eight years of the Iran-Iraq War. In July 1990 while negotiating with Kuwait, Iraq gathered 30,000 troops on the border. On July 31, 1990 or the 9th of *Av*, talks with Kuwait failed.[1] On August 2, 1990, Iraq invaded Kuwait and then Saddam Hussein threatened to invade Saudi Arabia. Since the world was dependent on oil, it was critical to protect the Persian Gulf region.

An international coalition of thirty-five countries led by the United States and United Kingdom moved over 500,000 troops into the Persian Gulf region. Reasons for war included the invasion of Kuwait, human rights abuses, use of chemical and biological weapons and development of nuclear weapons. The United Nations set a January 15, 1991 withdrawal and authorized force.

> The great duel, the mother of all battles has begun.[2]
> —Iraqi President Saddam Hussein, 1991

On January 17, 1991, the war to liberate Kuwait began. The coalition bombed strategic military targets giving air superiority in less than a week. Iraq retaliated by lobbing thirty-nine Scud missiles into Israel and forty-one into Saudi Arabia and Bahrain. They dumped 400 million barrels of crude oil into the Persian Gulf.

On February 24, the Iraqi army was worn down by a month of air bombings and the ground war began. While the Iraqi army protected the south and east borders, coalition forces invaded Southern Iraq from the west encircling Kuwait. After one hundred hours, Kuwait was liberated. The war ended on February 28, 1991 or the 14th of *Adar*, the Feast of *Purim*.

Prophecy

Revelation 8 says the sun, moon and stars were darkened by a third. When the Iraqi army retreated, they implemented a scorched-earth policy.[3] In Kuwait, 611 oil wells were set ablaze releasing thick black smoke. Day was as dark as night. The smoke impacted the climate throughout the Persian Gulf region, taking more than eight months to extinguish all the oil fires.[4]

Results

While many wars depended on national alliances, this war depended on world government. The United Nations gave approval for the war. Iraq War I was the first made for television war. The international coalition had a great military victory but lost the peace. No hope existed for the Iraqi people to overthrow their government. Uprisings in the Kurdish north and Shiite south encountered crushing defeats without international help.[5] Iraqi aircraft were restricted from no-fly zones. Saddam Hussein was contained but not for long. Iraq War I resulted in Iraq War II.

Despite Iraq's attempt to bring Israel into the war, the United States persuaded them to be neutral.[6] Of thirty-nine Scud missiles that landed in Israel, only two people were killed. Patriot missiles were given to intercept Scuds. A third of air power searched for Scud launchers. God protected His people by an eagle.

> He [God] shall cover you with his feathers, and under his wings shall you trust. You shall not be afraid for the terror by night; nor for the arrow that flies by day; Nor for the pestilence that walks in darkness; nor for the destruction that wastes at noonday. A thousand shall fall at your side, and ten thousand at your right hand; but it shall not come near you. Only with your eyes shall you behold and see the reward of the wicked (Psalm 91:4-8).

Three Woes

> And I beheld, and heard an angel flying through the midst of heaven, saying with a loud voice, Woe, woe, woe, to the inhabitants of the earth by reason of the other voices of the trumpet of the three angels, which are yet to sound! (Revelation 8:13).

The four trumpets of World War I, World War II, the Cold War and Iraq War I have sounded. There are three more trumpets to sound.

5. Fifth Trumpet—Unsealed

The fifth trumpet is the most amazing prophecy. Four trumpets give one or two verses that describe a couple of key details but this is the "mother of all trumpets." With eleven verses and twenty-four precise details, it is the longest and most specific trumpet judgment. A person living in the End Times can recognize the war and know exactly where and when we are. We saw it live!

History

The fifth trumpet was Iraq War II and judgment was against the unsealed. Iraq used chemical weapons in the Iran-Iraq War and genocide of Kurdish Iraqis. Saddam

Hussein aggressively attacked Iran, Kuwait, Saudi Arabia and Israel by starting the Iran-Iraq War, Iraq War I and supported the Palestinian terrorists. For twenty years, Iraq has destabilized the Middle East. The war was justified by crimes against humanity and weapons of mass destruction.

> Iraq admitted, among other things, an offensive biological warfare capability, notably … botulism, … anthrax; 25 biological-filled Scud warheads; and 157 aerial bombs…. If Saddam rejects peace and we have to use force, our purpose is clear. We want to seriously diminish the threat posed by Iraq's weapons of mass destruction program.
> —US President Bill Clinton, 1998[7]

Iraq had a history of using chemical and nuclear weapons.[8] In 1981, in a preemptive strike, Israel bombed the *Al Tuwaitha* nuclear materials testing reactor.[9] After Iraq War I, the United Nations required all long-range missiles, along with biological, chemical and nuclear materials destroyed and verified by weapons inspectors. By 1998, the Iraqi government refused to cooperate and the inspectors left. In October 2002, after the US Congress authorized force, the Iraqi government reluctantly allowed the inspectors to return.

> It should be the policy of the United States to support efforts to remove the regime headed by Saddam Hussein from power in Iraq and to promote the emergence of a democratic government to replace that regime.
> —Iraqi Liberation Act of 1998[10]

The United Kingdom and United States agreed to remove Saddam Hussein while China, France and Russia did not. The Oil for Food Program allowed Iraq to sell oil for food, medication and humanitarian aid but Iraq bought influence from China, France and Russia. UN Secretary-General Kofi Annan's program director Benon Sevan accepted nearly $150,000 in bribes.[11] Additionally, France sought power by restricting American and British foreign policy at the UN. "French opposition to the US is not about Iraq but about who runs the world."[12] Part of the debate for war was preemption. Do you attack your enemy before your enemy attacks you? After the 9/11 attacks, the answer was a resounding "yes." The only question left was, "When?"

On March 19, 2003, on the 15th of *Adar* during the Feast of *Purim*, the Iraq War began.[13] The first attack targeted Saddam Hussein and the Iraq leadership at Dora Farms. Two days later, "shock and awe" devastated key military resources. By April 9, 2003, Baghdad was captured by US forces.

After taking Baghdad and Tikrit, the war went from fighting to policing Iraq. The Iraqi military was defeated but dispersed into the civilian population. Former Baathists were joined by Sunni and Shiite militias and foreign groups controlled by Iran, Syria and Al-Qaeda.[14] While the coalition formed a new government and rebuilt infrastructure, insurgents assaulted people, planted roadside bombs, destroyed infrastructure and provoked religious wars. Since 2004, the war became more about Democrats and Republicans controlling Washington than about the war in Iraq.

Prophecy

Shock and Awe

> And the fifth angel sounded, and I saw a star fall from heaven unto the earth: and to him was given the key of the bottomless pit. And he opened the bottomless pit; and there arose a smoke out of the pit, as the smoke of a great furnace; and the sun and the air were darkened by reason of the smoke of the pit (Revelation 9:1-2).

In Revelation 9, John sees a star from heaven. During Iraq War I, there were problems with hardened targets. During the first attacks of Iraq War II, bunker-buster bombs aimed for Saddam Hussein and the leadership cut through buildings leaving huge pits.[15] Described as Hades, the bottomless pit was a huge crevice. Since oil fires worked well in the last war, the Iraqi army started oil trench fires near Baghdad. Smoke rose like a great furnace.[16] The initial "shock and awe" with explosion and fires appeared like Hell.

Geneva Convention

> And there came out of the smoke locusts upon the earth: and unto them was given power, as the scorpions of the earth have power. And it was commanded them that they should not hurt the grass of the earth, neither any green thing, neither any tree; but only those men which have not the seal of God in their foreheads (Revelation 9:3-4).

The locust-like creatures do not come out the deep pit but rather fly through the smoke. Regime change requires rebuilding Iraq after the war. The people and infrastructure are protected while the military focused on the Iraqi leadership and army, who are the unsealed. These were benevolent locusts that distinguished between targets, limited civilian casualties and followed rules of war according to the Geneva Convention.

Abu Ghraib Torture

> And to them it was given that they should not kill them, but that they should be tormented five months: and their torment was as the torment of a scorpion, when he strikes a man. And in those days shall men seek death, and shall not find it; and shall desire to die, and death shall flee from them (Revelation 9:5-6).

On August 25, 2003, *Abu Ghraib* opened for prisoners of war with valuable intelligence.[17] Operation Desert Scorpion captured key Iraqi leaders and Baath party insurgents. Interrogators were ordered to soften prisoners but conduct went beyond military orders. Because of a lack of supervision and confusion of interrogation rules, some techniques were used without permission.

In Muslim culture, honor is valued more than life itself. Honor killings against women were committed for adultery, divorce and victims of crime.[18] When martyrdom is valued, attacking one's honor is a fate worse than death.

> They said we will make you wish to die and it will not happen.
> —Ameen Saeed Al-Sheik, detainee 151362[19]

By January 13, 2004, the abuse photos were given to superiors. One picture was of electric shock torture which stings like a scorpion. After an investigation, seventeen people were suspended and nine people were court-martialed for abusing prisoners. Torture lasted five months.

Locusts, Horses, Crowns, Men, Women, Lions, Chariots, Iron, Scorpions

> And the shapes of the locusts were like unto horses prepared unto battle; and on their heads were as it were crowns like gold, and their faces were as the faces of men. And they had hair as the hair of women, and their teeth were as the teeth of lions. And they had breastplates, as it were breastplates of iron; and the sound of their wings was as the sound of chariots of many horses running to battle. And they had tails like unto scorpions, and there were stings in their tails: and their power was to hurt men five months (Revelation 9:7-10).

John took four verses and nine similes to describe this thing. Scholars say the creatures are either literal locusts or demonic beings but neither matches the account. John described something foreign to his first century but quite familiar to our twenty-first century.

Apache Helicopter[20]

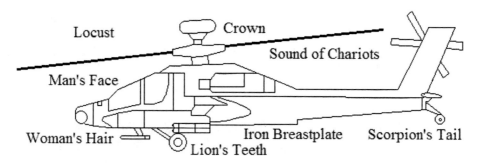

Locust   Crown
         Sound of Chariots
Man's Face
Woman's Hair   Iron Breastplate   Scorpion's Tail
         Lion's Teeth

I personally tend to think that God might utilize in his judgments some modern devices of man which the Apostle John was at a loss for words to describe nineteen centuries ago! In the case just mentioned, the locusts might symbolize an advanced kind of helicopter.
—Hal Lindsey, *There's A New World Coming*[21]

A helicopter looks like a locust in flight. When in battle, it flies low to the ground in attack formation. The radar dome looks like a crown. The pilot's face is visible through the window but he wears a helmet the shape of women's hair. The wheels with guns, missiles and rockets look like lion's teeth. A helicopter is heavily armored with a protective wall of steel. The loudest sound John had heard was an army of horse-drawn chariots but helicopters are known for their booming 120+ decibels.[22] The tail fin is like a scorpion's tail.

The first operational helicopter was developed in 1936 and later was used in World War II.[23] John described a specific helicopter. The Apache AH-64 is the United States Army's primary attack helicopter.[24] In 1986, it began service and was used in Iraq War I. By 1997, it was upgraded to the AH-64D Apache Longbow. The unique radar crown was added to make weapons more accurate. These enhanced helicopters were used in Afghanistan and Iraq.

Saddam the Destroyer

And they had a king over them, which is the angel of the bottomless pit, whose name in the Hebrew tongue is Abaddon, but in the Greek tongue has his name Apollyon (Revelation 9:11).

Saddam literally means Destroyer.[25] Throughout his reign, he was the servant of Satan and considered himself to be a modern-day Nebuchadnezzar.[26] Daniel 4 describes a king overcome by pride, judged by God and sent into the wilderness. Nebuchadnezzar swallowed his pride and returned to his throne but Saddam was exiled never to reign again.[27] On December 13, 2003, Saddam the Destroyer was the king literally found in a pit.

Feast of *Purim*

God associates Bible prophecies with Jewish holy days. The 9th of *Av* (July-August) had Israel's and the world's worst events. Iraq and Kuwait broke off peace talks on July 31, 1990 or the 9th of *Av* (Kadesh Barnea). Iraq War I started two days later and ended February 28, 1991 or the 14th of *Adar*. Twelve years and one day later, Iraq War II started March 19, 2003 or the 15th of *Adar*. *Purim* is a two-day celebration.

> … just like 12 years ago in the days of the Gulf War, it is again the festival of Purim and the miraculous redemption of the Jewish people from the hands of Haman which hovers over this conflict. This should not be lost on us.
> —Rabbi Nathan Lopes Cardozo, 2003[28]

> Who knows whether you are come to the kingdom for such a time as this? (Esther 4:14).

The book of Esther depicts God's deliverance of the Jewish people. During the reign of Xerxes or Ahasuerus, Esther became queen. Haman the Amalekite, chief administrator for Xerxes, plotted to kill the Jews. At the risk of her life, Esther saved her people. Haman was hanged and his people were judged. The Feast of *Purim* is a celebration of God's protection of His people, Israel.

> So they hanged Haman on the gallows that he had prepared for Mordecai (Esther 7:10).

Saddam the Destroyer was a type of evil Haman. He assisted Palestinian terrorists, shot Scud missiles into Israel, fought Iran and Kuwait, slaughtered his own people and plotted to destroy the Jews. Just like Haman, Saddam was hanged, his sons were killed and his nation was judged. He was executed on December 30, 2006 and buried on December 31 or the 10th of *Tevet* which is the day Babylon began the thirty-month siege of Jerusalem.

Trumpet 4 or 5

Some descriptions of the fifth trumpet match both Iraq wars. The sky was darkened and Apache helicopters were used. Each war included the Feast of *Purim*, Saddam Hussein, Iraq, the coalition and five months. Prophecy teacher Irvin Baxter interpreted Iraq War I as the fifth trumpet but left a void with the fourth trumpet.[29] However, the Apache helicopter radar dome was added in 1997.[30] After Saddam Hussein was overthrown, he was found in a literal pit. The fourth trumpet describes oil fires that darkened the sky at the end of Iraq War I. The fifth trumpet describes "shock and awe," *Abu Ghraib*, Apache helicopters and Saddam the Destroyer of Iraq War II.

Results

The Iraq War ended the reign of Saddam Hussein and Sunni control of Iraq. Achieving this goal created a major split between the United States and European Union led by France and Germany. After switching prime ministers, the United Kingdom moved back in line with the European Union. The coalition of France, Germany, China and Russia balanced the superpower of the United States. The European Union as part of the Union for the Mediterranean now covers an area greater than the ancient Roman Empire.[31]

> Resolution of the Arab-Israeli conflict is a strategic priority for Europe. Until this is achieved, there will be little chance of solving other problems in the Middle East. The EU's objective is a two-state solution with an independent, democratic, viable Palestinian state living side-by-side with Israel and its other neighbours.
> —European Union, *The EU and the Middle East Peace Process*[32]

The United States plays a critical part of God's End Time plan with seven wars of the seven trumpets. The European Union, Russia, United Nations and the United States formed the Quartet on the Middle East to guide the Israel-Palestine peace process.[33] These End Time powers describe Daniel's quartet of four beasts: lion (United Kingdom), eagle (United States), bear (Russia) and leopard (Germany).[34] On July, 16, 2002 or the eve of the 9th of *Av* (Kadesh Barnea), the Quartet announced the Roadmap for Peace that proposed a two-state solution to resolve the Israeli-Palestinian conflict. This division of land was originally proposed in 1947.[35]

> The Roadmap represents a starting point toward achieving the vision of two states, a secure State of Israel and a viable, peaceful, democratic Palestine. It is the framework for progress towards lasting peace and security in the Middle East.
> —US President George W. Bush, 2002[37]

Trumpet Judgments[36]

Trumpet	Prophecy	Event	Year/ Jewish Day	
1 Earth	Earth Burned No Man's Land	World War I	1914-1918 9th of *Av*	End Times
2 Sea	Ships Destroyed Burning Mountain Atomic Bomb	World War II	1938-1945 Tabernacles 9th of *Av* *Teshuvah*	
3 Rivers & Springs	Waters Bitter Nuclear Disaster Wormwood	Cold War/ Chernobyl	1986 Unleavened Bread	
4 Sun, Moon & Stars	Sky Darkened Oil Fires	Persian Gulf (Iraq War I)	1990-1991 9th of *Av* *Purim*	
5 Unsealed	Locusts Helicopters Destroyer	Iraq War (II) Saddam	2003-2010 *Purim* 10th of *Tevet*	
6 Humanity	Great Army Great Slaughter	Euphrates War (Iraq War III)	20?? 9th of *Av*?	Tribulation
7 World	Lightning, Thunder, Earthquake, Hail	Armageddon/ Second Coming	20?? 9th of *Av*? Atonement	

Israel was freed from Saddam the Destroyer but did not seek God for protection. In 2000, Israel became an associate member of the EU through the Union for the Mediterranean.[38] When Israel accepts the covenant of Daniel 9:27, they will join the EU.

The last American combat brigade left Iraq on August 19, 2010 or the 9th of *Elul* during *Teshuvah*, ending military involvement in Iraq.[39] The remainder of American military troops left by the end of 2011.

Revelation History

And the fourth angel sounded [Iraq War I], and [because of the Kuwait oil fires] the third part of the sun was smitten, and the third part of the moon, and the third part of the stars; so as the third part of them was darkened, and the day shined not for a third part of it, and the night likewise (Revelation 8:12).

And the fifth angel sounded [Iraq War II], and I saw a star [missile] fall from heaven unto the earth: and to him was given the key of the bottomless pit [with a bunker buster bomb]. And he opened the bottomless pit; and there arose a smoke out of the pit [oil fires], as the smoke of a great furnace [shock and awe]; and the sun and the air were darkened by reason of the smoke of the pit. And there came out of the smoke [these flying things that look like] locusts [helicopters] upon the earth: and unto them was given power, as the scorpions of the earth have power (Revelation 9:1-3).

And it was commanded them [because of nation building] that they should not hurt the grass of the earth, neither any green thing, neither any tree; but only those men [leaders and army] which have not the seal of God in their foreheads. And to them it was given that they should not kill them [following Geneva Convention rules of war], but that they should be tormented five months [at *Abu Ghraib* prison]: and their torment was as the torment of a scorpion, when he strikes a man [electric shock]. And in those days shall men seek death [Martyrs are rewarded], and shall not find it [Honor is valued more than life]; and shall desire to die [Dishonor is worse than death], and death shall flee from them (Revelation 9:4-6).

And [I don't know what these helicopter things were but] the shapes of the locusts were [in attack formation] like unto horses prepared unto battle; and on their heads were as it were crowns [radar domes] like gold, and [I saw] their faces were as the faces of men. And they had [helmet] hair as the hair of women, and their teeth [wheels, guns, missiles, rockets] were as the teeth of lions. And they had breastplates, as it were breastplates of iron; and the sound of their wings [loud helicopter blades] was as the sound of chariots of many horses running to battle. And they had tail [fins] like unto scorpions, and there were stings in their tails: and their power was to hurt men five months [at *Abu Ghraib*] (Revelation 9:7-10).

And they had a king over them, which is the angel [demon] of [Satan found in] the bottomless pit, whose name in the Hebrew tongue is Abaddon, but in the Greek

Seven Trumpets Timeline

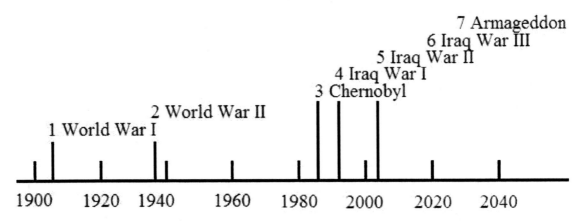

tongue has his name Apollyon [English is Destroyer and Arabic is Saddam] (Revelation 9:11-12).

Trumpets' Timeline

Of the first five trumpets that sounded, all five are wars that include issues of chemical or nuclear weapons and American involvement. With over twenty-five prophecies of the End Times, God's time is fulfilled on Jewish holy days. The trumpet judgments occur within a 120-year period.

You Are Here!

At the mall, there are maps that say, "You are here!" These are helpful when looking for a store. The map gives the right perspective on where you are and where you need to go.

One woe is past; and, behold, there come two woes more after (Revelation 9:12).

When are we in the End Times? Most prophecy teachers say we are waiting for the Rapture in Revelation 4:1. However, we are at Revelation 9:12 between the end of the fifth trumpet and the beginning of the sixth trumpet. This is still before the Rapture. The Tribulation begins with Revelation 10. With five trumpets complete, time is running out and we are almost home.

Breaking News: Revelation 9 Fulfilled!

In five trumpet judgments, God gives us specific details about five future wars. They deal with weapons of mass destruction, involve the United States and directly affect Israel. The fourth trumpet is Iraq War I and the Bible describes Kuwaiti oil fires. The fifth trumpet is Iraq War II and the Bible describes bunker-buster bombs, "shock and awe," oil fires, the Geneva Convention, *Abu Ghraib* torture, Apache helicopters and Saddam the Destroyer. God tells us specific details about specific events.

You are watching live on twenty-four-hour news channels, the world as described in Revelation 8-9. Although great turmoil exists, we live in exciting times when God fulfills His plan for the End Times. The fourth and fifth trumpets bring the United States to the Euphrates River. The sixth trumpet picks back up at the Euphrates River.

> If we are that weak, just think of who wants to come here first and take us over? The last thing I ever want to see is our country taken over because we're so financially weak, we can't do anything.
> —Businessman and US Presidential Candidate, Ross Perot, 2012[40]

As God prepares the world for the Tribulation, the End Time powers of China, the European Union, India, Islam and Russia plot to topple the United States and take the superpower title. Unfortunately, America rebels against God, causes the Tribulation and reaps national judgment of an economic depression combined with World War III. America is between Iraq and a hard place.

If five trumpets are fulfilled in the World Wars, Cold War and Iraq Wars, what do the last two trumpets tell us about the future of America, the Tribulation and the end of human rule?

Chapter 25

Iraq War III

I f the President of the United States had to tell the American people the truth about Iraq, would he? We fought Iraq War I to contain Saddam Hussein and lost the peace. We fought Iraq War II to overthrow Saddam Hussein and lost the country. Now we fight Iraq War III to get Iraq back but devastate our land.

In 2004, the majority of Americans voted to continue in Iraq but in 2008, they tired of war and the majority voted to leave. People do not want another Iraq War. A president will not tell you the truth about Iraq but a prophecy teacher must. America is going to fight a third war in Iraq.

The sixth trumpet is still future. This war is tied to the Rapture of the Church, the fall of the United States and the first half of the Tribulation. The sixth trumpet is described in more detail in the second volume, *America & the Rapture*. Here is an overview of the last war of the Church Age and the first war of the Tribulation.

What makes the United States fall so that Europe rules during the Tribulation?

6. Sixth Trumpet—Humanity

God's Judgment against Nations

After the Tower of Babel, God created countries to keep evil in check. Throughout history, we see God's judgment against nations. God sent ten plagues against Egypt. The Canaanite nations were expelled by Israel and then used to correct Israel's disobedience. Assyria conquered the northern kingdom of Israel. Babylon captured Assyria and the southern kingdom of Judah and was replaced by Media-Persia then Greece as the regional power. Jerusalem was destroyed and the Jews were scattered by Rome. In recent history, Napoleon's France and Hitler's Germany were defeated by the nations of Europe. America judged the Confederacy, Germany, Japan, the Soviet Union and Iraq. Sometimes the judge becomes the judged.

> Let every soul be subject unto the higher powers. For there is no power but of God: the powers that be are ordained of God. For he is the minister of God to you for good. But if you do that which is evil, be afraid; for he bears not the sword in vain: for he is the minister of God, a revenger to execute wrath upon him that does evil (Romans 13:1, 4).

God's plan for the world is six thousand years of human rule and one thousand years of God's rule. The Tribulation is the transition from 190+ nations to Jesus Christ. When we know world powers and Bible prophecy, we see God's plan to overthrow all nations with three End Wars.

> There is no question at all in my mind. If we keep going this way, some nation is going to head over here to take us. And boy, if they do, they picked the right time.
> —Businessman and US Presidential Candidate, Ross Perot, 2012[1]

God's Judgment against America

God begins the transition from human government to Christ's rule by starting with the world's only superpower. Broken families, lukewarm churches, bankrupt government, greedy corporations and a self-centered people demand chastisement from God. America's abandonment of God and spiritual weakness led to a materialistic focus. Before the Tribulation, God will bring judgment to the United States.

> And I [God] will make of you [Abraham] a great nation [Israel], and I will bless you, and make your name great; and you shall be a blessing: And I will bless them that bless you, and curse him that curses you: and in you shall all families of the earth be blessed (Genesis 12:2-3).

America has been a great ally for Israel and we have been blessed because of our actions but now we have turned away from God and Israel. The United States refuses to expand domestic oil, import more from peaceful, friendly nations and cut consumption. Because of our dependence on oil in the Middle East, America needs peace. The United States joins with the European Union, Russia and the United Nations into Daniel's quartet to appease Islamic oil-producing nations by forcing peace. However, stealing God's land brings the righteous judgment of God against America and the world.

In 2005, America forced Israel to surrender Gaza to Palestine. While Israel evacuated the settlements, on August 13, 2005 or the 9th of *Av* (Kadesh Barnea), Tropical Depression Ten forms, dissipates and reforms into Tropical Depression Twelve.[2] Hurricane Katrina devastates the Gulf Coast states of Alabama, Louisiana and Mississippi. Katrina was a direct judgment from God because of Gaza. When America divided Israel, God judged America.

Israeli Prime Minister Ariel Sharon suffered a massive stroke on January 4, 2006 that left him in a coma.[3] His Kadima party lost power in the 2009 Israeli election.[4] US President George W. Bush's Republican Party suffered major losses in the 2006 and 2008 elections. Neither Democrats nor Republican have changed this foreign policy to avoid our destruction.

> In the same day the Lord made a covenant with Abram, saying, Unto your seed have I given this land, from the river of Egypt unto the great river, the river Euphrates (Genesis 15:18).

God gave Israel the land from the Nile to the Euphrates, including the Sinai Peninsula, Gaza Strip, Judea and Samaria (West Bank) and Golan Heights. Since 1947, United States foreign policy supported the division of Israeli land.[5] We have no right to take land God gave to Israel and give it away. When America curses Israel, God curses America. The covenant that takes Judea and Samaria (West Bank) and gives the land to Palestine causes the fall of the United States, the Tribulation and Armageddon.

> I will gather all nations and bring them down to the Valley of Jehoshaphat [in Jerusalem]. There I will enter into judgment against them concerning my inheritance, my people Israel, for they scattered my people among the nations and divided up my land (Joel 3:2 NIV).

Prophecy

> And the sixth angel sounded, and I heard a voice from the four horns of the golden altar which is before God, saying to the sixth angel which had the trumpet, Loose the four angels which are bound in the great river Euphrates. And the four angels were loosed, which were prepared for an hour, and a day,

and a month, and a year, to slay the third part of men. And the number of the army of the horsemen were two hundred thousand thousand [200 million]: and I heard the number of them (Revelation 9:13-16).

The sixth trumpet will be Iraq War III and judgment will be against humanity. The Euphrates River flows through Turkey, Syria and Iraq. In 2012, the United States removed the remaining military troops from Iraq. About ten years from now despite current politics, America will return to Iraq.

Clashing Armies

With over a billion people, China, India and Islam can assemble an army of 200 million people. India has a population of 1.2 billion people but not the aggressive nature to start this war.[6] Islam has a billion people and a combative nature.[7] However, Islam is not the leader of Iraq War III because Ezekiel says it attacks Israel in the Russian-Islamic War.[8]

Persia [Iran], Ethiopia [or Sudan], and Libya with them; all of them with shield and helmet (Ezekiel 38:5).

China has a population of 1.3 billion people, military, economy and a need to start the war.[9] Many scenarios can lead to war including Iran, Iraq, Israel, North Korea, Syria and Taiwan. America's debt and impact on the world's economy control of oil in the Middle East and interference in China's control of the Far East will influence their decision to go to war. China's economy and defense spending has made them rise to superpower contender. In the book, *Showdown: Why China Wants War with the United States*, China needs a limited war to become the next superpower.[10] Of all major super-powers throughout history, only the Roman Empire collapses without a major war.

If the Americans draw their missiles and position-guided ammunition on to the target zone on China's territory, I think we will have to respond with nuclear weapons, ... we [...] will prepare ourselves for the destruction of all of the cities east of Xi'an [in central China]. Of course the Americans will have to be prepared that hundreds ... of cities will be destroyed by the Chinese.
—Major General Zhu Chenghu, Dean at China's National Defense University, 2005[11]

Opposing China in the war is the United States. India is brought in to balance China's population. This war includes the three most populated nations. America may develop a coalition from the Far East that includes Australia, Japan and South Korea. The

European Union is the clear winner of the war because they do not directly participate while three powerful nations fall.

> For the time is come that judgment must begin at the house of God: and if it first begin at us, what shall the end be of them that obey not the gospel of God? (1 Peter 4:17).

Possible Scenario

Although Iraq War III is still future, fulfilled prophecy, the Jewish calendar and current events tell a possible scenario. In July or August, Daniel's quartet announces the peace treaty that takes Judea and Samaria (West Bank) from Israel and gives the land to Palestine. The plan includes sharing Jerusalem and the temple mount. After seventy years of conflicts and wars, the treaty is hailed as "Peace for our time."[12]

About the 9th of *Av* (July/August), China challenges the United States by invading Iraq to control oil needed for their growing economy. This begins as a conventional war with an overwhelming force of millions of troops. China assumes the United States will give up Iraq instead of starting World War III. If China is not expelled, they replace America as the superpower and rule the world. America retaliates with conventional weapons and brings India into the war with millions of troops. The war escalates as the battlefield widens from Iraq to India and China.

About fifty days later on the 1st of *Tishri* (Trumpets), Jesus Christ will rapture His Church. World War III is the future event that requires God's timely rescue mission of His people before the Tribulation. The Church is delivered from the wrath of sin at the cross and the wrath of God against the world.

> Therefore let us not sleep, as do others; but let us watch and be sober. For God has not appointed us to wrath, but to obtain salvation by our Lord Jesus Christ (1 Thessalonians 5:6, 9).

On the 10th of *Tishri* during the Day of Atonement, the foreign minister and future dictator of the European Union confirms the Quartet's treaty with Israel and Palestine. The Tribulation begins.

After millions of citizens disappear, the United States uses tactical nuclear weapons to weaken the Chinese armies. The east-west war escalates from conventional to nuclear to a MAD (Mutual Assured Destruction) war as nuclear powers bomb cities. According to Revelation 9, the war includes a 200 million-man army and a casualty rate of ~2.5 billion people. With a total population reaching nearly three billion, China, India and the United States sustain the brunt of casualties.

About 3½ years later on the 10th of *Nisan* (Passover Lamb), the Antichrist becomes king of the world. During Unleavened Bread, the great peacemaker ends Iraq War III.

> The second woe is past; and the third woe comes quickly (Revelation 11:14)

This is the best understanding of the future sixth trumpet. More prophecy questions and timing issues still need to be answered. However, some or all of the Tribulation described in Revelation 9-20 could be fulfilled in the 2020's.

Results

Iraq War III begins the dramatic transition from man's rule to Jesus Christ's rule. As the result of the all-out nuclear war, China, India and the United States go from leading powers to shadows of their current self. Without America, Daniel's quartet becomes John's trio. The Russian bear merges with the German leopard and the British lion to become the dreadful and terrible fourth beast.[13] The European Union and United Nations become one and make the Antichrist emperor of this one-world government. The United States' eagle is absent as a leader during the Tribulation.

> And the beast which I saw was like unto a leopard [Germany], and his feet were as the feet of a bear [Russia], and his mouth as the mouth of a lion [United Kingdom]: and the dragon gave him his power, and his throne, and great authority (Revelation 13:2).

Israel gives up Judea and Samaria (West Bank) to Palestine but gains a few years of peace to build the third Jewish temple. They join the European Union as member and become a protected nation. Islam takes Judea and Samaria and lives to fight another day.

When World War III ends, 3½ years of the Tribulation is complete. With the final seven bowls, the wrath of God is poured out against Satan, Antichrist and their followers.

End Time Wars

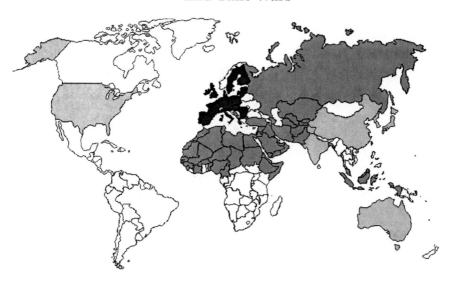

7. Seventh Trumpet—Armageddon

> And the seventh angel sounded; and there were great voices in heaven, saying, The kingdoms of this world are become the kingdoms of our Lord, and of his Christ; and he shall reign for ever and ever. And the temple of God was opened in heaven, and there was seen in his temple the ark of his testament: and there were lightnings, and voices, and thunderings, and an earthquake, and great hail (Revelation 11:15, 19).

The seventh trumpet is Armageddon and judgment is against the world. All the nations of the world bring a great coalition army against Israel. At the Second Coming, Jesus Christ redeems a remnant of Israel, conquers Satan, the Antichrist and their armies then rules the earth for one thousand years.

Three End Wars

During the Tribulation, God uses three End Wars to overthrow all nations and prepares for the Millennium reign of Jesus Christ. Once the four horses and the five trumpet judgments are moved into the Church Age, three major world wars describe three major events of the Tribulation.

1. World War III (Iraq War III)

Iraq War III is the sixth trumpet and judgment is against humanity. This war includes End Time powers of China, India and the United States with other Far East nations. The war begins right before the Tribulation and ends 3½ years into the Tribulation. Iraq War III is described in Revelation 9:13-21 and 11:14 within the first half of the Tribulation in Revelation 10-11.

> Loose the four angels which are bound in the great river Euphrates. And the four angels were loosed, which were prepared for an hour, and a day, and a month, and a year, to slay the third part of men (Revelation 9:14-15).

2. World War IV (Russian-Islamic War)

The Russian-Islamic War (Gog and Magog) is the final battle of the War on Terrorism. Russia and radical Islamic nations of Iran, Libya, Sudan, Turkey and others attack Israel. Fighting Israel defies the Antichrist's power so he must respond. The war begins at the middle of the Tribulation and lasts three years. Jesus Christ says those in Judea (West Bank) must flee.[14] The Russian-Islamic War is described in Ezekiel 38-39 and Daniel 11:36-45 within the second half of the Tribulation in Revelation 13-19.

> And at the time of the end shall the king of the south [Islamic nations] push at him [Antichrist]: and the king of the north [Russia] shall come against him like a whirlwind, with chariots, and with horsemen, and with many ships; and he shall enter into the countries, and shall overflow and pass over (Daniel 11:40).

3. World War V (Armageddon)

After Russia, Islam and Antichrist fight against each other, they join forces to annihilate Israel. About the 9th of *Av* (Kadesh Barnea), all the world's armies gather for the Battle of Armageddon at the valley of Megiddo in northern Israel. At first, Israel is devastated as two-thirds of the people are slaughtered and half of Jerusalem is taken captive. On the 10th of *Tishri* (Atonement) at the Second Coming, Jesus Christ restores Israel and removes its enemies. Armageddon is described in Daniel 11:36-45 and Zechariah 12-14 in the last months of the Tribulation in Revelation 13-19.

For I will gather all nations against Jerusalem to battle; and the city shall be taken, and the houses rifled, and the women ravished; and half of the city shall go forth into captivity, and the residue of the people shall not be cut off from the city. Then shall the Lord go forth, and fight against those nations, as when he fought in the day of battle (Zechariah 14:2-3).

The seven years of the Tribulation period are described in the third volume, *Tribulation*.

God's Plan for Our Time Unsealed, Fulfilled and Revealed

Humanity paints an optimistic picture of the world. Despite economic deficits, political corruption, warring nations and global warming, new technologies and social-minded governments help people live longer and enjoy life. The global village evolves into a future utopia. The future is bright with no end in sight.

If we see reality, the Islamic green horse threatens world peace. The red Russian bear is finished hibernating and back to its old Soviet ways. The European Union, led by France, Germany and the United Kingdom, dominates the world's agenda through its weak but collective regional power. America's foreign policy turns against Israel to appease our oil interests. But watch out for that giant red Chinese dragon as it raises its ugly head on the way to the Euphrates.

Through prophecy and current events, Scripture gives a different perspective of the world. The seven churches, the seven world powers, the four horses on the run and five wars of the seven trumpet judgments tell us we are in the twilight of human rule. It is time for major regime change and the dawning of a new day.

Our sovereign God gives people one more opportunity for salvation as the world transitions from Gentile rule to the rule of Jesus Christ. In a span of seven years, all nations fall like dominos with Iraq War III, Russian-Islamic War and Armageddon. Yet before Satan rules the world and all Hell breaks loose on earth, Christians hear the sound of the last *shofar* on that glorious day of the Jewish Feast of Trumpets.

Does this make End Time prophecy relevant to you?

Midway

Chapter 26

What Kind of People Ought You to Be?

B efore 1914, a man living in Austria-Hungry understood the signs of the times. He saw World War I coming to Europe and encouraged his children to leave their homeland. His two youngest sons followed his advice, traveled to Canada and settled in America. About one hundred years later, his great-grandson tells the world that Iraq War III is coming and we are about to leave.

Many Scriptures are given to prove that the End Times are here. God's plan for our time tells us we are one hundred years into the End Times. The four horses are on the run and five wars of the seven trumpets have sounded. The nations prepare for the next war but God prepares for the reign of Jesus Christ.

This book is written to break through the confusion of symbolism, tradition and many End Time views. The point is not to pick a Rapture date, then wait on a hill or in a bunker till Jesus Christ returns. Prophecy is not given to just know and understand. Knowledge and understanding require action. We must apply God's Word to our hearts so we change our lives to impact our churches and the world.

It is important to view current events in the context of the End Times. Many people view the black clouds of militant China and radical Islamic terrorism as approaching storms. The Doomsday Clock sits at 11:55 PM because of Middle East troubles and the spread of nuclear weapons.[1] Americans think a nuclear attack is likely in five years.[2] People seek a political savior to solve the world's problems. Instead of a Christian worldview, we need a Revelation worldview that understands God's plan for His people and the transition to Jesus Christ's rule.

You may be the only Jesus people see. However, the world hears a jumbled mess from Christians. We shine a dim light for those searching for answers. Our God gave the Word and the Holy Spirit to give us answers. Knowing the world's future, we should not be occupied by the world's system. Use your spiritual gifts to minister in your local churches and reach out to people you meet. Share End Time prophecy with other believers. God's plan to redeem the world and reign over the world includes us. Because God told us His plan for our time, what kind of people ought you to be?

Scoffers and Believers[3]

> Knowing this first, that there shall come in the last days scoffers, walking after their own lusts, and saying, Where is the promise of his coming? for since the fathers fell asleep, all things continue as they were from the beginning of the creation (2 Peter 3:3-4).

Peter says people will ridicule Jesus Christ's coming. They do not believe Jesus Christ came the first time. The world is distracted by the lives of Christians instead of the message of Christ. Some Christians focus on changing the behavior of the lost. Jesus Christ confronted religious leaders but most refused to change. He comforted sinners because they recognized their faults and just needed to repent. We are the messengers but the Holy Spirit must change people's hearts and lives. When you hear people mock the End Times, another prophecy is fulfilled.

In Jesus Christ's First Coming, His focus was on a remnant of Israel that would accept their Messiah. As a result, He associated with tax collectors and prostitutes. His primary responsibility was training twelve disciples. These twelve were doubters, deniers and betrayers who were more interested in their places in the kingdom than their present mission. Eleven finally got it after He arose. The truth of the resurrection and the power of the Holy Spirit transformed them into willing servants who sacrificed their lives for the Gospel.

The scoffers can be Christians. We are responsible to know the Bible and that will take a lifetime. We must take what is said, compare it with the Bible and discern what is true. Jesus Christ cannot come any day in the next one hundred years but He will call us home on Trumpets in the next twenty years. Iraq proves that. We must share this message with other Christians and encourage their ministry.

When we say, "Jesus Christ is coming soon," scoffers respond, "They have been saying that for years." That part is true. It has been more than 1985 years since the cross. God did not break His promise but God's plan will occur in God's time.

The scoffers continue, "All things continue as they always have been." Humanity took millions of years to evolve and it will take millions of years to end. They assume that the world will continue forever. However, everything has a beginning and an end. They choose to forget God's judgments since creation.

> For this they willingly are ignorant of, that by the word of God the heavens were of old, and the earth standing out of the water and in the water: Whereby the world that then was, being overflowed with water, perished: But the heavens and the earth, which are now, by the same word are kept in store, reserved unto fire against the day of judgment and perdition of ungodly men (2 Peter 3:5-7).

Humans have a short attention span. Because of our increasingly faster-paced world and faster-paced culture, our attention span is becoming shorter. We forget the lessons of history. The rat race of life makes it easy to get mired in the world and get off-track from God's mission. We are not rats and this world's system is the wrong race. Despite all the racket in this world, God continues to speak in a still small but clear voice. Judgment day is coming!

> This I say therefore, and testify in the Lord, that you henceforth walk not as other Gentiles walk, in the vanity of their mind, And be renewed in the spirit of your mind; And that you put on the new man, which after God is created in righteousness and true holiness (Ephesians 4:17, 23-24).

Peter reminds us of history. God created the world and humanity fell. After 1656 years, humanity rebelled against God. To save the world, God had to destroy humanity. Noah built an ark to preserve his family and the animals while giving humanity a second chance. God sent a worldwide flood to destroy the earth. Many heard Noah say, "Judgment is coming." Despite knowing the future, they rejected the truth and were caught by surprise.

> As the days of Noah were, so shall also the coming of the Son of man be (Matthew 24:37).

It has been ~4330 years since the great flood. This time God will not destroy the earth by flood but by fire. It is not just any fire. Three End Wars of Iraq War III, Russian-Islamic War and Armageddon are nuclear world wars.[4] Jesus Christ said the days of Noah are similar to the End Times and judgment follows. We see the wars on the horizon. The only question is "When?" As God gave Noah a 120-year warning before the flood so God is giving us a 120-year warning before the fire.

> But, beloved, be not ignorant of this one thing, that one day is with the Lord as a thousand years, and a thousand years as one day. The Lord is not slack concerning his

promise, as some men count slackness; but is longsuffering to us-ward, not willing that any should perish, but that all should come to repentance (2 Peter 3:8-9).

God's time is not our time. When He created the vast universe, He created time and space. God is limited by neither. He told the apostle John, "I am the beginning and the end."[5] Our God is eternally present in time and space. That is something we cannot comprehend. Humanity's rule over the earth is limited to six thousand years. Bible chronology tells us we are at the end of that time. No wonder so many prophecies are being fulfilled in our time.

God is never early and never late but always fulfills His promises on time. As clearly seen in Jewish holy days, a specific time exists to God's specific plan to redeem the world and then to judge the world. He is longsuffering. How many of us pray, "Lord come quickly," without consideration for the lost. Every day results in people who will enter Heaven for eternity. It will take longer than we want but He still redeems the lost in the End Times.

But the day of the Lord will come as a thief in the night; in which the heavens shall pass away with a great noise, and the elements shall melt with fervent heat, the earth also and the works that are therein shall be burned up (2 Peter 3:10).

The Day of the Lord is God's one thousand years. It is preceded by seven years of Tribulation. To those who are not watching, the Second Coming comes suddenly and as a surprise like a thief in the night.

Some say after the Second Coming, no millennium will occur because the earth will burn up. Peter does not tell the entire story but summarizes key points. He describes three future nuclear wars during the Tribulation periods.[5] After the Tribulation when a remnant survives, God restores the earth and removes the curse during the reign of Jesus Christ on earth.

The wolf and the lamb shall feed together, and the lion shall eat straw like the bull: and dust shall be the serpent's meat (Isaiah 65:25).

For about 4000 years, God promised His people the Messiah would come and He did. About 2500 years ago, Ezekiel wrote that Israel would be a nation in a day and that happened in 1948. The apostle John described exact details of the World Wars, Cold War and Iraq Wars; five trumpets are history. God told us the Messiah is coming again to judge the world and it will happen in God's time.

Seeing then that all these things shall be dissolved, what manner of persons ought you to be in all holy conversation and godliness, Looking for and hasting unto the coming of the day of God, wherein the heavens being on fire shall be dissolved, and the elements shall melt with fervent heat? Nevertheless we, according to his promise, look for new heavens and a new earth, wherein dwells righteousness (2 Peter 3:11-13).

Everything that is temporary will be destroyed. If we invest our lives in houses, cars, careers, entertainment and retirement, they will be burned up and we will lose it all. If we invest in our relationship with God, God's Word, God's ministry and people, they will last for eternity. You cannot take it with you but you can invest your time, talents and treasures by sending eternal things ahead.

Lay up for yourselves treasures in heaven, where neither moth nor rust does corrupt, and where thieves do not break through nor steal (Matthew 6:20).

Peter asks the question to Christians. "What manner of persons ought you to be?" The first step is salvation in Jesus Christ. Next we are to grow in our relationship with God through worship, studying His Word, listening to what He says and talking with Him in prayer. We apply the truth we learn to our hearts and our lives. As children of God, we are holy people in word and deed and invest our lives in the kingdom of God. At the same time, we share our lives in a good local Christ-centered Bible church. There we fellowship and grow with other believers and use our spiritual gifts to encourage, teach and disciple one another in our walk with God. The best testimony for Christianity is love for one another. Time passes quickly when we are busy doing what God has called us to do.

The earth will be burned up but we are promised a better future. We have victory over sin, death and the grave and are given eternal life with God. We have confidence that God will win the final victory over Satan and Antichrist. Our ultimate future is when Jesus Christ reigns forever on earth and in Heaven.

Wherefore, beloved, seeing that you look for such things, be diligent that you may be found of him in peace, without spot, and blameless. And account that the longsuffering of our Lord is salvation; even as our beloved brother Paul also according to the wisdom given unto him has written unto you; As also in all his epistles, speaking in them of these things; in which are some things hard to be understood, which they that are unlearned and unstable twist, as they do also the other scriptures, unto their own destruction (2 Peter 3:14-16).

The only way to have peace with God is through Jesus Christ. Then God becomes Lord of our lives and the Holy Spirit creates righteousness in our hearts. Each day, we choose to follow Him instead of this condemned world. God's longsuffering delay is another opportunity for salvation to those who are lost. Additionally, it is time for Christians to prepare our lives for eternity.

These spiritual truths can be hard to understand and require diligent study. Beware of false teachers who manipulate Scripture. They make detours and stumbling blocks so that you become discouraged and fall. Discernment is critical within the church. Everything said or written in the church and the world must be compared to Scripture. The rejection of Jesus Christ's salvation brings ruin to false teachers. But Peter and Paul were united in preaching the same truth of Jesus Christ's redemption and God's ultimate victory over His foes.

> You therefore, beloved, seeing you know these things before, beware lest you also, being led away with the error of the wicked, fall from your own steadfastness. But grow in grace, and in the knowledge of our Lord and Savior Jesus Christ. To him be glory both now and for ever. Amen (2 Peter 3:17-18).

As God gave Noah's world plenty of warning so God has given us End Time prophecy to know the future. Plenty of signs lead to the Rapture and Tribulation. False teachers seek to lead you away from your secure faith in God. Grow stronger in the grace and knowledge of Jesus Christ by growing your relationship with God. Stay committed to Him by applying His Word, prayer and fellowship with His people. No surprise will occur to those who daily walk with God, know His Word and watch for His soon return while they minister.

Wake up and Live in the Day[6]

> If there be any other commandment, it is briefly comprehended in this saying, namely, You shall love your neighbor as yourself. Love works no ill to his neighbor: therefore love is the fulfilling of the law (Romans 13:9-10).

It is important that we go back to the basics of Christian living. We are commanded to love God with all our being and to love our neighbor as ourselves. Selfless love fulfills the Law and displays God's amazing mercy and grace to others. Because God loves us, we love one another.

> And that, knowing the time, that now it is high time to awake out of sleep: for now is our salvation nearer than when we believed. The night is far spent, the day is at hand: let us therefore cast off the works of darkness, and let us put on the armor of light. Let

us walk honestly, as in the day; not in rioting and drunkenness, not in chambering and wantonness, not in strife and envying. But put on the Lord Jesus Christ, and make not provision for the flesh, to fulfill the lusts thereof (Romans 13:11-14).

Now that we know our time is the end of the End Times, we need to wake up. The phrase "awake out of sleep" is a clear reference to the Rapture. God is sounding the trumpets of alarm to wake up His people. At the Last Trump on the Feast of Trumpets, the dead in Christ are awakened out of their sleep. It is time to wake up and get to work before the "Last Trump."

Since we are Christians, the redemption part of salvation is complete through Jesus Christ. The next step is our sanctification as we live and grow day by day in Jesus Christ. The final step of salvation is at the Rapture. God awakens the living and dead in Christ for everlasting life. Not only do we receive new bodies but God removes our old sinful natures, guilt and shame. The completion of our salvation is so near. The night is about over and soon it will be the dawn of that new and glorious day. That day we see Jesus Christ face-to-face.

Paul tells us we are children of the day and not the night so we should watch and be sober. All people sin but since Christians are alive in Christ, we strive to grow and with the Holy Spirit's help, remove sin from our lives. We put away drunkenness and strife of the night and we live in the righteousness of Christ in the light of the day. Everyone enjoys a good party but now our efforts must focus on that future celebration with God and God's people in Heaven.

Each day, we put on the armor of light. Ephesians 6 describes the whole armor of God: truth, righteousness, peace, faith, salvation and the Word of God. This battle is not a fight against people but rather a spiritual war for the hearts and minds of people. The best weapons we have are truth and love. We put on Jesus Christ and allow the Holy Spirit to live through us. Then others will see the light of Christ in us. In these final days, it is important to live in Christ as children of the day.

Minister to One Another[7]

But the end of all things is at hand: be therefore sober, and watch unto prayer. And above all things have fervent charity among yourselves: for charity shall cover the multitude of sins. Use hospitality one to another without grudging (1 Peter 4:7-9).

Because we are at the end of the End Times, we should be God-focused on God's mission. No one can better keep us informed than our Commander-in-chief. Be in constant communion with God. Examine yourself first then assist others in the Church. Love each other selflessly. Love and forgiveness are powerful tools to unite all believers. Give mercy and grace as mercy and grace were given to you. Serve one another without complaining.

> As every man has received the gift, even so minister the same one to another, as good stewards of the manifold grace of God. If any man speak, let him speak as the oracles of God; if any man minister, let him do it as of the ability which God gives: that God in all things may be glorified through Jesus Christ, to whom be praise and dominion for ever and ever. Amen (1 Peter 4:10-11).

God has designed the local church for us to practice our faith so we apply it out in the community where we live. Since we the Church are going to spend eternity together, we better learn to get along together here on earth. Serve and minister to one another with your spiritual gifts. The Holy Spirit supplies these gifts and abilities and gives the power to do God's work. Be good stewards of the gifts and talents that God has given you. Do good works out of the motivation of love of God, to glorify God and to encourage His people.

Prophecy Must Change Our Hearts and Lives

First and foremost, prophecy is about knowing and understanding the character and nature of God. He is sovereign over all creation and we see His plan being fulfilled today. From the beginning, it is a plan of redemption for the world. We must apply the truth from the Word of God to our hearts and lives. We grow our faith, trust, confidence and love for God.

Through the Holy Spirit, God's Word must change our hearts and lives because this world is about to drastically change. Now is the time to see God and join Him in His plan. We must grow in our relationships with God, use our spiritual gifts and talents in the local church, encourage, serve and disciple other Christians, invest our time and resources in God's ministry and reach the lost. The blessed hope is that He will return for His people. Bible prophecy is useless unless we apply it to our hearts and live these principles each day. Live today like a 21st Century Revelation Christian with the end in sight.

After knowing the end of this age, how does this change your heart and life to wake up, follow God, serve in His Church and reach people for the Kingdom of God?

Chapter 27

The End of the Beginning

God reveals Himself in prophecy. He is full of mercy, grace and love and is longsuffering as the Savior of humanity. He reveals Himself as prophet, priest and king. He is sovereign, sitting on the throne in Heaven but personally involved in each person's individual life. He reveals Himself as holy and righteous, the God of justice and judgment for those who accept His offer of salvation and for those who keep rejecting Him.

God's Word

God reveals His Word to those who seek truth. When you study Genesis, Daniel, Matthew or Revelation, interpret the Bible the same way. He has preserved His Word so when we correctly apply basic Bible principles, understand symbols and know history then prophecy is clearly understood from beginning to end. He promises to bless us when we know the book of Revelation.

God's Time

God reveals His time. Creation, Jewish feasts and history, major events on Jewish holy days, Daniel's seventy weeks, the life of Christ and Bible chronology tell us about time. The cross is the cornerstone of the timeline. So many prophecies are being fulfilled today. We may not know the dates of the Rapture and Second Coming but we know the days are the Feast of Trumpets and Day of Atonement.

God's Plan for Our Time

The book, *21st Century Revelation,* starts with a premise that we are at the end of the End Times. Once we see God in prophecy, get beyond symbolism, correct a few mistakes of tradition and know what God is telling us in His Word, we understand Bible prophecy and God's plan for our time. The End Times are focused on the time before the Rapture. During the Laodicean period, seven powers fight to become the only superpower. Four horses are on the run and five of seven trumpets have sounded. Now we know where and when we are in prophecy.

Further, the End Times are a time of global upheaval. The world's political, religious and economic systems transform in preparation for the Tribulation. Through the World Wars, Cold War and Iraq Wars, God warns us that Jesus Christ is about to return for His Church, restore Israel and judge the world.

We Are Close to the End!

1. God's character and nature gives man a choice and judgment day.
2. The Word of God reveals the time of God and the plan of God.
3. God's time is four thousand years before the cross and three thousand years after.
4. Bible chronology points to the end of man's six-thousand-year rule.
5. Key events of the last one hundred years occur on Jewish holy days.
6. The end of the Laodicean period is the end of the Church Age.
7. Seven End Time powers are ready for the Tribulation.
8. Four horses of the apocalypse are on the run today.
9. Seven wars of the seven trumpets occur in a 120-year period.
10. The United States is described in over one hundred Bible prophecies.

Wake up, Laodicean Church! It is time to see God's plan for our time and get to work. Christians are a part of God's plan in a local church to use our gifts and abilities, to love one another, work together, make disciples and tell others about Jesus Christ.

Super Signs—Israel and So Much More

A super sign is a key event that fulfills a specific prophecy during the End Times. The most important super sign is when Israel became an independent nation after more than two thousand years. Super signs such as the World Wars, Iraq Wars and the rise and fall of the United States are predicted in Scripture. The new Roman Empire, the division and reunification of Germany and the emergence of Islam are all a part of God's plan. We have been in the End Times for one hundred years.

The introduction of this book includes a chart of super signs that happen during the End Times and Tribulation. These signs are more than generic "wars and rumors of wars" since they are described in Scripture. God tells us specific events before they happen so we can know the signs of the times, wake up, serve in His Church and be ready to meet the Lord in the air.

**The closer we get to the end of the age,
the clearer the picture becomes.**

Here are the super signs of the End Times with Bible prophecy and Scripture references. The birth of the United States is a super sign that happens before 1900. Over twenty other super signs occur before the Rapture. Other events occur during the Tribulation.

Super Signs of the End Times

Year	Fulfillment	Prophecy	Scripture
1776	Birth of the United States	Eagle's Wings Torn from the Lion	Daniel 7:4
~1900	End Times Begin	Laodicean Period	Revelation 3:14-21
1914 -1918	World War I	1st Trumpet — Earth	Revelation 8:7
1917	Rise of the United States	3rd Seal — Black Horse	Revelation 6:5-6
1917	Rise of Communism	2nd Seal — Red Horse	Revelation 6:3-4
1938 -1945	World War II	2nd Trumpet — Sea	Revelation 8:8-9
1945	Germany Divided	Leopard Fatal Wound	Daniel 7:6 Revelation 13:2-3
1948	Israel Reborn	Valley of Dry Bones	Ezekiel 36-37
1950	European Union (Revived Roman Empire)	Lion/Bear/Leopard	Daniel 7:1-7 Revelation 13:2
1957	Germany Joins EU	Leopard	Daniel 7:6 Revelation 13:2
1967	Jerusalem Reunited	Immovable Rock	Zechariah 12:1-3
1973	United Kingdom Joins EU	Lion/Leopard	Daniel 7:4 Revelation 13:2
1979	Rise of Islam	4th Seal — Green Horse	Revelation 6:7-8

1945 -1989 1986	Cold War Chernobyl Accident	3rd Trumpet—Rivers Wormwood	Revelation 8:10-11
1989	Iron Curtain Falls Russia Hibernates	2nd Seal—Red Horse	Daniel 7:5 Revelation 6:3-4
1990 -1991	Iraq War I (Persian Gulf War)	4th Trumpet—Sky	Revelation 8:12-13
1990	Reunification of Germany	Leopard Fatal Wound Healed	Daniel 7:6 Revelation 13:2-3
1997	EU-Russia Partnership	Lion/Bear/Leopard	Daniel 7:5 Revelation 13:2
2000	Israel Associate Member of EU	World Government	Daniel 9:27 Revelation 13:7
2002	The Quartet on the Middle East (European Union, Russia, United Nations, United States)	Lion, Eagle, Bear, Leopard	Daniel 7:1-7
2003 -2010	Iraq War II Saddam Hussein	5th Trumpet—Unsealed Destroyer	Revelation 9:1-12
20??	English Official Language of European Union	Mouth of the Lion	Revelation 13:2
20??	Iraq War III	6th Trumpet—Humanity	Revelation 9:13-21
20??	Rapture	Feast of Trumpets *Yom Teruah* Last Trump	1 Corinthians 15 1 Thessalonians 4:16-17
20??	Tribulation Begins Israel Joins EU	Confirmation of the Covenant	Daniel 9:27
20??	Israel Builds Temple	Temple of God	Revelation 11:1-2
20??	Fall of the United States	Eagle Missing	Daniel 7:4 Revelation 13:2
20??	Russia Joins EU	Lion/Leopard/Bear Merge	Daniel 7:5 Revelation 13:2
20??	EU & United Nations Merge	World Government	Revelation 13:7

20??	World Political, Religious & Economic System	Antichrist, False Prophet & Mark of the Beast	Revelation 6:2-6 Revelation 13:1-18
20??	Apostasy & False Religions Merge	White Horse & Green Horse	Revelation 13:11-15
20??	False Religion & European Union	Woman & the Beast	Revelation 17:1-18
20??	Russian-Islamic War	Gog and Magog	Ezekiel 38-39
20??	Battle of Armageddon	6th-7th Seal, 7th Trumpet & 7th Bowl	Revelation 6:12-17, 11:15-19, 16:16-21
20??	Second Coming	Day of Atonement *Yom Kippur*	Revelation 19:1-21
20??	Reign of Christ	Tabernacles *Sukkot*	Revelation 20:1-5

The United States is the current superpower and participates in many of these events. The focus of future events is moving from America to Iraq, then Europe and finally Israel. The fulfillment of these prophecies proves the Word of God is true, alive and relevant for our time.

21st Century Revelation: World Wars, Iraq Wars & End Wars
A current understanding of God's plan for our time

God gave us His Son to die for our sin so that we can have a personal relationship with Him. He gave us the Holy Spirit to live within us to guide and empower us. He gave us His Word, which tells us about Himself and how we should live. He gave us a Church of believers to disciple us, put our faith into practice and work together to share redemption with the world. He tells us specific events in the future before they happen and then fulfills those events before our eyes.

God is not waiting for the Tribulation but is now implementing His plan for our time. We can know the prophecies of the End Times, understand the symbols that point to Jesus Christ's return, recognize the signs of the times and put it all together. That gives us confidence in

God—not only for His plan for the world but also for His individual plan for our lives. It is time the Church wakes up and gets to work.

About 1985 years ago, Jesus Christ said He would return for His people. We see God working through current events. The horses are on the run and the trumpets are sounding. We must be ready to meet our Savior and Lord Jesus Christ. The Rapture is about to occur and then the Tribulation begins. Then within seven years, God restores Israel, conquers all nations and Jesus Christ reigns on earth.

Hallelujah Chorus

And He shall reign forever and ever
King of kings and Lord of lords
King of kings and Lord of lords
And He shall reign forever and ever
Forever and ever, forever and ever
Hallelujah! Hallelujah! Hallelujah! Hallelujah!
Hal-le-lu-jah!
—George Frideric Handel, Messiah, 1741[14]

The Rapture is just the end of the beginning.

Surely I come quickly. Amen. Even so, come, Lord Jesus (Revelation 22:20).

Appendix

Invitation

Y ou are invited into a personal relationship with my Lord and Savior Jesus Christ.

1. **Everyone is a sinner.**

   For all have sinned, and come short of the glory of God (Romans 3:23).

2. **The result of sin is death.**

   For the wages of sin is death (Romans 6:23).

3. **God loves us and gave us His Son.**

   For God so loved the world, that he gave his only begotten Son, that whosoever believes in him should not perish, but have everlasting life (John 3:16).

4. **Jesus Christ gives us eternal life.**

   But the gift of God is eternal life through Jesus Christ our Lord (Romans 6:23).

5. **While we were sinners, Christ died for us.**

   But God commended his love toward us, in that, while we were yet sinners, Christ died for us (Romans 5:8).

6. Salvation is not by works but by God's mercy.

Not by works of righteousness which we have done, but according to his mercy he saved us (Titus 3:5).

7. Confess and believe.

That if you will confess with your mouth the Lord Jesus, and will believe in your heart that God raised him from the dead, you will be saved. For with the heart man believes unto righteousness; and with the mouth confession is made to salvation (Romans 10:9-10).

8. Call on Jesus Christ to be saved.

For whosoever shall call upon the name of the Lord shall be saved (Romans 10:13).

Would you like to accept Jesus Christ as your Savior? Then say a simple prayer to God. Just saying words will not save you. Believing in Jesus Christ and His work at the cross then receiving Him as Savior will save you.

God, I have sinned against You and deserve punishment for my failings. I believe Jesus Christ, the Son of God, died on the cross in my place for my sins. Today, I trust in Jesus Christ and His free gift of salvation. I accept God's love, grace and mercy and know He has forgiven all my sins. Now Jesus Christ is my Savior and I make Him Lord of my life.

After you accept Jesus Christ, follow up on your new relationship with God. Read the Bible, starting with the Gospels then the New Testament. Pray by talking with God. Make a public profession of your faith through baptism. Join with other Christians in a local Bible-believing church. There you can learn more about God and use your talents and gifts to minister to other people.

9. Now you are the child of God.

Behold, what manner of love the Father has bestowed upon us, that we should be called the sons [or children] of God (1 John 3:1).

About the Author

I, Robert "Cook" Szakacs, grew up in a Christian family with loving parents who encouraged and prepared us to succeed in whatever we chose to do. We were part of a Presbyterian Bible church and Methodist Christian school.

My family, church and school reinforced a love of God and country. We participated in Bible conferences at church and on vacation. At home, we watched the evening news and discussed Bible principles and current events. We were involved in the local political process and marched on Washington. I still remember a sixth-grade Bible study on the first half of Daniel. My classes on Genesis, Life of Christ and US History were essential to the writing of this book.

I studied at a Baptist college with plenty of Bible services throughout the week. Some favorite sermons were about prophecy and America. I received Jesus Christ as Savior and a degree in Computer Science. A computer programmer is a unique profession for a prophecy writer/teacher. When pulling prophecies together, there is an incredible logical design to God's time and plan.

All churches I have been a member of were independent Bible churches that focused on a personal relationship with God. After moving to Texas, I matured from passive attendance to active participation. My emphasis changed from the worship service to smaller Bible studies in which Christians teach Christians and mutually share our lives. I am challenged to seek truth in the Bible beyond the surface.

**One day, I asked God to love His Word more
and this book is the result of that prayer.**

The study of prophecy has been an amazing journey. Church and school gave a good biblical foundation. My dad told me the Feast of Trumpets is the Rapture. I followed up with a personal study of the Jewish feasts. In the fall of 2002 during the Iraq War debate, my pastor taught a Bible study on Revelation and I broke through the symbols. I read books and watched shows by Jack Van Impe, Tim LaHaye, Hal Lindsey, Perry Stone and others. Irvin Baxter described America's vital role in End Time events and Bill Bonnett explained a thorough chronology.

I asked God to love His Word more and ever since, my cup runs over. Having a little extra time, I decided to consolidate what I learned into a different kind of prophecy book. Instead of rehashing the traditional Protestant view or explaining just pieces of the puzzle, I wrote this comprehensive study incorporating corrected traditional teachings with the Jewish calendar, Bible chronology, American history and current world events. While writing, I recognized that the revelation of Jesus Christ must begin with an understanding of God and God's Word.

Now we see how God uses America's vital role as leader of the free world. End Time powers are conspiring to topple the United States and rule the world. The four horses and six wars of the seven trumpets are preparing the political, religious and economic systems for the Tribulation. Within a seven-year period, all nations will fall as the next superpower rules the world. Then Jesus Christ will conquer the Antichrist and reign on earth. As we see God at work around us, this message makes prophecy relevant for us today.

I write this book for the Laodicean church. My responsibility is to help wake up the Church and encourage the body but also watch the emerging global political, religious and economic apocalypse and warn the Saints. Stop being distracted by the world's system. Understand the truth of our time. Lend mutual support to each other as we work together for the Kingdom. The horses are on the run and the trumpets are sounding. What type of people should we be?

Although Moses had his burning bush and Paul had his road to Damascus, I have this amazing journey spending time in the presence of God and studying His Word. Writing the book is half the battle. Time is limited. So, I begin the rest of my life sharing this message of God's Word to the Church. This journey will end at the Rapture in the presence of my Savior and Lord Jesus Christ.

Appendix C

Prophecy Fulfilled

In Daniel 11:3-35, God gave Daniel prophecies of the Greek Empire and Greek civil wars between Seleucid (North) in Syria and Ptolemy (South) in Egypt that fought for control of the Middle East and especially Judea. A person living at the time could read Scripture, interpret the passage literally and understand the signs of the times.

Wars of Diadochi (Succession)

And when he [Alexander the Great] shall stand up, his kingdom shall be broken, and shall be divided toward the four winds of heaven; [The Greek empire divides into four regions under his generals Cassandar of Greece, Lysimachus of Asia Minor (Turkey), Seleucus I of Syria and Ptolemy I of Egypt[1]] and not to his posterity [Alexander's brother Philip III and son Alexander IV are assassinated], nor according to his dominion which he ruled: for his kingdom shall be plucked up, even for others beside those. [The appointed regents fall.] And the king of the south [Ptolemy I of Egypt] shall be strong, and one of his princes [Ptolemy's general Seleucus I of Syria]; and he [Seleucus I] shall be strong above him [Ptolemy I], and have dominion; his [Seleucus] dominion shall be a great dominion. [Greek Egypt starts strong but Greek Syria becomes stronger] (Daniel 11:4-5).

And in the end of years [253 BC at the end of the Second Syrian War[2]] they shall join themselves together; for the king's [Ptolemy II] daughter [Berenice] of the south [Egypt]; shall come to the king of the north [Antiochus II of Syria] to make an agreement: [Because of the peace treaty, Antiochus II divorces his wife Laodice for Berenice] but she [Berenice] shall not retain the power of the arm; neither shall he [Antiochus II] stand, nor his arm [because the deal backfires]; but she shall be given up [After Ptolemy II died, Antiochus II divorces Berenice and remarries Laodice]. and they that brought her [Berenice's Egyptian attendants], and he that begot her

Greek Kings of the North and South[3]

Seleucid Kingdom North (Syria)			Ptolemaic Kingdom South (Egypt)	
Date (BC)	King	War	Date (BC)	King
311-305 S 305-281 K	Seleucus I	Wars of Diadochi	323-305 S 305-283 K	Ptolemy I
291-281 C 281-261 K	Antiochus I	Syrian War I	285-283 C 283-246 K	Ptolemy II
261-246	Antiochus II	Syrian War II		
246-225	Seleucus II	Syrian War III	246-222	Ptolemy III
225-223	Seleucus III			
223-187	Antiochus III the Great	Syrian War IV	221-205	Ptolemy IV
		Syrian War V	204-181	Ptolemy V
187-175	Seleucus IV			
175-164	Antiochus IV	Syrian War VI	186-145	Ptolemy VI
163-161	Antiochus V			
161-150	Demetrius I			

C—Co-Rule, K—King, S—Satrap

[Ptolemy II dies], and he that strengthened her [Antiochus II] in these times. [Laodice does not trust Antiochus II so she plots to have him poisoned and Berenice and son killed. Her son, Seleucus II, becomes king] (Daniel 11:6).

Syrian War III

But out of a branch of her roots [Berenice's brother], shall one [Ptolemy III] stand up in his estate, which shall come with an army, and shall enter into the fortress of the king of the north [Seleucus II of Syria], and shall deal against them, and shall prevail: [As revenge for his sister's death, Ptolemy III attacks Syria, kills Laodice and loots the region all the way to Babylon. Seleucus II flees to Asia Minor.[4]] And shall also carry captives into Egypt their gods, with their princes, and with their precious vessels of silver and of gold; [He takes 40,000 talents of silver, 4000 talents of gold and 2500 idols.] and he shall continue more years than the king of the north [Seleucus II of

Syria]. [Ptolemy III lives four years longer than Seleucus II.]. So the king of the south [Ptolemy III of Egypt] shall come into his kingdom [Seleucus II of Syria], and shall return into his own land [Egypt]. [By 245 BC, Ptolemy III gains the Syrian coast but Seleucus II forces Ptolemy to retreat] (Daniel 11:7-9).

Syrian War IV

But his sons [Seleucus III and Antiochus III the Great] shall be stirred up, and shall assemble a multitude of great forces: and one [Antiochus the Great] shall certainly come, and overflow, and pass through: [In 219 BC, he takes the Syrian coastline, Tyre and Judea[5]]: then shall he return, and be stirred up, even to his fortress. And the king of the south [Ptolemy IV of Egypt] shall be moved with rage, and shall come forth and fight with him, even with the king of the north [Antiochus the Great]: and he shall set forth a great multitude; but the multitude shall be given into his [Ptolemy IV] hand. [In 217 BC, Ptolemy IV defeats Antiochus the Great at the Battle of Raphia in Gaza and takes back Judea.[6]] And when he has taken away the multitude, his heart shall be lifted up; and he shall cast down many ten thousands: but he shall not be strengthened by it. [In 213 BC, Ptolemy IV kills 40,000 Jews in Alexandria, Egypt] (Daniel 11:10-12).

Syrian War V

For the king of the north [Antiochus the Great of Syria] shall return [about fifteen years later], and shall set forth a multitude greater than the former, and shall certainly come after certain years with a great army and with much riches. And in those times there shall many stand up against the [child] king of the south [Ptolemy V of Egypt]: [King Philip of Macedonia joins Antiochus the Great against Egypt[7]] also the robbers of your people shall exalt themselves to establish the vision; but they shall fall. [Some Jews rebel against Egypt but Ptolemy V's general Scopas crushes the Jewish rebellion in 200 BC] (Daniel 11:13-14).

So the king of the north [Antiochus the Great] shall come, and cast up a mount, and take the most fenced cities [of Sidon]: and the arms of the south [Egypt dealing with their own civil war and regency issue] shall not withstand, neither his chosen people, neither shall there be any strength to withstand. But he [Antiochus the Great] that comes against him [Ptolemy V] shall do according to his own will, and none shall stand before him: and he shall stand in the glorious land [Judea], which by his hand shall be consumed. [In 197 BC, at the Battle of Panium in the Golan Heights of northern Israel, Antiochus the Great captures Judea, Lebanon and Syria from Egypt.[8] Judea's liberation from Greek Egypt results in greater persecution by Greek Syria] (Daniel 11:15-16).

He [Antiochus the Great of Syria] shall also set his face to enter with the strength of his whole kingdom, and upright ones with him; thus shall he do: [In 195 BC, He plans to overthrow Egypt by diplomatic means[9]] and he shall give him [Ptolemy V] the daughter of women [Cleopatra I the ancestor of Cleopatra VII consort of Julius Caesar], corrupting her: [He gives his daughter to undermine Egypt] but she shall not stand on his side, neither be for him [as she chooses her husband over her father] (Daniel 11:17).

After this shall he [Antiochus the Great] turn his face unto the isles, and [in 192 BC, teaming up with the famous Carthaginian General and enemy of Rome, Hannibal] shall take many [invading up the coast of Asia Minor and the Greek islands]: but a prince [Roman general Scipio Asiaticus[10]] for his own behalf shall cause the reproach offered by him to cease; without his own reproach, he shall cause it to turn upon him. [In 190 BC, the Romans defeat him at the battle of Magnesia in Western Asia Minor and force him to pay tribute of 15,000 talents of silver.] Then he shall turn his face toward the fort of his own land: but he shall stumble and fall, and not be found. [In 187 BC, Antiochus the Great dies while plundering a pagan temple in Persia] (Daniel 11:18-19).

[Rome's defeat of Greek Syria results in a great amount of tribute owed.] Then shall stand up in his estate a raiser of taxes [Seleucus IV] in the glory of the kingdom: [He sent the tax collector Heliodorus to seize the gold in the Jewish temple.[11]]; but within a few days he shall be destroyed, neither in anger, nor in battle. [Heliodorus leads a coup, assassinates Seleucus IV and tries to become king but dies] (Daniel 11:20).

Daniel 11 continues in chapter 8, Prophecy Fulfilled.

Appendix D

Jewish Feast Dates

2000-2040[1]

Roman Year	Jewish Year	Kadesh Barnea	Trumpets	Atonement	Tabernacles
		Kadesh Barnea	*Rosh Hashanah*	*Yom Kippur*	*Sukkot*
		9th of *Av*	1st-2nd of *Tishri*	10th of *Tishri*	15th of *Tishri*
2000 L	5761	8/9	9/29-30	10/8	10/13
2001	5762	7/28	9/17-18	9/26	10/1
2002	5763 L	7/17	9/6-7	9/15	9/20
2003	5764	8/6	9/26-27	10/5	10/10
2004 L	5765 L	7/26	9/15-16	9/24	9/29
2005	5766	8/13	10/3-4	10/12	10/17
2006	5767	8/2	9/22-23	10/1	10/6
2007	5768 L	7/23	9/12-13	9/21	9/26
2008 L	5769	8/9	9/29-30	10/8	10/13
2009	5770	7/29	9/18-19	9/27	10/2
2010	5771 L	7/19	9/8-9	9/17	9/22
2011	5772	8/8	9/28-29	10/7	10/12
2012 L	5773	7/28	9/16-17	9/25	9/30
2013	5774 L	7/15	9/4-5	9/13	9/18
2014	5775	8/4	9/24-25	10/3	10/8
2015	5776 L	7/25	9/13-14	9/22	9/27

2016 L	5777	8/13	10/2-3	10/11	10/16
2017	5778	7/31	9/20-21	9/29	10/4
2018	5779 L	7/21	9/9-10	9/18	9/23
2019	5780	8/10	9/29-30	10/8	10/13
2020 L	5781	7/29	9/18-19	9/27	10/2
2021	5782 L	7/17	9/6-7	9/15	9/20
2022	5783	8/6	9/25-26	10/4	10/9
2023	5784 L	7/26	9/15-16	9/24	9/29
2024 L	5885	8/12	10/2-3	10/11	10/16
2025	5786	8/2	9/22-23	10/1	10/6
2026	5787 L	7/22	9/11-12	9/20	9/25
2027	5788	8/11	10/1-2	10/10	10/15
2028 L	5789	7/31	9/20-21	9/29	10/4
2029	5790 L	7/21	9/9-10	9/18	9/23
2030	5791	8/7	9/27-28	10/6	10/11
2031	5792	7/28	9/17-18	9/26	10/1
2032 L	5793 L	7/17	9/5-6	9/14	9/19
2033	5794	8/3	9/23-24	10/2	10/7
2034	5795	7/24	9/13-14	9/22	9/27
2035	5796	8/13	10/3-4	10/12	10/17
2036 L	5797	8/2	9/21-22	9/30	10/5
2037	5798 L	7/20	9/9-10	9/18	9/23
2038	5799	8/9	9/29-30	10/8	10/13
2039	5800	7/30	9/18-19	9/27	10/2
2040 L	5801 L	7/18	9/7-8	9/16	9/21

Calendar Notes

- L (Leap Year) The Roman calendar adds day February 29 about every four years. The Jewish calendar adds month *Adar* I every two or three years.
- The Feast of Trumpets is celebrated on two days.

- The crescent new moon is about sixteen hours after the astronomical new moon.
- The Jewish holy days start at evening at sunset of the date listed.
- Since 398, the Jewish calendar follows a nineteen-year rule-based perpetual calendar not set by observation. The new moon and year may be off a day.
- Jerusalem is seven hours earlier than United States' Eastern Time.

Appendix E

Chronology of Jesus Christ

T his is the sequence of key events in the birth, ministry, death, burial and resurrection of Jesus Christ.[1]

Year	Event	Scripture
63 BC	Hasmonean Independence Ends[2] Judea Protectorate of Rome Rome Appoints Antipater King Herodian Dynasty Begins	
41 BC	Rome Appoints Herod the Great, King of the Jews over Judea, Samaria and Galilee	
31 BC	Octavius Defeats Anthony in Egypt, Reign Begins[3]	
27 BC	Octavius Named Augustus Senate Gives Title of Emperor[4]	
23 BC	Herod Rebuilds Temple 18th Year of Herod[5]	John 2:19-20
22 BC	Main Temple Complete[6]	
8 BC	Caesar Augustus Census Decree 28 BC, 8 BC, 14 AD[7]	Luke 2:1-3
Sivan June	Zechariah—Abijah Division Priest at Temple—10th Week Angel Visits Zechariah	Luke 1:5-22 1 Chronicles 24:10
Sivan June	Elizabeth Pregnant	Luke 1:23-25
Kislev	Angel Visits Mary	Luke 1:26-33

Kislev 25-*Tevet* 3 December 24/25 Gregorian	Mary Visits Elizabeth Mary Pregnant *Hanukkah*	Luke 1:39-44
	Mary Returns to Nazareth	Luke 1:56
	Angel Sent to Joseph	Matthew 1:18-21
7 BC *Nisan* April	John the Baptist Born Passover	Luke 1:57-65
Sivan *Tishri* *Kislev*	Triple Conjunction of Jupiter and Saturn in Pieces May 27, October 6 and December 1[8]	
	Joseph and Mary Travel from Nazareth to Bethlehem	Luke 2:4-5
7 BC *Tishri* 15 October 7/8 Julian October 5/6 Gregorian	Jesus Christ Born Tabernacles Roman Census Taken Conjunction	Luke 2:6-7
	Shepherds Visit Bethlehem	Luke 2:8-20
Tishri 23 October 15/16	Jesus Christ's Circumcision *Simhat Torah* Rejoicing of the *Torah*	Luke 2:21
Heshvan 25 November 16/17	Jesus Christ's Dedication Simeon and Anna	Luke 2:22-24
	Joseph, Mary and Jesus Travel North to Nazareth	Luke 2:39-40
6 BC *Shevat* February	Conjunction of Jupiter, Saturn and Mars[9]	
	Joseph, Mary and Jesus Travel from Nazareth to House in Bethlehem	Matthew 2:11
5 BC ~*Adar-Sivan* ~March 9-June 16	Star of Bethlehem Comet Recorded by Chinese and Koreans[10]	

~*Sivan* ~May-June	Wise Men Travel to Jerusalem and Bethlehem	Matthew 2:1-12
	Joseph, Mary and Jesus Flee South to Egypt	Matthew 2:13-15
	Herod's Decree	Matthew 2:16-18
4 BC *Adar* 13 March 13	Fast of Esther[11] Partial Lunar Eclipse	
4 BC *Adar-Nisan* March-April	Herod the Great Dies[12] Judea Divided among Sons	Matthew 2:19-23
4 BC October	James Ussher, 1654 Jesus Christ's Birth[13]	
1 BC December 25	Dionysius Exiguus, 532 Jesus Christ Birth[14]	
	Joseph, Mary and Jesus Leave Egypt for Nazareth	Matthew 2:19-23
~6 AD	Rome Appoints Governor of Judea[15]	Luke 2:41-50
6 AD *Nisan* 14	Jesus at Passover—12.5	Luke 2:41-50
10 AD	Augustus—Emperor Tiberius—Co-Regent[16]	
14 AD	Tiberius—Sole Reign[17]	
18 AD	Joseph Caiaphas—High Priest Annas—Father-in-Law[18]	Luke 3:2 John 18:12-13
22 AD	Pontius Pilate—Governor 12th Year of Tiberius[19]	Luke 3:1
24 AD *Nisan*	John the Baptist Begins Ministry 15th Years from Co-Regency	Luke 3:1
Tishri 15	Jesus Begins Ministry— ~30 Tabernacles Birthday (30)	Luke 3:23
25 AD	46th Year of Temple Rebuilding	John 2:19-20

Nisan 14	Passover 1	John 2:23
?	4 Months to Harvest	John 4:35
?	Unknown Feast	John 5:1
Tishri 15	Tabernacles Birthday (31)	
26 AD *Nisan* 14	Passover 2	John 6:4
Tishri 15	Tabernacles Birthday (32)	John 7:2
Kislev 25	Dedication (*Hanukkah*)	John 10:22
27 AD *Nisan* 9 Friday, April 4	Triumphal Entry Public Presentation of the Messiah	Daniel 9:25-26 John 12:12-19
Nisan 10 Saturday, April 5	Lamb Taken for Passover Jewish Leaders Choose Jesus Christ	Exodus 12:1-14 Mark 11:18
Nisan 14 Wednesday, April 9	Last Supper, Betrayal, Trial, Passover 3 and Crucifixion	John 13-19
Nisan 15 Thursday, April 10	Unleavened Bread High Sabbath	
Nisan 16 Friday, April 11	Spices Bought after Sabbath	Mark 16:1
Nisan 17 Saturday, April 12	Regular Sabbath	
Nisan 18* Sunday, April 13	Firstfruits Resurrection	Leviticus 23:10-11 John 20:1-10
Iyar 28* Thursday, May 23	Ascension Jerusalem Day 1967[20]	Acts 1:9
Sivan 9* Sunday, June 1	Pentecost	Acts 2:-4

*Julian dates with Sadducees' interpretation of feasts.

Appendix F

Endnotes

Many preachers, teachers and scholars of the past and present have preserved, translated and explained the Word of God to develop our Christian heritage and current understanding of the Bible. I am very thankful to these people for their impact on Christianity. From that point, I have the opportunity to review their work and build from there.

If I reference a source or state that I agree or disagree on one point with a person, ministry, organization or doctrinal theory, it does not indicate I agree or disagree on all points.

The majority of Scripture is from the Authorized King James Version. Some obsolete words have been altered to assist reading and understanding. A few words have not changed to exalt our sovereign God.

- **Bibliography**

  [1] Holy Bible, Authorized King James Version, 1611, *Bible Gateway*, <http:// www. biblegateway .com>, October 1, 2012.

  [2] Baxter, Irvin, End Time Ministries, *Endtime*, <http://www.endtime.com>, October 1, 2012.

  [3] Baxter, Irvin, Politics and Religion, *Endtime*, <http://www.endtime.com/ Radio. aspx>, October 1, 2012.

  [4] Bonnett, Bill, Chronology of Man, *Abdicate*, http://abdicate.net/book.aspx>, October 1, 2012.

  [5] Bonnett, Bill, "Linear Chronology of Man According to the Scriptures," *Abdicate*, <http://abdicate.net/chron.aspx>, October 1, 2012.

  [6] Chumney, Edward, Seven Festivals of the Messiah, *Hebraic Heritage Ministries*, <http://www. hebroots.org/sevenfestivals.htm>, October 1, 2012.

  [7] Guzik, David, Commentary on the Bible, *Enduring Word*, <http:// www.enduring-word.com/library_commentaries.html>, October 1, 2012.

  [8] "Hebcal Jewish Calendar," *Hebcal*, <http://www.hebcal.com/>, October 1, 2012.

[9] Henry, Matthew, <u>Matthew Henry Commentary on the Whole Bible</u>, 1706-1721, *Blue Letter Bible*, <http://cf.blueletterbible.org/commentaries/>, October 1, 2012.

[10] Jamieson, Robert, et al., <u>Commentary Critical and Explanatory on the Whole Bible</u>, 1871, *Blue Letter Bible*, <http://cf. blueletterbible.org/ commentaries/>, October 1, 2012.

[11] LaHaye, Tim and Hindson, Ed, <u>The Popular Encyclopedia of Bible Prophecy</u>, (Eugene, OR: Harvest House, 2004).

[12] LaHaye, Tim, <u>Prophecy Study Bible</u>, (Chattanooga, TN: AMG Press, 2000).

[13] Lindsey, Hal, "The Hal Lindsey Report," *Hal Lindsey*, <http://www. hallindsey. com/>, October 1, 2012.

[14] Scofield, Cyrus, <u>Reference Notes, 1917 Edition</u>, *Bible Study Tools*, <http:// www. biblestudytools. com/commentaries/scofield-reference-notes/>, October 1, 2012.

[15] Van Impe, Jack, Jack Van Impe Ministries International, *JVIM*, <http:// www. jvim. com/>, October 1, 2012.

[16] Wesley, John, <u>Wesley's Explanatory Notes</u>, 1754-1765, *Bible Study Tools*, <http:// www.bible studytools.com/commentaries/wesleys-explanatory-notes/>, October 1, 2012.

[17] *Wikipedia*, <http://en.wikipedia.org/wiki/Main_Page>, October 1, 2012.

- **Book Cover**
  - Five photos depict the World Wars, Cold War and Iraq Wars described by John the Apostle in the book of Revelation.

[1] "Trench Warfare," *Wikipedia*, <http://en.wikipedia.org/wiki/Trench _warfare>, October 1, 2012.

[2] "Nagasaki," *Wikipedia*, <http://en.wikipedia.org/wiki/Nagasaki>, October 1, 2012.

[3] "Chernobyl Disaster," *Wikipedia*, <http://en.wikipedia.org/wiki/Chernobyl _Disaster>, October 1, 2012.

[4] "Kuwaiti Oil Fires," *Wikipedia*, <http://en.wikipedia.org/wiki/Kuwaiti_oil _fires>, October 1, 2012.

[5] "Iraq War," *Wikipedia*, <http://en.wikipedia.org/wiki/Iraq_War>, October 1, 2012.

1. Does Prophecy Matter?

[1] Konig, George, "27% of the Bible Is Prophecy," Konig, <http://www.konig. org/ wc24.htm>, October 1, 2012.

Payne, J. Barton, <u>Encyclopedia of Biblical Prophecy</u>, (San Francisco: Harper and Row, 1973).

[2] Reagan, David R, "The Passion in Prophecy," *Lamb Lion*, <http:// lamblion .com/ articles/articles_first7.php>, October 1, 2012.

[3] Blackaby, Henry and King, Claude, <u>Experiencing God, Knowing and Doing the Will of God</u> (Lifeway Press, 2003) 225.

[4] Young, Darrel, "Why Study Bible Prophecy?," *Focus on Jerusalem*, October 2003, <http://focusonjerusalem.com/whystudybibleprophecy.html>, October 1, 2012.

[5] Krauthammer, Charles, "France's Game," March 17, 2003, *Time*, <http:// www.time.com/time/magazine/article/0,9171,1101030324-433251,00 .html>, October 1, 2012.

[6] Joel 3:2.

[7] Revelation 9:13-16.

[8] Ezekiel 37-39.

2. End Times Defined

[1] LaHaye, Tim and Hindson, Ed, <u>The Popular Encyclopedia of Bible Prophecy</u>. LaHaye, Tim, "Glossary of Prophetic Terms," <u>Prophecy Study Bible</u>, 1407-1409. Van Impe, Jack, <u>Jack Van Impe's Dictionary of Prophetic Terms</u>, 1998, *JVIM*, <http://www. jvim.com/>, October 1, 2012.

[2] Konig, George, "27% of the Bible is Prophecy," *Konig*, <http://www.konig .org/ wc24.htm>, October 1, 2012. Payne, J. Barton, <u>Encyclopedia of Biblical Prophecy</u>.

[3] "Judea and Samaria," *Wikipedia*, <http://en.wikipedia.org/wiki/Judea_and_ Samaria>, October 1, 2012.

[4] LaHaye, Tim, "Pretribulation Rapture," <u>Prophecy Study Bible</u>, 1481.

3. The Throne of God

[1] Henry, Matthew, "Daniel 7," <u>Matthew Henry Commentary</u>, *Blue Letter Bible*, <http://cf. blueletterbible.org/commentaries/>, October 1, 2012.

[2] Guzik, David, "Isaiah 3," *Enduring Word*, <http://www.enduringword.com/ library_commentaries.htm>, October 1, 2012.

[3] "Throne," *Bible Gateway*, <http://www.biblegateway.com/ keyword/>, October 1, 2012.

[4] Exodus 39.

[5] Wesley, John, "Revelation 4," <u>Wesley's Explanatory Notes</u>, 1754-1765, *Bible Study Tools*, <http://www.bible studytools.com/commentaries/ wesleysexplanatory-notes/>, October 1, 2012.

[6] Jamieson, Robert, et al., "Revelation 4," <u>Commentary Critical and Explanatory on the Whole Bible</u>, *Blue Letter Bible*, <http://cf. blueletter bible.org/commentaries/>, October 1, 2012.

[7] Guzik, David, "Revelation 4," <u>David Guzik's Commentary</u>, *Enduring Word*, <http:// www.enduringword.com/library_commentaries.htm>, October 1, 2012.

[8] Matthew 17:1-9.

[9] Wesley, John, "Revelation 1," <u>Wesley's Explanatory Notes</u>, 1754-1765, *Bible Study Tools*, <http://www.bible studytools.com/commentaries/ wesleys-explanatory-notes/>, October 1, 2012.

[10] LaHaye, Tim, "John's Vision of Christ," <u>Prophecy Study Bible</u>, 1360.

[11] Wesley, John, "Revelation 1," <u>Wesley's Explanatory Notes</u>, *Bible Study Tools*, <http://www.bible studytools.com/commentaries/ wesleys-explanatory-notes/>, October 1, 2012.
"*Aggelos,*" *Blue Letter Bible*, <http://cf.blueletter bible.org/lang/lexicon/ lexicon. cfm?strongs=G32>, October 1, 2012.

[12] Guzik, David, "Revelation 19," <u>David Guzik's Commentary</u>, *Enduring Word*, <http://www.enduringword.com/library_ commentaries.htm>, October 1, 2012.

[13] Jamieson, Robert, et al., "Revelation 19," *Blue Letter Bible*, <http://cf. blueletterbible.org/commentaries/>, October 1, 2012.

4. The Revelation of Jesus Christ

[1] Matthew 1:21.

[2] John 14:6.

[3] "Repent," *Bible Gateway*, <http://www.biblegateway.com/keyword/>, October 1, 2012.

[4] Daniel 2:26-28.

[5] Daniel 10:1-12.

[6] Genesis 5:24.

[7] Genesis 22:1-14.

[8] Genesis 32:24-30.

[9] Exodus 3:1-8.

[10] 2 Kings 2:9-12.

[11] Matthew 14:25-31.

[12] Matthew 17:1-9.

[13] 2 Corinthians 12:1-4.

5. Study the Bible

[1] Wallace, Daniel, *Bible*, <http://www.bible.org/page.php?page_id=1503>, October 1, 2012.

[2] LaHaye, Tim, "How to Study the Bible," <u>Prophecy Study Bible</u> 639.

[3] Weathers, John, <u>Genesis</u>, Harford Christian School, September 1975.

[4] Daniel 2-4.

[5] Weathers, John, <u>Genesis</u>, Harford Christian School.

[6] MacArthur, John, "How to Enjoy Bible Study," *Grace to You*, <http:// www.gty.org/ Resources/Articles/2429>, October 1, 2012.

[7] Matthew 7:7.

6. Symbols Revealed

[1] "Apocalypse," *Merriam-Webster*, <http://www.merriam-webster.com/ dictionary/ Apocalypse>, October 1, 2012.

[2] LaHaye, Tim and Hindson, Ed, <u>The Popular Encyclopedia of Bible Prophecy</u> 27-31.

[3] LaHaye, <u>The Popular Encyclopedia of Bible Prophecy</u> 27-31.

[4] "Who's on First?," *Wikipedia*, <http://en.wikipedia.org/wiki/Who's_on _first>, October 1, 2012.

[5] "Symbols in Bible Prophecy," *Teaching Hearts*, <http://www.teaching hearts.org/ dre00symbols.html>, October 1, 2012.

[6] "Numbers in the Bible," *Teaching Hearts*, <http://teachinghearts.org/ dre17httnumber.html>, October 1, 2012.

[7] Arthur, Kay, <u>How to Study Your Bible</u> (Eugene, OR: Harvest House, 1994) 95-101. LaHaye, Tim, "How to Study Bible Prophecy," <u>Prophecy Study Bible</u> xiii.

[8] "Lion," *Bible Gateway*, <http://www.biblegateway.com/ keyword/>, October 1, 2012.

[9] Mullins, Jim, <u>The Revelation of Jesus Christ</u> 2002 12-13.

[10] Kelly, Jack, "Revelation 4," *Grace through Faith*, <http://gracethrufaith .com/ revelation-times/revelation-4/Revelation 4>, October 1, 2012.

[11] "Four Gospels," *Spirit and Truth*, <http://www.spiritandtruth.org/teaching/ Book_of_Revelation/commentary/htm/topics/four_gospels.html>, October 1, 2012.

[12] "Exploring the Gospels," *Life of Christ*, <http://www.lifeofchrist.com/life/ gospels/ print.asp>, October 1, 2012.

[13] Kelly, Jack, "Revelation 4," *Grace through Faith*, <http://gracethrufaith .com/ revelation-times/revelation-4/Revelation 4>, October 1, 2012.

[14] Numbers 2.
Kelly, Jack, "Revelation 4".

[15] Kelly, Jack, "Revelation 4".

7. Prophets and Prophecy

[1] Hindson, Ed, "The Office of the Prophet," <u>Prophecy Study Bible</u> 312.

[2] Anderson, Jim, "False Prophecy," <u>Prophecy Study Bible</u> 222. Noorbergen, Rene, "Test of a True Prophet," *Bible Plus*, <http:// bibleplus.org/ prophecy/visions-egw/ tests_of_a_true_prophet.htm>, October 1, 2012.

[3] Isaiah 8:16, Isaiah 29:10-13, Revelation 22:10.

[4] MacArthur, John, "How to Enjoy Bible Study," *Grace to You*, <http://www. gty.org/ Resources/Articles/2429>, October 1, 2012.

[5] Konig, George, "27% of the Bible is Prophecy," *Konig*, <http://www.konig .org/ wc24.htm>, October 1, 2012.
Payne, J. Barton, <u>Encyclopedia of Biblical Prophecy</u>.

[6] LaHaye, Tim, "How to Study Bible Prophecy," <u>Prophecy Study Bible</u> xiii.

[7] Authur, Kay, <u>How to Study Your Bible</u> 95-101. LaHaye, Tim, "How to Study Bible Prophecy," <u>Prophecy Study Bible</u> xiii.

[8] Kelly, Jack, "Revelation 4," *Grace Through Faith*, <http://gracethrufaith .com/ revelation-times/revelation-4/Revelation 4>, October 1, 2012.

[9] Van Impe, Jack, "Methods of Interpretation," <u>Jack Van Impe's Dictionary of Prophetic Terms</u>, *JVIM*, <http://www. jvim.com/>, October 1, 2012.

[10] Mayden, Joe, Christ Chapel Bible Church, April 2011.

8. Prophecy Fulfilled

[1] Malick, David, "An Introduction to the Book of Daniel," *Bible*, <http:// www.bible. org/page.php?page_id=924>, October 1, 2012.

[2] "Bible Timeline," *Bible Study*, <http://www.biblestudy.org/beginner/bible-timeline. html>, October 1, 2012.

[3] Daniel 7:1-28, Revelation 13:1-3.

[4] Josephus, Flavius, <u>The Antiquities of the Jews</u>, Book 11, Chapter 8, Paragraph 5, *Christian Classics Ethereal Library*, <http://www.ccel.org /ccel/josephus/ complete>, October 1, 2012.

[5] "Bible Prophecy - Verify History," *All about the Truth*, <http:// www.all abouttruth. org/bible-prophecy.htm>, October 1, 2012.

[6] Van Impe, Jack, <u>Final Mysteries Unsealed</u> (Nashville: Word Publishing, 1998) 189.

[7] "Cyrus the Great," *Wikipedia*, <http://en.wikipedia.org/wiki/Cyrus_the _ Great>, October 1, 2012.

[8] "Greco-Persian Wars," *Wikipedia*, <http://en.wikipedia.org/wiki/Greco-Persian_ Wars>, October 1, 2012.

[9] "Persian Kings," *Wikipedia*, <http://en.wikipedia.org/wiki/List_of_kings_ of_Persia>, October 1, 2012.

[10] Walvoord, John, "History from Darius to the Time of the End," *Bible*, <http://www. bible.org/page.php?page_id=5662>, October 1, 2012.

[11] Josephus, Flavius, <u>The Antiquities of the Jews</u>, Book 11, Chapter 8, Paragraph 5, *Christian Classics Ethereal Library*, <http://www.ccel.org /ccel/josephus/ complete>, October 1, 2012.

[12] "Kings of Macedon," *Wikipedia*, <http://en.wikipedia.org/wiki/List_of_ Kings_of_ Macedon>, October 1, 2012.

[13] "Diadochi," *Wikipedia*, <http://en.wikipedia.org/wiki/Diadochi>, October 1, 2012.

[14] "Antiochus IV," *Wikipedia*, <http://en.wikipedia.org/wiki/Antiochus_IV>, October 1, 2012.

[15] "Antiochus IV," *Wikipedia*.

[16] "Syrian Wars," *Wikipedia*, <http://en.wikipedia.org/wiki//Syrian_Wars>, October 1, 2012.

[17] "Syrian Wars," *Wikipedia*.

[18] "Antiochus IV," *Wikipedia*, <http://en.wikipedia.org/wiki/Antiochus_IV>, October 1, 2012.

[19] "Syrian Wars," *Wikipedia*, <http://en.wikipedia.org/wiki/Syrian_Wars>, October 1, 2012.

[20] "Gaius Popillius Laenas," *Wikipedia*, <http://en.wikipedia.org/wiki/Gaius_ Popillius_Laenas>, October 1, 2012.

[21] "Maccabean Revolt," *Wikipedia*, <http://en.wikipedia.org/wiki/Maccabean_ Revolt>, October 1, 2012.

[22] Daniel 8:9-14.

[23] "Antiochus IV," *Wikipedia*, <http://en.wikipedia.org/wiki/Antiochus_IV>, October 1, 2012.

[24] "Siege of Jerusalem 63 BC," *Wikipedia*, <http://en.wikipedia.org/wiki/Siege _of_Jerusalem_(63_BC)>, October 1, 2012.

9. In the Beginning, God

[1] "Ultimate Fate of the Universe," *Wikipedia*, <http://en.wikipedia.org/wiki/ Ultimate_fate_of_the_universe>, October 1, 2012.

[2] "Global Warming," *Wikipedia*, <http://en.wikipedia.org/wiki/Global_ warming>, October 1, 2012.

[3] "Tolerance," *Wikipedia*, <http://en.wikipedia.org/wiki/Tolerance>, October 1, 2012.

[4] Daniel 2-4.

[5] "Great Disappointment," *Wikipedia*, <http://en.wikipedia.org/wiki/The_ Great_ Disappointment>, October 1, 2012.

[6] "Young Earth Creationism," *Wikipedia*, <http://en.wikipedia.org/wiki/ Young_ Earth_Creationism>, October 1, 2012.

[7] "Numbers in the Bible," *Teaching Hearts*, <http://teachinghearts.org/ dre17httnumber.html>, October 1, 2012.

[8] "Sabbath," *Bible Gateway*, <http://www.biblegateway.com/ keyword/>, October 1, 2012.

9 Reagan, David, "What Year Is It and Does It Really Matter?," *Lamb Lion*, <http://www.lamblion.com/articles/articles_jewishlife3.php>, October 1, 2012.

10 Babylonian Talmud, Book 9, Chapter 1, *Sacred Texts*, <http://www.sacred-texts.com/jud/t09/zar03.htm#page_1>, October 1, 2012.

11 "Millennialism," *Wikipedia*, <http://en.wikipedia.org/wiki/Millennialism>, October 1, 2012.

12 Reagan, David, "What Year Is It and Does It Really Matter?," *Lamb Lion*, <http://www.lamblion.com/articles/articles_jewishlife3.php>, October 1, 2012.

13 Thiel, Bob, "Does God Have a 6000 Year Plan," COG Writer, <http://www.cogwriter.com/six_thousand_year_plan_6000.htm>, October 1, 2012.

14 "Israel," *Wikipedia*, <http://en.wikipedia.org/wiki/Israel>, October 1, 2012.

15 "Dionysius Exiguus," Wikipedia, <http://en.wikipedia.org/wiki/Dionysius_Exiguus>, October 1, 2012.

16 "Ussher Chronology," *Wikipedia*, <http://en.wikipedia.org/wiki/Ussher chronology>, October 1, 2012.
Bonnett, Bill, "Linear Chronology of Man According to the Scriptures," *Abdicate*, <http://abdicate.net/chron.aspx>, October 1, 2012.

17 "James Ussher," *Wikipedia*, <http://en.wikipedia.org/wiki/James_Ussher>, October 1, 2012.

18 Hebcal Jewish Calendar, *Hebcal*, <http://www.hebcal.com/hebcal/>, October 1, 2012.

19 First, Michael, Jewish History in Conflict: A Study of the Major Discrepancy between Rabbinic and Conventional Chronology (New York: Jason Aronson, Inc., 1997) 3.
Reagan, David, "What Year Is It and Does It Really Matter?," *Lamb Lion*, <http://www.lamblion.com/articles/articles_jewishlife3.php>, October 1, 2012.

10. Seven Days of God

1 Kelly, Jack, "Revelation 4," *Grace through Faith*, <http://gracethrufaith.com/revelation-times/revelation-4/Revelation 4>, October 1, 2012.

2 Rich, Tracey, "Jewish Calendar: A Closer Look," *Judaism 101*, <http://www.jewfaq.org/calendr2.htm>, October 1, 2012.

3 Exodus 12, Leviticus 23.
Rich, Tracey, "Jewish Calendar," *Judaism 101*, <http://www.jewfaq.org/calendar.htm>, October 1, 2012.
Rich, Tracey, "Jewish Holidays," *Judaism 101*, <http://www.jewfaq.org/holiday0.htm>, October 1, 2012.

4 "Jewish Calendar," *Wikipedia*, <http://en.wikipedia.org/wiki/Jewish_calendar>, October 1, 2012.

[5] "Hillie II," *Wikipedia*, <http://en.wikipedia.org/wiki/Hillie_II>, October 1, 2012.

[6] "Jewish Calendar," *Wikipedia*, <http://en.wikipedia.org/wiki/Jewish_ calendar>, October 1, 2012.

[7] *"Anno Mundi,"* *Wikipedia*, <http://en.wikipedia.org/wiki/Anno_Mundi>, October 1, 2012.

[8] Chumney, Edward, Seven Festivals of the Messiah, Chapter 7, Hebraic Heritage Ministries, <http://www.hebroots.org/sevenfestivals_chap7.htm>, October 1, 2012.

[9] Rood, Michael, *Hebrew Calendar*, <http://michaelrood.tv/biblical-hebrew-calendar>, October 1, 2012.

[10] Rich, Tracey, "Jewish Holidays," *Judaism 101*, <http://www.jewfaq.org/ holiday0.htm>, October 1, 2012.

[11] Chumney, Edward, Seven Festivals of the Messiah, Chapter 2, Hebraic Heritage Ministries, <http://www.hebroots.org/sevenfestivals_chap2.htm>, October 1, 2012. "Jewish Holidays," *Wikipedia*, <http://en.wikipedia.org/wiki/Jewish_ holidays>, October 1, 2012.

[12] Chumney, Edward, Seven Festivals of the Messiah, Chapter 2, Hebraic Heritage Ministries, <http://www.hebroots.org/sevenfestivals_chap2.htm>, October 1, 2012.

[13] "The Resurrection of Yeshua and the Festivals of Firstfruits," Anno Mundi Books, <http://www.annomundi.com/bible/firstfruits1.htm>, October 1, 2012.

11. The Feast of Trumpets

[1] Larsen, David, "John Nelson Darby: Pioneer of Dispensational Premillennialism," *Pre-Trib Research Center*, <http://www.pre-trib .org/article-view.php?id=177#_ednref15>, October 1, 2012.

[2] LaHaye, Tim and Hindson, Ed, The Popular Encyclopedia of Bible Prophecy, 316-320.

[3] LaHaye, The Popular Encyclopedia of Bible Prophecy, 316-320.

[4] Larsen, David, "John Nelson Darby: Pioneer of Dispensational Premillennialism," Pre-Trib Research Center, <http://www.pre-trib .org/article-view.php?id=177#_ednref15>, October 1, 2012.

[5] Chumney, Edward, Seven Festivals of the Messiah, Chapter 2, Hebraic Heritage Ministries, <http://www.hebroots.org/sevenfestivals_chap2.htm>, October 1, 2012.

[6] "Forty Days," *Bible Gateway*, <http://www.biblegateway. com/keyword/>, October 1, 2012.

[7] Marcus, Yossi, "Blow the Shofar During Elul," Ask Moses, <http://www.askmoses.com /article/283,544/Why-do-we-blow-the-shofar-every-day-during-the-month-of-Elul.html>, October 1, 2012.

[8] "A Glossary of Basic Jewish Terms and Concept," *Orthodox Union*, <http://www. ou.org/about/ judaism/tw.htm>, October 1, 2012.

[9] Rich, Tracey, "*Rosh Hashanah*" *Judaism 101*, <http://www.jewfaq. org/holiday2. htm>, October 1, 2012.

[10] Chumney, Edward, Seven Festivals of the Messiah, Chapter 7, *Hebraic Heritage Ministries*, <http://www.hebroots.org/sevenfestivals_chap7.htm>, October 1, 2012.

[11] Chumney, Edward, Seven Festivals of the Messiah, Chapter 7.

[12] Rich, Tracey, "Rosh Chodesh" *Judaism 101*, <http://www.jewfaq.org/ chodesh. htm>, October 1, 2012.

[13] Note: The astronomical new moon (no moon) is when the moon is between the earth and sun. The Jewish new moon is the first visible crescent.

[14] Chumney, Edward, Seven Festivals of the Messiah, Chapter 7, *Hebraic Heritage Ministries*, <http://www.hebroots.org/sevenfestivals_chap7.htm>, October 1, 2012.

[15] Silberberg, Naftali, "Two Days of *Rosh Hashanah*," *Ask Moses*, <http:// www. askmoses.com/article/617,19380/Why-are-there-two-days-of-Rosh-Hashanah-even-in-Israel.html>, October 1, 2012.

[16] Rich, Tracey, "*Rosh Hashanah*," *Judaism 101*, <http://www.jewfaq.org/ holiday2. htm>, October 1, 2012.

[17] Numbers 10:3, 5, 9, Exodus 19:16, 19.
Hecht, Mendy, "What Is a Shofar," *Ask Moses*, <http://www.askmoses. com/ article/618,150/What-is-a-shofar.html>, October 1, 2012.
Note: This is a partial list of shofar blast before the Musaf.

[18] Hecht, Mendy, "What Is a Shofar," *Ask Moses*, <http://www.askmoses. com/ article/618,150/What-is-a-shofar.html>, October 1, 2012.

[19] Hecht, "What Is a Shofar," *Ask Moses*.

[20] "Decoding the Shofar," *My Jewish Learning*, <http://www. myjewishlearning. com/holidays/Rosh_Hashana/Overview_Rosh_ Hashanah_Community/Sounding_ Shofar/DecodingShofar.htm>, October 1, 2012.

[21] "One Hundred Sounds," *Chabad*, <http://www.chabad.org/holidays/Jewish NewYear/template_cdo/aid/4387/jewish/100-Sounds.htm>, October 1, 2012.

[22] Chumney, Edward, Seven Festivals of the Messiah, Chapter 6, *Hebraic Heritage Ministries*, <http://www.hebroots.org/sevenfestivals_chap6.htm>, October 1, 2012.

[23] Chumney, Edward, Seven Festivals of the Messiah, Chapter 7, *Hebraic Heritage Ministries*, <http://www.hebroots.org/sevenfestivals_chap7.htm>, October 1, 2012.

[24] Genesis 30:6.

[25] Rich, Tracey, "*Rosh Hashanah*," *Judaism 101*, <http://www.jewfaq.org/ holiday2. htm>, October 1, 2012.

[26] Chumney, Edward, <u>Seven Festivals of the Messiah</u>, Chapter 7, *Hebraic Heritage Ministries*, <http://www.hebroots.org/sevenfestivals_chap7.htm>, October 1, 2012.

[27] Rich, Tracey, "*Rosh Hashanah,*" *Judaism 101*, <http://www.jewfaq.org/ holiday2. htm>, October 1, 2012.

[28] "First Night of *Rosh Hashanah,*" Chabad, <http://www.chabad.org/ holidays/ JewishNewYear/template_cdo/aid/4380/jewish/First- Night-of-Rosh-Hashanah. htm>, October 1, 2012.

[29] "Various Customs of *Rosh Hashanah,*" *Orthodox Union*, <http://www.ou .org/ chagim/roshhashannah/customs.html>, October 1, 2012.

[30] Genesis 29:26-28, Judges 14:15-17.

12. Fall Jewish Feasts

[1] Rich, Tracey, "Days of Awe," *Judaism 101*, <http://www.jewfaq.org/ holiday3.htm>, October 1, 2012.

[2] Chumney, Edward, <u>Seven Festivals of the Messiah</u>, Chapter 8, *Hebraic Heritage Ministries*, <http://www.hebroots.org/sevenfestivals_chap8.htm>, October 1, 2012.

[3] Chumney, Edward, <u>Seven Festivals of the Messiah</u>, Chapter 8.

[4] Rich, Tracey, "*Yom Kippur,*" *Judaism 101*, <http://www.jewfaq.org/ holiday4.htm>, October 1, 2012.

[5] Exodus 34:28-29.

[6] Chumney, Edward, <u>Seven Festivals of the Messiah</u>, Chapter 8, *Hebraic Heritage Ministries*, <http://www.hebroots.org/sevenfestivals_chap8.htm>, October 1, 2012.

[7] Rich, Tracey, "Sacrifices and Offerings," *Judaism 101*, <http://www. jewfaq.org/ qorbanot.htm>, October 1, 2012.

[8] "Scapegoat," *Wikipedia*, <http://en.wikipedia.org/wiki/Scapegoat>, October 1, 2012.

[9] Chumney, Edward, <u>Seven Festivals of the Messiah</u>, Chapter 8, *Hebraic Heritage Ministries*, <http://www.hebroots.org/sevenfestivals_chap8.htm>, October 1, 2012.

[10] Chumney, Edward, <u>Seven Festivals of the Messiah</u>, Chapter 8.

[11] Jamieson, Robert, et al., "Leviticus 25," *Blue Letter Bible*, <http://cf. blueletter-bible.org/commentaries/>, October 1, 2012.

[12] Chumney, Edward, <u>Seven Festivals of the Messiah</u>, Chapter 9, *Hebraic Heritage Ministries*, <http://www.hebroots.org/sevenfestivals_chap9.htm>, October 1, 2012.

[13] Rich, Tracey, "*Sukkot,*" *Judaism 101*, <http://www.jewfaq.org/ holiday5 .htm>, October 1, 2012.

[14] Chumney, Edward, <u>Seven Festivals of the Messiah</u>, Chapter 9, *Hebraic Heritage Ministries*, <http://www.hebroots.org/sevenfestivals_chap9.htm>, October 1, 2012.

[15] Chumney, Edward, <u>Seven Festivals of the Messiah</u>, Chapter 9.

[16] Chumney, Edward, <u>Seven Festivals of the Messiah</u>, Chapter 9.

[17] Chumney, Edward, <u>Seven Festivals of the Messiah</u>, Chapter 9.

[18] Chumney, Edward, <u>Seven Festivals of the Messiah</u>, Chapter 9.

[19] Rich, Tracey, "Shemini Atzeret and Simchat Torah," *Judaism 101*, <http:// www. jewfaq.org/holiday6.htm>, October 1, 2012

[20] Rich, Tracey, "Shemini Atzeret and Simchat Torah".

[21] "John Wilbur Chapman," *Wikipedia*, <http://en.wikipedia.org/wiki/ John_Wilbur_ Chapman>, October 1, 2012.

13. Minor Feasts, Major Events

[1] "Jewish Holidays," *Wikipedia*, <http://en.wikipedia.org/wiki/Jewish_ holidays>, October 1, 2012.

[2] Exodus 32.

[3] II Kings 25:3-6.

  <u>Talmud Taanit</u>, Chapter 4, Paragraph 5, *Jewish Virtual Library*, <http:// www. jewishvirtuallibrary.org/jsource/Talmud/taanit4.html>, October 1, 2012.

[4] Numbers 13-14.

  "Mishnah Ta'anit 4:6-7: Days of National Mourning," The Center of Online Jewish Studies, <http://cojs.org/cojswiki/Mishnah_ Ta%E2%80% 99anit_ 4:6-7:_Days_of_ National_Mourning>, October 1, 2012.

[5] Bonnett, Bill, <u>Chronology of Man</u>, *Abdicate*, *<http*://abdicate.net/ book .aspx>, 140-141, October 1, 2012.

[6] Bonnett, Bill, <u>Chronology of Man</u>, 140-141.

[7] *"Hanukkah," Wikipedia*, <http://en.wikipedia.org/wiki/*Hanukkah*>, October 1, 2012.

[8] "10th of *Tevet*," *Wikipedia*, <http://en.wikipedia.org/wiki/10th_of_*Tevet*>, October 1, 2012.

[9] Esther 9:31.

[10] Exodus 17:8:16.

[11] 1 Samuel 15:1-35.

[12] Bonnet, Bill, <u>Chronology of Man</u>, *Abdicate*, *<http*://abdicate.net/book .aspx>, 140-141, October 1, 2012.

[13] Hebcal Jewish Calendar, *Hebcal*, <http://www.hebcal.com/hebcal/>, October 1, 2012.

[14] "Alhambra Decree," *Wikipedia*, <http://en.wikipedia.org/wiki/Alhambra_ decree>, October 1, 2012.

[15] "Christopher Columbus," *Wikipedia*, <http://en.wikipedia.org/wiki/ Christopher_ Columbus>, October 1, 2012.

[16] "American Independence Day," *Wikipedia*, <http://en.wikipedia.org/wiki/ American_Independence_Day>, October 1, 2012.

[17] "United States Constitution," *Wikipedia*, <http://en.wikipedia.org/wiki/ Us_ constitution>, October 1, 2012.

[18] "William McKinley," *Wikipedia*, <http://en.wikipedia.org/wiki /William_ McKinley, William>, October 1, 2012.

[19] "*Titanic*," *Wikipedia*, <http://en.wikipedia.org/wiki/Titanic>, October 1, 2012.
Note: An observed new moon on March 18, 1912 may delay *Nisan* one day.

[20] "World War I," *Wikipedia*, <http://en.wikipedia.org/wiki/World War II>, October 1, 2012.

[21] "Edmund Allenby," *Wikipedia*, <http://en.wikipedia.org/wiki/Edmund_ Allenby>, October 1, 2012.

[22] "British Mandates of Palestine," *Wikipedia*, <http://en.wikipedia.org/wiki/ British_Mandate_for_Palestine>, October 1, 2012.

[23] "Munich Agreement," *Wikipedia*, <http://en.wikipedia.org/wiki/Munich_ Agreement>, October 1, 2012.

[24] "World War II," *Wikipedia*, <http://en.wikipedia.org/wiki/World_War_II>, October 1, 2012.

[25] "Treblinka," *Wikipedia*, <http://en.wikipedia.org/wiki/Treblinka>, October 1, 2012.

[26] "Atomic Bombing of Hiroshima and Nagasaki," *Wikipedia*, <http://en. wikipedia. org/wiki/Atomic_bombings_of_Hiroshima_and_ Nagasaki>, October 1, 2012.

[27] "Nuremberg Trials," *Wikipedia*, <http://en.wikipedia.org/wiki/Nuremberg_ Trials>, October 1, 2012.

[28] "Jewish Holidays," *Wikipedia*, <http://en.wikipedia.org/wiki/ Jewish_ holidays>, October 1, 2012.

[29] "Cuban Missile Crisis," *Wikipedia*, <http://en.wikipedia.org/wiki/Cuban_ Missile_Crisis>, October 1, 2012

[30] "Chernobyl Disaster," *Wikipedia*, <http://en.wikipedia.org/wiki/ Chernobyl_disaster>, October 1, 2012.

[31] "Persian Gulf War," *Wikipedia*, <http://en.wikipedia.org/wiki/ Persian_ Gulf_War>, October 1, 2012.

[32] "September 11 Attacks," *Wikipedia*, <http://en.wikipedia.org/wiki/ September_11_ attacks>, October 1, 2012.

[33] "Afghanistan War," *Wikipedia*, <http://en.wikipedia.org/wiki/ Afghanistan_ War>, October 1, 2012.

[34] "Quartet on the Middle East," *Wikipedia*, <http://en.wikipedia.org/wiki/ Quartet_ on_the_Middle_East>, October 1, 2012.

[35] "Disengagement Plan," *Wikipedia*, <http://en.wikipedia.org/wiki/ Disengagement_ plan>, October 1, 2012.

[36] "Tropical Depression Ten (2005)," *Wikipedia*, <http://en.wikipedia.org/ wiki/ Tropical _Depression _Ten_(2005)>, October 1, 2012.

[37] "Iraq War," *Wikipedia*, <http://en.wikipedia.org/wiki/Iraq_War>, October 1, 2012.

[38] Esther 9:20-22.

[39] "Libya Civil War," *Wikipedia*, <http://en.wikipedia.org/wiki/Libya_civil_ war>, October 1, 2012.
Marcus, Jonathan, "Libya: French plane fires on military vehicle," *BBC News*, <http://www.bbc.co.uk/news/world-africa-12795971, March 19, 2011>, October 1, 2012.

[40] Ezekiel 38-39.

[41] Daniel 9:27, Revelation 9:13-16.

[42] Daniel 9:27.

[43] Revelation 13:5

[44] Revelation 11:3-13.

[45] Revelation 11:14.

[46] Ezekiel 38-38, Matthew 24:15-16.

[47] Bonnet, Bill, <u>Chronology of Man</u>, *Abdicate*, *<http*://abdicate.net/book .aspx>, 115-117, 126, 140-141, October 1, 2012.
Hebcal Jewish Calendar, *Hebcal*, <http://www.hebcal.com/hebcal/>, October 1, 2012.

14. Israel's Time Out

[1] Exodus 34.

[2] Exodus 1:5, Numbers 1:46.

[3] Numbers 12-13.

[4] Bonnett, Bill, "Linear Chronology of Man According to the Scriptures," *Abdicate*, <http://abdicate.net/chron. aspx>, October 1, 2012.

[5] Bonnett, "Linear Chronology of Man According to the Scriptures," *Abdicate*.

[6] Daniel 2:37-45.

[7] "Antiochus IV," *Wikipedia*, <http://en.wikipedia.org/wiki/Antiochus_IV>, October 1, 2012.

[8] "Hasmonean Kingdom," *Wikipedia*, <http://en.wikipedia.org/wiki/ Hasmonean>, October 1, 2012.

[9] Coleman, William, <u>Today's Handbook of Bible Times & Customs</u> (Ada, MI: Bethany House Publishers, 1984) 207-208.

[10] Coleman, William, <u>Today's Handbook of Bible Times & Customs</u>, 207-208.

[11] Numbers 11:16.
"Sanhedrin," *Wikipedia*, <http://en.wikipedia.org/wiki/Sanhedrin>, October 1, 2012.

[12] Bonnett, Bill, "Linear Chronology of Man According to the Scriptures," *Abdicate*, <http://abdicate.net/ chron. aspx>, October 1, 2012.

[13] Van Impe, Jack, "Methods of Interpretation," <u>Jack Van Impe's Dictionary of Prophetic Terms</u>, *JVIM*, <http://www. jvim.com/>, October 1, 2012.

[14] Larkin, Clarence, "Mountain Peaks of Prophecy," <http://clarencelarkin charts.com/ Clarence_Larkin_6.html>, October 1, 2012.

[15] LaHaye, Tim, "Dispensations," <u>Prophecy Study Bible</u>, 4, 10.

[16] LaHaye, Tim, "Dispensations," <u>Prophecy Study Bible</u>, 4, 10.

[17] Price, Randall, "Daniel's Seventy Weeks," <u>Prophecy Study Bible</u>, 912.

[18] Allred, Dawn, September 2006.

15. Daniel's Seventy Weeks

[1] Bonnett, Bill, "Linear Chronology of Man According to the Scriptures," *Abdicate*, <http://abdicate.net/chron.aspx>, October 1, 2012.

[2] Jeremiah 25:11-13, Jeremiah 29:10.

[3] Matthew 6:9-10.

[4] Daniel 9:4-19.

[5] Leviticus 26.

[6] *"Pesha," Blue Letter Bible*, <http://cf.blueletterbible.org/lang/lexicon/ lexicon. cfm?Strongs=H06588&t=kjv>, October 1, 2012.

[7] *"Kala," Blue Letter Bible*, <http://cf.blueletterbible.org/lang/lexicon/ lexicon. cfm?Strongs=H03607&t=kjv>, October 1, 2012.

[8] Guzik, David, "Daniel 9," <u>David Guzik's Commentary</u>, *Enduring Word*, <http:// www.enduringword.com/library_commentaries.htm>, October 1, 2012.

[9] *"Kaphar," Blue Letter Bible*, <http://cf.blueletterbible. org/lang/lexicon/ lexicon. cfm?Strongs=H03722&t=kjv>, October 1, 2012.

[10] Guzik, David, "Daniel 9," <u>David Guzik's Commentary</u>, *Enduring Word*, <http:// www.enduringword.com/library_commentaries.htm>, October 1, 2012.

[11] Bonnett, Bill, "Linear Chronology of Man According to the Scriptures," *Abdicate*, <http://abdicate.net/hron.aspx>, October 1, 2012.

[12] Ezra 2:64-65.

[13] Ezra 6:15.

"Second Temple," *Wikipedia, http://en.wikipedia.org/wiki/ Second_Temple>, October 1, 2012.*

[14] Ezra 4:1-24.

[15] Jamison, et al, "Ezra 4," *Blue Letter Bible*, <http://cf. blueletterbible.org/ commentaries/>, October 1, 2012.

[16] Ezra 8:1-14.

[17] "*Mashiyach*," *Blue Letter Bible*, <http://cf.blueletterbible.org/lang/lexicon/ lexicon. cfm?Strongs=H04899&t=kjv>, October 1, 2012.

[18] Guzik, David, "Revelation 4," David Guzik's Commentary, *Enduring Word*, <http:// www.enduringword.com/library_commentaries.htm>, October 1, 2012.

[19] Reagan, David, "What Year Is It and Does It Really Matter?," *Lamb Lion*, <http:// www.lamblion.com/articles/articles_jewishlife3. php>, October 1, 2012.
Miller, Rachel, "How the Rabbis Calculated the Age of the World," *My Jewish Learning*, <http://www.myjewishlearning.com/holidays/ About_ Jewish_Holidays/ Solar_and_Lunar/CountingYears/YossiChart.htm>, October 1, 2012.

[20] "Iranian Calendar," *Wikipedia*, <http://en.wikipedia.org/wiki/Iranian_ Calendar>, October 1, 2012.

[21] Revelation 11:2, 13:5.

[22] "Persian Calendar," *Wikipedia*, <http://en.wikipedia.org/wiki/Persian_ calendar>, October 1, 2012.

[23] "Daniel's Visions, Accuracy of his Prophecies," Discover Revelation, <http://www. discoverrevelation.com/18.html>, October 1, 2012.

[24] Jamieson, Robert, et al., "Daniel 9," *Blue Letter Bible*, <http://www. blueletterbible. org/ commentaries>, October 1, 2012.

[25] Bonnett, Bill, "Linear Chronology of Man According to the Scriptures," *Abdicate*, <http://abdicate.net/chron. aspx>, October 1, 2012.

[26] Matthew 2:16, Acts 18:2.

[27] "Caligula," *Wikipedia*, <http://en.wikipedia.org/wiki/Caligula>, October 1, 2012.

[28] "Nero," *Wikipedia*, <http://en.wikipedia.org/wiki/Nero>, October 1, 2012.

[29] "Zealot," *Wikipedia*, <http://en.wikipedia.org/wiki/Zealot>, October 1, 2012.

[30] "First Jewish-Roman War," *Wikipedia*, <http://en.wikipedia.org/wiki/First_ Jewish-Roman_War>, October 1, 2012.

[31] "First Jewish-Roman War," *Wikipedia*.

[32] "First Jewish-Roman War," *Wikipedia*.

[33] Young, Darrell, "Fall of Jerusalem," *Focus on Jerusalem*, <http:// focusonjerusalem.com/thefallofjerusalem.html>, October 1, 2012.

[34] "Destruction of Jerusalem," *Bible History*, <http://www.bible-history.com/ jerusalem/firstcenturyjerusalem_destruction_of_jerusalem_in_70_a_d_. html>, October 1, 2012.

[35] LaHaye, Tim, Prophecy Study Bible, 914.

[36] Chumney, Edward, Seven Festivals of the Messiah, Chapter 7, Hebraic Heritage Ministries, <http://www.hebroots.org/sevenfestivals_chap7.htm>, October 1, 2012.

[37] "Nero," *Wikipedia*, <http://en.wikipedia.org/wiki/Nero>, October 1, 2012.

[38] Revelation 17:12-13.

[39] LaHaye, Tim, "Daniel's Outline of the Future," <u>Prophecy Study Bible</u>, 914.

[40] "Alexander the Great," *Wikipedia*, <http://en.wikipedia.org/wiki/ Alexander_the_ Great>, October 1, 2012.

[41] *"Hanukkah," Wikipedia*, <http://en.wikipedia.org/wiki/*Hanukkah*>, October 1, 2012.

[42] LaHaye, Tim, "Daniel's Outline of the Future," <u>Prophecy Study Bible</u>, 914.

[43] Ezekiel 36-39, Zechariah 12-14.

16. The Life of Christ

[1] "Caesar Augustus," *Wikipedia*, <http://en.wikipedia.org/wiki/Caesar_ Augustus>, October 1, 2012.

[2] Augustus, Caesar, <u>The Deeds of the Divine Augustus</u>, *Massachusetts Institute of Technology*, <http://classics.mit.edu/Augustus/ deeds.html>, October 1, 2012.

[3] Augustus, <u>The Deeds of the Divine Augustus</u>, *Massachusetts Institute of Technology*.

[4] 1 Chronicles 24 assigns priestly duties to the twenty-four descendants of Aaron. The division of Abijah drew the eighth lot so they serve on Passover, Weeks, week 10, Tabernacles and week 35.

[5] 1 Chronicles 24:1-19.

[6] "Pregnancy," *Wikipedia*, <http://en.wikipedia.org/wiki/Pregnancy>, October 1, 2012.

[7] "Six Millennium Catalog of Phases of the Moon," *NASA*, <http://eclipse. gsfc.nasa. gov/phase/phases-0099.html>, October 1, 2012.
The Gregorian calendar is set to the First Council of Nicaea in 325 AD. There is a two days difference between Julian and Gregorian calendars.

[8] "Controversy over Elijah's Return," *Wikipedia*, <http://en.wikipedia. org/wiki/ Elijah>, October 1, 2012.

[9] Luke 1:17.

[10] "Star of Bethlehem," *Wikipedia*, <http://en.wikipedia.org/wiki/Star_of_ Bethlehem>, October 1, 2012.
Parpola, Simo, "The Magi and the Star," <u>Bible Review</u>, December 2001, 16-23, 52, 54. "Triple Conjunction of Jupiter and Saturn," Son of Man, <http://www. sonof-man.org /triple.htm>, October 1, 2012.
"Six Millennium Catalog of Phases of the Moon," *NASA*, <http://eclipse. gsfc.nasa. gov/phase/phases-0099.html>, October 1, 2012.
There is a two day error between Julian and Gregorian calendars.

[11] "Star of Bethlehem," *Wikipedia*. Parpola, "The Magi and the Star," <u>Bible Review</u>, 16-23, 52, 54.

"Triple Conjunction of Jupiter and Saturn," Son of Man. "Six Millennium Catalog of Phases of the Moon," *NASA*.

[12] John 1:4-9, Luke 2:10.
Chumney, Edward, <u>Seven Festivals of the Messiah</u>, Chapter 9, *Hebraic Heritage Ministries*, <http://www.hebroots.org/sevenfestivals_chap9.htm>, October 1, 2012.

[13] Matthew 1:23, John 1:14.

[14] Zechariah 14:16.

[15] "*Skenoo*," *Blue Letter Bible*, <http://cf.blueletterbible.org/lang/lexicon/ lexicon.cfm?Strongs=G4637&t=kjv>, October 1, 2012.

[16] Steel, Duncan, <u>Marking Time: The Epic Quest to Invent the Perfect Calendar</u> (New York: J. Wiley, 2000) 330.
Science and Christian Belief, Vol 5, (October 1995): 83-101.

[17] Steel, Duncan, <u>Marking Time: The Epic Quest to Invent the Perfect Calendar</u>, 330.
Humphreys, Colin, "The Star of Bethlehem," October 1995, *Astronomy & Cosmology*, <http://www.asa3.org/ASA/topics/Astronomy-Cosmology/ S&CB%20 10-93Humphreys.html>, October 1, 2012.

[18] Kidger, Mark, "Star of Bethlehem," Comet and Asteroid Observing, <http://www. astrosurf.com/comets/Star_of_Bethlehem/English/ Chinese.htm>, October 1, 2012.

[19] Matthew 2:1, Luke 1:5.

[20] Josephus, Flavius, <u>The Antiquities of the Jews</u>, Book 17, Chapter 6, Paragraph 4, *Christian Classics Ethereal Library*, <http://www.ccel.org/ ccel/josephus/ complete>, October 1, 2012.

[21] Josephus, <u>The Antiquities of the Jews</u>.

[22] Bonnett, Bill, "Linear Chronology of Man According to the Scriptures".
Miller, Rachel, "How the Rabbis Calculated the Age of the World".
Reagan, David, "What Year Is It and Does It Really Matter?".

[23] "Six Millennium Catalog of Phases of the Moon," NASA, <http://eclipse.gsfc.nasa. gov/phase/phases0001.html>, October 1, 2012.

[24] Jonah 1:17, Matthew 12:39-40, Revelation 11:11-12.

[25] "First Council of Nicaea," *Wikipedia*, <http://en.wikipedia.org/wiki/First_ Council_of_Nicaea>, October 1, 2012.

[26] "The Resurrection of Yeshua and the Festivals of Firstfruits," Anno Mundi Books, <http://www.annomundi.com/bible/firstfruits1.htm>, October 1, 2012.

17. Basic Bible Chronology

[1] Josephus, Flavius, <u>The Antiquities of the Jews</u>, Book 2, Chapter 15, Paragraph 2, *Christian Classics Ethereal Library*, <http://www.ccel.org/ ccel/josephus/ complete>, October 1, 2012.

[2] Bonnett, Bill, "Linear Chronology of Man According to the Scriptures," *Abdicate*, <http://abdicate.net/chron.aspx>, October 1, 2012.

[3] 2 Samuel 2:4, 5:3-5, 5:6-7, 6:1-2.

[4] Bonnett, Bill, "Linear Chronology of Man According to the Scriptures," *Abdicate*, <http://abdicate.net/chron.aspx>, October 1, 2012.

[5] Bonnett, "Linear Chronology of Man According to the Scriptures," *Abdicate*.

[6] Isaiah 44:28.

[7] Jeremiah 25:11.

[8] "Kings of Persia," *Wikipedia*, <http://en.wikipedia.org/wiki/Kings_of_ Persia>, October 1, 2012.

[9] Bonnett, Bill, "Linear Chronology of Man According to the Scriptures," *Abdicate*, <http://abdicate.net/chron.aspx>, October 1, 2012.
"Byzantine Empire," Wikipedia, <http://en.wikipedia.org/wiki/ Eastern_ Roman_ Empire>, October 1, 2012.

[10] Bonnett, Bill, "Linear Chronology of Man According to the Scriptures," *Abdicate*.

[11] Bonnett, Bill, "Linear Chronology of Man According to the Scriptures," *Abdicate*.

[12] Bonnett, Bill, "Linear Chronology of Man According to the Scriptures," *Abdicate*.

[13] *"Pax Romana,"* Wikipedia, <http://en.wikipedia.org/wiki/Pax_romana>, October 1, 2012.

[14] "In the Fullness of Time: Christianity in the Roman Empire," *History of Western Civilization*, <http://mason.gmu.edu/~ddonald/typeassignment/ index3.htm>, October 1, 2012.

[15] "Jewish-Roman Wars," *Wikipedia*, <http://en.wikipedia.org/wiki/Jewish- Roman_ wars>, October 1, 2012.

[16] "Alexander the Great," *Wikipedia*, <http://en.wikipedia.org/wiki/ Alexander_the_ great>, October 1, 2012

[17] "In the Fullness of Time: Christianity in the Roman Empire," History of Western Civilization, <http://mason.gmu.edu/~ddonald/typeassignment/ index3.htm>, October 1, 2012.

[18] "In the Fullness of Time: Christianity in the Roman Empire," *History of Western Civilization*.

[19] Coleman, William, Today's Handbook of Bible Times & Customs, 207-208.

[20] Coleman, Today's Handbook of Bible Times & Customs, 207-208.

[21] Revelation 13:1-17.

18. Spring Forward or Fall Back?

[1] "Julian Calendar," *Wikipedia*, <http://en.wikipedia.org/wiki/Julian_ Calendar>, October 1, 2012.

[2] "Julian Calendar," *Wikipedia*.

[3] Steel, Duncan, <u>Marking Time: The Epic Quest to Invent the Perfect Calendar</u>, 166.

[4] "Why Leap Years Are Used," *Time and Date*, <http://www.timeanddate .com/date/ leapyear.html>, October 1, 2012.

[5] Steel, Duncan, <u>Marking Time: The Epic Quest to Invent the Perfect Calendar</u>, 169.

[6] Meyer, Peter, "The Julian and Gregorian Calendars," *Hermetic System*, <http://www. hermetic. ch/cal_stud/cal_art.html#Julian_Calendar>, October 1, 2012.

[7] Josephus, Flavius, <u>The Antiquities of the Jews</u>, Book 17, Chapter 6, Paragraph 4, *Christian Classics Ethereal Library*, <http://www.ccel.org/ ccel/josephus/ complete>, October 1, 2012.

[8] "Six Millennium Catalog of Phases of the Moon," *NASA*, <http://eclipse .gsfc.nasa. gov/phase/phases-0099.html>, October 1, 2012.
   Note: Julian year 4 BC is astronomical year -3.

[9] "Dionysius Exiguus," *Wikipedia*, <http://en.wikipedia.org/wiki/Dionysius_ Exiguus>, October 1, 2012.

[10] "James Ussher," *Wikipedia*, <http://en.wikipedia.org/wiki/James_Ussher>, October 1, 2012.

[11] Josephus, Flavius, <u>The Antiquities of the Jews</u>, Book 17, Chapter 6, Paragraph 4, *Christian Classics Ethereal Library*, <http://www.ccel.org/ ccel/josephus/ complete>, October 1, 2012.

[12] Steel, Duncan, <u>Marking Time: The Epic Quest to Invent the Perfect Calendar</u>, 112.

[13] Bonnett, Bill, <u>Chronology of Man</u>, *Abdicate*, <http://abdicate.net/book .aspx>, 93, October 1, 2012.

[14] Bedwell, Wayne, "The Original Calendar for Our Day," Section 3, Paragraph 7, *Studies in the Word*, <http://www. studiesintheword.org/ original_calendar. htm#SECTION3>, October 1, 2012.

[15] "Hebrew Calendar," *Wikipedia*, <http://en.wikipedia.org/wiki/Hebrew_ calendar>, October 1, 2012.

[16] "Hebrew Calendar," *Wikipedia*.

[17] "Hebrew Calendar," *Wikipedia*.

[18] Hebcal Jewish Calendar, *Hebcal*, <http://www.hebcal.com/hebcal/>, October 1, 2012.

[19] "Yose Ben Halafta," *Wikipedia*, <http://en.wikipedia.org/wiki/Yose_ben_ Halafta>, October 1, 2012.

[20] Bonnett, Bill, "Linear Chronology of Man According to the Scriptures," *Abdicate*, <http://abdicate.net/chron.aspx>, October 1, 2012.

Miller, Rachel, "How the Rabbis Calculated the Age of the World," *My Jewish Learning*, <http://www.myjewishlearning.com/holidays/ About_ Jewish_Holidays/ Solar_and_Lunar/CountingYears/YossiChart.htm>, October 1, 2012.

Reagan, David, "What Year Is It and Does It Really Matter?," *Lamb Lion*, <http://www.lamblion.com/articles/articles_jewishlife3.php>, October 1, 2012.

[21] First, Michael, <u>Jewish History in Conflict: A Study of the Major Discrepancy Between Rabbinic and Conventional Chronology</u>, 3.
Reagan, David, "What Year Is It and Does It Really Matter?".

[22] First, Michael, <u>Jewish History in Conflict: A Study of the Major Discrepancy Between Rabbinic and Conventional Chronology</u>.
Reagan, David, "What Year Is It and Does It Really Matter?".

[23] Nehemiah 10:2-9.

[24] Reagan, David, "What Year Is It and Does It Really Matter?".

[25] "Sedar Olam Rabba," *Wikipedia*, <http://en.wikipedia.org/wiki/ Seder_Olam_ Rabba>, October 1, 2012.
Bonnett, Bill, <u>Chronology of Man</u>, *Abdicate*, <http://abdicate.net/ book.aspx>, 15-16, October 1, 2012.

[26] Bonnett, Bill, "Linear Chronology of Man According to the Scriptures," *Abdicate*, <http://abdicate.net/chron.aspx>, October 1, 2012.
Bill Bonnett dates the year as 4003 AM but that is two years off from the cross.

[27] Bonnett, Bill, "Linear Chronology of Man According to the Scriptures".
Miller, Rachel, "How the Rabbis Calculated the Age of the World".
Reagan, David, "What Year Is It and Does It Really Matter?".

[28] "AD," *Wikipedia*, <http://en.wikipedia.org/wiki/Anno_Domini>, October 1, 2012.

[29] "Feast of Trumpets," *Wikipedia*, <http://en.wikipedia.org/wiki/Feast_of _ Trumpets>, October 1, 2012.

[30] Billings, Josh, "Prophecy," *Quoteland*, <http://www.quoteland.com>, October 1, 2012.

[31] "Harold Camping," *Wikipedia*, <http://en.wikipedia.org/wiki/Harold_ Camping>, October 1, 2012.

19. Church Age & End Times

[1] Blackaby, Henry and King, Claude, <u>Experiencing God, Knowing and Doing the Will of God</u>, 225.

[2] Towns, Elmer, "The Seven Churches," <u>Prophecy Study Bible</u>, 1365.

[3] LaHaye, Tim, "<u>The Seven Churches</u>," Prophecy Study Bible, 1359

[4] Henry, Matthew, "Revelation 2-3," <u>Matthew Henry Commentary</u>, *Blue Letter Bible*, <http://cf.blueletterbible.org/commentaries/>, October 1, 2012.

[5] Henry, "Revelation 2," <u>Matthew Henry Commentary</u>.

[6] Henry, "Revelation 2," <u>Matthew Henry Commentary</u>.

[7] "Edict of Milan," *Wikipedia*, <http://en.wikipedia.org/wiki/Edict_of_Milan >, October 1, 2012.

[8] "Theodosius I," *Wikipedia*, < http://en.wikipedia.org/wiki/Theodosius_I >, October 1, 2012.

[9] Numbers 22-24, 31

[10] Henry, "Revelation 2," <u>Matthew Henry Commentary</u>.

[11] LaHaye, Tim, <u>Revelation Illustrated and Made Plain</u> (Grand Rapids, MI: Zondervan, 1999) 44.

[12] Graham, Billy, <u>Approaching Hoofbeats: The Four Horsemen of the Apocalypse</u> (Waco, TX: Word Books, 1983) 54.

[13] Henry, "Revelation 3," <u>Matthew Henry Commentary</u>.

[14] Henry, "Revelation 3," <u>Matthew Henry Commentary</u>.

[15] Towns, Elmer, "The Seven Churches," <u>Prophecy Study Bible</u>, 1365.

[16] Henry, "Revelation 3," <u>Matthew Henry Commentary</u>.

20. Players in the Game

[1] Lindsey, Hal, <u>There's a New World Coming, A Prophetic Odyssey</u> (Santa Ana, CA: Vision House, 1973) 8.

[2] "King of the Hill Game," *Wikipedia*, <http://en.wikipedia.org/wiki/King_of_the_Hill_(game)>, October 1, 2012.

[3] "The Rules of Risk," Parker Brothers is a division of Hasbro.

[4] *Independence Day*, dir. Roland Emmerich, DVD, 1996.

[5] Acton, Lord John, *Wikiquote*, <http://en.wikiquote.org/wiki/John_Dalberg-Acton,_1st_Baron_Acton>, October 1, 2012.

[6] Rosenberg, Joel, <u>Epicenter</u> (Carol Stream, IL: Tindale House Publishers, 2006) 15.

[7] "List of Countries by GDP (2010)," *Wikipedia*, <http://en.wikipedia.org/ wiki/ List_of_countries_by_GDP_(PPP)>, October 1, 2012. American English spelling.

[8] "United Nations Security Council," *Wikipedia*, <http://en.wikipedia.org/ wiki/ United_Nations_Security_ Council>, October 1, 2012.

[9] "Group of Eight," *Wikipedia*, <http://en.wikipedia.org/wiki/Group_of_8>, October 1, 2012.

[10] "Group of Twenty," *Wikipedia*, <http://en.wikipedia.org/wiki/Group_ of_20>, October 1, 2012.

[11] "NATO," *Wikipedia*, <http://en.wikipedia.org/wiki/NATO>, October 1, 2012.

[12] "National Energy Policy, 2001," *White House*, <http://www.whitehouse.gov/ energy/Overview. pdf>, October 1, 2012.

[13] "Sovereign Wealth Funds," *Wikipedia*, <http://en.wikipedia.org/wiki/ Sovereign_ wealth_fund>, October 1, 2012.

[14] "Major Foreign Holders of Treasury Securities," *US Treasury*, <http:// www. treasury.gov/resource-center/data-chart-center/tic/Documents/ mfh.txt>, October 1, 2012.

Organization of Petroleum Exporting Countries (OPEC): Algeria, Bahrain, Gabon, Iran, Iraq, Kuwait, Libya, Nigeria, Oman, Qatar, Saudi Arabia, United Arab Emirates, Venezuela.

Caribbean: Bahamas, Bermuda, British Virgin Islands, Cayman Islands, Netherlands Antilles, Panama.

[15] *We Just Decided To*," The Newsroom, HBO, June 24, 2012.

[16] "Superpower," *Wikipedia*, <http://en.wikipedia.org/wiki/Superpower>, October 1, 2012.

[17] Graham, Billy, Approaching Hoofbeats: The Four Horsemen of the Apocalypse, 171.

[18] Lincoln, Abraham, "Proclamation Appointing a Nation Fast Day," *Quote World*, <http://www.quoteworld.org/quotes/10233>, March 30, 1963, October 1, 2012.

[19] "Russia," *Wikipedia*, <http://en.wikipedia.org/wiki/Russia>, October 1, 2012.

[20] "Quartet on the Middle East," *Wikipedia*, <http://en.wikipedia.org/wiki/ Quartet_ on_the_Middle_East>, October 1, 2012.

[21] "BRIC," *Wikipedia*, <http://en.wikipedia.org/wiki/BRIC>, October 1, 2012.

[22] "Petroleum Production (2009) and Consumption (2008)," *Wikipedia*, <http:// en.wikipedia.org/wiki/Petroleum>, October 1, 2012.

[23] "Petroleum Production (2009) and Consumption (2008)," *Wikipedia*.

[24] Ezekiel 38.

[25] Singleton, Malik, "OECD Report Says China's Economy Will Overtake US Economy By 2016", International Business Times, March 22, 2013, < http:// www.ibtimes.com/oecd-report-says-chinas-economy-will-overtake-us-econ-omy-2016-1146333, March 31, 2013.

[26] "Peoples Republic of China," *Wikipedia*, <http://en.wikipedia.org/wiki/ People's_ Republic_of_China>, October 1, 2012.

[27] "China," *CIA World Factbook*, <https://www.cia.gov/library/publications/ the-world-factbook/geos/ch.html>, October 1, 2012.

[28] "CIA Chief Says China's Rapid Military Buildup Troubling," *American Free Press*, April 30, 2008, <http://ca.news.yahoo.com/s/afp/080430/world/ us_china_mili-tary_intelligence_1>, October 1, 2012.

29 "List of Countries by Population," *Wikipedia*, <http://en.wikipedia.org/wiki/List_of_countries_by_population>, October 1, 2012.
American English spelling.

30 "Lawmakers Fight against China Trade Rule," *CNN*, <http://money.cnn.com/2005/02/09/news/international/china_trade/>, October 1, 2012.

31 "India," *Wikipedia*, <http://en.wikipedia.org/wiki/India>, October 1, 2012.

32 "Nuclear Nations," *Wikipedia*, <http://en.wikipedia.org/wiki/Nuclear_ nations>, October 1, 2012.

33 "Israel," *Wikipedia*, <http://en.wikipedia.org/wiki/Israel>, October 1, 2012.

34 "Euro-Mediterranean Partnership," *European Union*, <http://eeas.europa .eu/euromed/index_en.htm>, October 1, 2012.

35 "Quartet on the Middle East," *Wikipedia*, <http://en.wikipedia.org/wiki/ Quartet_on_the_Middle_East>, October 1, 2012.

36 "Supranationalism," *Wikipedia*, <http://en.wikipedia.org/wiki/ Supranationalism>, October 1, 2012.

37 "Trade Bloc," *Wikipedia*, <http://en.wikipedia.org/wiki/Trade_bloc>, October 1, 2012.
"Monetary Union," *Wikipedia*, <http://en.wikipedia.org/wiki/Monetary_ Union>, October 1, 2012.

38 American English spelling.

39 American English spelling.

40 "Trade Bloc," *Wikipedia*, <http://en.wikipedia.org/wiki/Trade_bloc>, October 1, 2012.

41 "European Union," *Wikipedia*, <http://en.wikipedia.org/wiki/European_ union>, October 1, 2012.

42 Churchill, Winston, "Speech at the University of Zurich," 1946, *Council of Europe*, <http://assembly.coe.int/Main.asp?link=/AboutUs/zurich_e.htm>, October 1, 2012.

43 "European Union," *CIA World Factbook*, <https://www.cia.gov/library/ publications/the-world-factbook/geos/ee.html>, October 1, 2012.

44 Krauthammer, Charles, "France's Game," *Time,* March 17, 2003, <http:// www.time.com/time/magazine/article/0,9171,1101030324-433251,00 .html>, October 1, 2012.

45 "European Union," *Wikipedia*, <http://en.wikipedia.org/wiki/European_ union>, October 1, 2012.

46 "Cooperation and Partnership Agreement," *European Union*, <http://eeas .europa.eu/russia/index_en.htm> , October 1, 2012.

47 "Euro-Mediterranean Partnership," European Union, <http://www.eeas .europa.eu/euromed/index_en.htm>, October 1, 2012.
"European Neighbourhood Policy," *Wikipedia*, <http://en.wikipedia.org/ wiki/

European_Neighbourhood_Policy>, October 1, 2012.

"Union for the Mediterranean," *Wikipedia*, <http://en.wikipedia.org/wiki/ Union_for_ the_Mediterranean>, October 1, 2012.

[48] "Eurosphere," *Wikipedia*, <http://en.wikipedia.org/wiki/Eurosphere>, October 1, 2012.

Leonard, Mark, <u>Why Europe Will Run the 21st Century</u> (Fourth Estate, 2005).

[49] "European Union," *Wikipedia*, <http://en.wikipedia.org/wiki/European_ union>, October 1, 2012.

[50] "European Debt Crisis," *Wikipedia*, <http://en.wikipedia.org/wiki/ European_sovereign_debt_crisis>, October 1, 2012.

"PIIGS," *Wikipedia*, <http://en.wikipedia.org/wiki/PIIGS>, October 1, 2012.

[51] "North American Free Trade Agreement," *Wikipedia*, <http://en.wikipedia .org/ wiki/North_American_Free_Trade_Agreement>, October 1, 2012.

[52] "Security and Prosperity Partnership of North America," *Wikipedia*, <http:// en.wikipedia.org/wiki/Security_and_Prosperity_Partnership_of_North_ America>, October 1, 2012.

[53] "How Dependent Are We on Foreign Oil," May 1, 2008, Energy Information Administration, <http://tonto.eia.doe.gov/energy_in_brief/ foreign_oil_ dependence.cfm>, October 1, 2012.

[54] "Fox, Vicente," March 21, 2000, *PBS News Hour*, <http://www.pbs.org/ newshour/ bb/latin_america/jan-june00/fox_3-21.html>, October 1, 2012.

[55] "Organisation of Islamic Cooperation," *Wikipedia*, <http://en.wikipedia.org/ wiki/ Organisation_of_Islamic_Cooperation>, October 1, 2012.

American English spelling.

[56] "Nuclear Nations," *Wikipedia*, <http://en.wikipedia.org/wiki/Nuclear_ nations>, October 1, 2012.

[57] "Organisation of the Islamic Conference," *Wikipedia*, <http://en.wikipedia .org/ wiki/Organisation_of_the_Islamic_Conference>, October 1, 2012.

[58] "Catholic Church," *Wikipedia*, <http://en.wikipedia.org/wiki/Catholic_ Church>, October 1, 2012.

[59] "United Nations," *Wikipedia*, <http://en.wikipedia.org/wiki/United_ Nations>, October 1, 2012.

[60] "Superpower," *Wikipedia*, <http://en.wikipedia.org/wiki/Superpower>, October 1, 2012.

21. Four Horses on the Run

[1] Guzik, David, "Daniel 4," <u>David Guzik's Commentary</u>, *Enduring Word*, <http:// www.enduringword.com/library_commentaries.htm>, October 1, 2012.

[2] "Four Horsemen of the Apocalypse," *Got Questions*, <http://www.got questions.org/four-horsemen-apocalypse.html>, October 1, 2012.

[3] Baxter, Irvin, Politics and Religion, *Endtime*, <http://www.endtime.com/ Radio.aspx>, October 1, 2012.

[4] "Karl Marx," *Wikipedia*, <http://en.wikipedia.org/wiki/Karl_Marx>, October 1, 2012.

[5] "Red," *Merriam-Webster*, <http://www.merriam-webster.com/dictionary/ red>, October 1, 2012.

[6] Van Impe, Jack, "Horses," Jack Van Impe's Dictionary of Prophetic Terms, *JVIM*, <http://www. jvim.com/>, October 1, 2012.

[7] James 1:19.

[8] Revelation 9:13-21, Ezekiel 38-39.

[9] "Black," *Merriam-Webster*, <http://www.merriam-webster.com/dictionary/ black>, October 1, 2012.

[10] "Wall Street Crash of 1929," *Wikipedia*, <http://en.wikipedia.org/wiki/ Wall_Street_Crash_of_1929>, October 1, 2012.

[11] "Black Friday," *Wikipedia*, <http://en.wikipedia.org/wiki/Black_Friday_ (shopping)>, October 1, 2012.

[12] Baxter, Irvin, Politics and Religion, *Endtime*, <http://www.endtime .com/ Radio.aspx>, October 1, 2012.

[13] Guzik, David, "2 Kings 6," David Guzik's Commentary, Enduring Word, <http:// www.enduringword.com/library_commentaries.htm>, October 1, 2012.

[14] "Spanish Armada," *Wikipedia*, <http://en.wikipedia.org/wiki/ Spanish_ Armada>, October 1, 2012.

[15] "*Chloros*," Blue Letter Bible, <http://cf. blueletterbible.org/lang/lexicon/ lexicon.cfm?Strongs=G5515&t=kjv>, October 1, 2012.

[16] "*Chloros*–Revelation 6:8," Bible Gateway, <http://www.biblegateway .com/>, October 1, 2012.

[17] Baxter, Irvin, Politics and Religion, *Endtime*, <http://www.endtime.com/ Radio.aspx>, October 1, 2012.

[18] "Symbols of Islam," *Wikipedia*, <http://en.wikipedia.org/wiki/Symbols_of_ Islam>, October 1, 2012.

[19] "Organisation of Islamic Cooperation," *Wikipedia*, <http://en.wikipedia.org/ wiki/Organisation_of_Islamic_Cooperation>, October 1, 2012.

[20] "Islam," *Wikipedia*, <http://en.wikipedia.org/wiki/Islam>, October 1, 2012.

[21] "Islam," *Wikipedia*.

[22] "Islamic_Terrorism," *Wikipedia*, <http://en.wikipedia.org/wiki/Islamic_ Terrorism>, October 1, 2012.

[23] "Afghanistan War," *Wikipedia*, <http://en.wikipedia.org/wiki/Afganistan_ War>, October 1, 2012.

"Iraq War," *Wikipedia*, <http://en.wikipedia.org/wiki/Iraq_War>, October 1, 2012.

[24] "Arab Spring," *Wikipedia*, <http://en.wikipedia.org/wiki/Arab_Spring>, October 1, 2012.

[25] "Mahmoud Ahmadinejad," *Wikipedia*, <http://en.wikipedia.org/wiki/ Mahmoud_Ahmadinejad>, October 1, 2012.

[26] Evans, Mark, The Final Move Beyond Iraq (Lake Mary, FL: Frontline, 2007) 111.

[27] "Twelfth Iman," *Wikipedia*, <http://en.wikipedia.org/wiki/Twelfth_imam>, October 1, 2012.

[28] Ezekiel 38:1-8.

[29] "White," *Merriam-Webster*, <http://www.merriam-webster.com/dictionary/ white>, October 1, 2012.

[30] "Constantine I," *Wikipedia*, <http://en.wikipedia.org/wiki/Constantine_I>, October 1, 2012.

[31] "Theodosius I," Wikipedia, <http://en.wikipedia.org/wiki/Theodosius_I>, October 1, 2012.

"Roman Question," Wikipedia, <http://en.wikipedia.org/wiki/Roman_Question>, October 1, 2012

[32] "Umayyad conquest of Hispania," *Wikipedia*, <http://en.wikipedia.org/wiki/ Umayyad_conquest_of_Hispania>, October 1, 2012.

[33] "Catholic Church by Country," Wikipedia, <http://en.wikipedia.org/wiki/ Catholic_Church_by_country>, October 1, 2012.

"Communist State," Wikipedia, <http://en.wikipedia.org/wiki/Communist_ countries>, October 1, 2012.

"Core Countries," Wikipedia, <http://en.wikipedia.org/wiki/Core_ countries>, October 1, 2012.

"Islamic by Country," Wikipedia, <http://en.wikipedia.org/wiki/List_of_ countries_by_Muslim_population>, October 1, 2012.

[34] "Prophecy of the Popes," Wikipedia, <http://en.wikipedia.org/wiki/ Prophecy_of_the_Popes>, October 1, 2012

[35] Graham, Billy, Approaching Hoofbeats: The Four Horsemen of the Apocalypse, 10.

[36] "Four Freedoms," *Wikipedia*, <http://en.wikipedia.org/wiki/Four_ Freedoms>, October 1, 2012.

[37] "Four Freedoms," *Wikipedia*.

22. Keys to the Trumpets

[1] "*Apsinthion*," *Blue Letter Bible*, <http://cf. blueletterbible.org/lang/lexicon/ lexicon. cfm?Strongs=G894&t=kjv>, October 1, 2012.

[2] "Revelation 8:11 Latin Vulgate," *Bible Database*, <http://www.bibledbdata .org/ onlinebibles/vulgate/66_008.htm>, October 1, 2012.

[3] "Grand Wormwood," Wikipedia, <http://en.wikipedia.org/wiki/Grand_ worm-wood>, October 1, 2012.
"Mugwort," Wikipedia, <http://en.wikipedia.org/wiki/Mugwort>, October 1, 2012.

[4] "Wormwood," *Merriam-Webster*, <http://www.merriam-webster.com/ dictionary/ Wormwood>, October 1, 2012.

[5] "Grand Wormwood," *Wikipedia*, <http://en.wikipedia.org/wiki/Grand_ wormwood>, October 1, 2012.
"Mugwort," *Wikipedia*, <http://en.wikipedia.org/wiki/Mugwort>, October 1, 2012.

[6] Katzer, Gernot, "Mugwort (Artemisia vulgaris L.)," *Gernot Katzer's Spice Pages*, <http://www.uni-graz.at/~katzer/engl/Arte_vul.html>, October 1, 2012.
"Chernobyl City," *Wikipedia*, <http://en.wikipedia.org/wiki/Chernobyl_ (city)>, October 1, 2012.

[7] "Wormwood," *CyberMova English-Ukrainian Dictionary*, <http:// cybermova.com/ cgi-bin/onlinedic.pl>, October 1, 2012

[8] Van Impe, Jack, "Wormwood," Jack Van Impe's Dictionary of Prophetic Terms, *JVIM*, <http://www. jvim.com/>, October 1, 2012.

[9] "Wormwood (Star)," *Wikipedia*, <http://en.wikipedia.org/wiki/ Wormwood_(star)>, October 1, 2012.

[10] Schmemann, Serg, "The Talk of Moscow; Chernobyl Fallout: Apocalyptic Tale and Fear," July 26, 1986, New York Times, <http://www.nytimes.com/ 1986/07/26/ world/the-talk-of-moscow-chernobyl-fallout-apocalyptic-tale-and-fear.html>, October 1, 2012.

[11] "Biological Classification," *Wikipedia*, <http://en.wikipedia.org/wiki/ Biological_ classification>, October 1, 2012.

[12] "Apollo," *Wikipedia*, <http://en.wikipedia.org/wiki/Apollo>, October 1, 2012.

[13] Gottlieb, Bruce, "What's the Name of Saddam Hussein?," November 16, 1998, Slate, <http://www.slate.com/id/1001998/>, October 1, 2012.

[14] Gottlieb, "What's the Name of Saddam Hussein?".

[15] "Saddam Hussein," *Wikipedia*, <http://en.wikipedia.org/wiki/Saddam_ Hussein>, October 1, 2012.

[16] Sax, Eddie, "Saddam Destroyer Debate: Is His Name Really In the Bible?," Endtime Magazine, January/February 2004.

[17] Arnold, Michael, "Under Saddam's Eye," *Jerusalem Post*, December 13, 1997.

[18] "A Saddam by Any Other Name?," December 17, 2003, CBS News, <http://www.cbsnews.com/stories/2003/12/17/iraq/main589004.html>, October 1, 2012.

[19] "Radical Cleric Sadr Blames U.S. for Iraq Violence," March 30, 2007, *Reuters*, <http://www.reuters.com/article/2007/03/31/us-iraq-sadr-idUSYAT04407020070331>, October 1, 2012.

[20] "Saddam Hussein," *Wikipedia*, <http://en.wikipedia.org/wiki/Saddam_ Hussein>, October 1, 2012.

[21] LaHaye, Tim, "Glossary of Prophetic Terms," Prophecy Study Bible, 1407-1409.

[22] Baxter, Irvin, Politics and Religion, *Endtime*, <http://www.endtime.com/ Radio.aspx>, October 1, 2012.

[23] LaHaye, Tim, "An Outline of Revelation," Prophecy Study Bible, 1358.

[24] Ice, Thomas, "Israel's Fall Feasts and Date-Setting of the Rapture," July 1992, *Pre-Trib Research Center*, <http://www.pre-trib.org/article-view.php? id=234>, October 1, 2012.

[25] Baxter, Irvin, Politics and Religion, *Endtime*, <http://www.endtime.com/ Radio.aspx>, October 1, 2012.

[26] Ice, Thomas, "Four Approaches to Prophetic Fulfillment," Prophecy Study Bible, 1192.

[27] Baxter, Irvin, Politics and Religion, *Endtime*, <http://www.endtime.com/ Radio.aspx>, October 1, 2012.

23. World Wars, Cold War

[1] LaHaye, Tim, "Is the United States in Bible Prophecy?," National Liberty Journal, February 1997, 16.

[2] Baxter, Irvin, Politics and Religion, *Endtime*, <http://www.endtime.com/ Radio.aspx>, October 1, 2012.

[3] "Seal of the US Department of the Treasury," *Wikipedia*, <http://en. wikipedia.org/wiki/Seal_of_the_United_States_Department_of_the_ Treasury>, October 1, 2012.

[4] "Great Seal of the United States," *Wikipedia*, <http://en.wikipedia.org/wiki/ Great_Seal_of_the_United_States>, October 1, 2012.

[5] "United Kingdom," *Wikipedia*, <http://en.wikipedia.org/wiki/United_ Kingdom>, October 1, 2012.

[6] "Spanish Armada," *Wikipedia*, <http://en.wikipedia.org/wiki/ Spanish_ Armada>, October 1, 2012.

[7] "British Empire," *Wikipedia*, <http://en.wikipedia.org/wiki/British_ empire>, October 1, 2012.

[8] "American Revolutionary War," *Wikipedia*, <http://en.wikipedia.org/wiki/ American_Revolutionary_War>, October 1, 2012.

[9] Baxter, Irvin, <u>Politics and Religion</u>, *Endtime*, <http://www.endtime.com/ Radio.aspx>, October 1, 2012.

[10] Van Impe, Jack, "Judgments: Seals, Trumpets and Vials," <u>Jack Van Impe's Dictionary of Prophetic Terms</u>, *JVIM*, <http://www. jvim.com/>, October 1, 2012.

[11] "World War I," *Wikipedia*, <http://en.wikipedia.org/wiki/World_ War_I>, October 1, 2012.

[12] "Scorched Earth," *Wikipedia*, <http://en.wikipedia.org/wiki/Scorched_ Earth>, October 1, 2012.

[13] "League of Nations," *Wikipedia*, <http://en.wikipedia.org/wiki/League_of_ Nations>, October 1, 2012.

[14] "Balfour Declaration," *Wikipedia*, <http://en.wikipedia.org/wiki/Balfour_ Declaration_of_1917>, October 1, 2012.

[15] LaHaye, Tim and Jenkins, Jerry, <u>Are We Living in the End Times</u>, (Wheaton, Illinois: Tyndale House Publishers, Inc., 1999), 43.

[16] "William McKinley," *Wikipedia*, <http://en.wikipedia.org/wiki/William_ McKinley>, October 1, 2012.

[17] "World War I," *Wikipedia*, <http://en.wikipedia.org/wiki/World_War_I>, October 1, 2012.

[18] Genesis 6:3.

[19] "Munich Agreement," *Wikipedia*, <http://en.wikipedia.org/wiki/Munich_ Agreement>, October 1, 2012.

[20] "World War II," *Wikipedia*, <http://en.wikipedia.org/wiki/World_War_II>, October 1, 2012.

[21] "Battle of the Atlantic (World War II)," *Wikipedia*, <http://en.wikipedia .org /wiki/ Battle_of_the_Atlantic_(World_War_II)>, October 1, 2012.

[22] "Pacific War," *Wikipedia*, <http://en.wikipedia.org/wiki/Pacific_War>, October 1, 2012.

[23] "The Seven Trumpets," <u>The Little Book of Prophecy and Truth</u>, 2006, <http://www.prophecyandtruth.com/book.htm#trumpets>, October 1, 2012.

[24] LaHaye, Tim and Hindson, Ed, <u>The Popular Encyclopedia of Bible Prophecy</u>, 393.

[25] "Atomic Bombings of Hiroshima and Nagasaki," *Wikipedia*, <http://en .wikipedia. org/wiki/Atomic_bombings_of_Hiroshima_and_Nagasaki>, October 1, 2012.

[26] "Atomic Bombings of Hiroshima and Nagasaki".

[27] "Holocaust," *Wikipedia*, <http://en.wikipedia.org/wiki/Holocaust>, October 1, 2012.

[28] "Warsaw Ghetto," *Wikipedia*, <http://en.wikipedia.org/wiki/Warsaw_ghetto>, October 1, 2012.

[29] Bonnett, Bill, Chronology of Man, Abdicate, <http://abdicate.net/book .aspx>, 140-141, October 1, 2012.

"Treblinka," Wikipedia, <http://en.wikipedia.org/wiki/Treblinka>, October 1, 2012.

[30] "Nuremberg Trials," *Wikipedia*, <http://en.wikipedia.org/wiki/Nuremberg_ Trials>, October 1, 2012.

[31] "Nuremberg Trials," *Wikipedia*.

[32] "Israel," *Wikipedia*, <http://en.wikipedia.org/wiki/Israel>, October 1, 2012.

[33] "Chernobyl Disaster," Wikipedia, <http://en.wikipedia.org/wiki/Chernobyl_ Disaster>, October 1, 2012.

"Meltdown in Chernobyl," Seconds from Disaster, Season 1, Episode 7, National Geographic Channel, August 17, 2004.

[34] "Disaster at Chernobyl," Zero Hour, Season 1, Episode 1, *History Channel*, 2004.

[35] "Global Radiation Exposures," *The Hiroshima International Council*, <http://www. hiroshima-cdas.or.jp/HICARE/en/10/hi04.html>, October 1, 2012.

[36] "Chernobyl Disaster," *Wikipedia*, <http://en.wikipedia.org/wiki/Chernobyl_ Disaster>, October 1, 2012.

[37] "Liquidators," *Wikipedia*, <http://en.wikipedia.org/wiki/Liquidators>, October 1, 2012.

[38] "Prypiat, Ukraine," *Wikipedia*, <http://en.wikipedia.org/wiki/Prypiat>, October 1, 2012.

[39] "Forsmark Nuclear Power Plant," *Wikipedia*, <http://en.wikipedia.org/wiki/ Forsmark_Nuclear_Power_Plant>, October 1, 2012.

[40] Tracz, Orysia Paszczak, "The Things We Do," The Ukranian Weekly, May 16, 2004, <http://www.ukrweekly.com/old/archive/2004/200417.html>, October 1, 2012.

[41] "Chernobyl City," *Wikipedia*, <http://en.wikipedia.org/wiki/Chernobyl_ (city)>, October 1, 2012.

Katzer, Gernot, "Mugwort (Artemisia vulgaris L.)," *Gernot Katzer's Spice Pages*, <http://www.uni-graz.at/~katzer/engl/Arte_vul.html>, October 1, 2012.

[42] "Cooperation and Partnership Agreement," European Union, <http://eeas .europa. eu/russia/index_en.htm>, October 1, 2012.

[43] Daniel 7:4-6, Revelation 13:2-3.

[44] European Commission, External Relations, Euro-Mediterranean Partnership, <http://ec.europa.eu/external_relations/euromed/index_en .htm>, October 1, 2012.

"Union for the Mediterranean," *Wikipedia*, <http://en.wikipedia.org/wiki/ Union_for_the_Mediterranean>, October 1, 2012.

24. Between Iraq and a Hard Place

[1] "Persian Gulf War," *Wikipedia*, <http://en.wikipedia.org/wiki/Gulf_War>, October 1, 2012.

[2] "Persian Gulf War," *Wikipedia*.

[3] "Kuwait Oil Fires," *Wikipedia*, <http://en.wikipedia.org/wiki/Kuwaiti_oil_ fires>, October 1, 2012.

[4] Ibrahimm, Youssef M., "Most Oil Fires Are out in Kuwait, but Its Environment Is Devastated," *New York Times*>, October 19, 1991, <http:// query. nytimes. com/gst/ fullpage.html?res=9D0CE3DF1E3BF 93AA257 53C1A967958260>, October 1, 2012.

[5] "Persian Gulf War," *Wikipedia*, <http://en.wikipedia.org/wiki/Gulf_War>, October 1, 2012.

[6] "Persian Gulf War," *Wikipedia*.

[7] Clinton, Bill, "Text of Clinton Statement on Iraq," February 17, 1998, *CNN*, <http:// www.cnn.com/ALLPOLITICS/1998/02/17/transcripts/clinton. iraq/>, October 1, 2012.

[8] "Iraq War," *Wikipedia*, <http://en.wikipedia.org/wiki/Iraq_War>, October 1, 2012.

[9] "*Tuwaitha*," *Wikipedia*, <http://en.wikipedia.org/wiki/Tuwaitha>, October 1, 2012.

[10] "Iraqi Liberation Act," The Library of Congress, *Thomas*, <http://thomas .loc.gov/ cgi-bin/query/z?c105:H.R.4655.ENR:>, October 1, 2012.

[11] "Oil for Food Program," *Wikipedia*, <http://en.wikipedia.org/wiki/Oil_ for_food>, October 1, 2012.

[12] Krauthammer, "France's Game," *Time*.

[13] "2003 Invasion of Iraq," *Wikipedia*, <http://en.wikipedia.org/wiki/ Invasion_of_ Iraq>, October 1, 2012.

[14] "Iraqi Insurgency," *Wikipedia*, <http://en.wikipedia.org/wiki/Iraqi_ Insurgency>, October 1, 2012.

[15] "Bunker Buster Bomb," *Wikipedia*, <http://en.wikipedia.org/wiki/Bunker_ buster_bomb>, October 1, 2012.

[16] "2003 Invasion of Iraq," *Wikipedia*, <http://en.wikipedia.org/wiki/2003_ Invasion_ of_Iraq>, October 1, 2012.

[17] "*Abu Ghraib* Torture and Prisoner Abuse," *Wikipedia*, <http://en.wikipedia .org/ wiki/Abu_Ghraib_torture_and_prisoner_abuse>, October 1, 2012.

[18] "Honor Killing," *Wikipedia*, <http://en.wikipedia.org/wiki/Honor_Killing>, October 1, 2012.

[19] "*Abu Ghraib* Torture and Prisoner Abuse," *Wikipedia*, <http://en.wikipedia .org/ wiki/Abu_Ghraib_torture_and_prisoner_abuse>, October 1, 2012.

[20] "Apache Helicopter," *Wikipedia*, <http://en.wikipedia.org/wiki/Apache_ helicopter>, October 1, 2012.
Apache AH-64D developed by Hughes Helicopter, purchased by McDonnell Douglas and merged with Boeing.

[21] Lindsey, Hal, There's a New World Coming, A Prophetic Odyssey, 53.

[22] "Frequently Asked Questions," *Dangerous Decibels*, <http://www .dangerousdecibels.org/education/information-center/faq/>, October 1, 2012.

[23] "Helicopter," *Wikipedia*, <http://en.wikipedia.org/wiki/Helicopter>, October 1, 2012.

[24] "Apache Helicopter," *Wikipedia*, <http://en.wikipedia.org/wiki/ Apache_ helicopter>, October 1, 2012.

[25] *Gottlieb, Bruce,* "What's the Name of Saddam Hussein?," November 16, 1998, *Slate*, <http://www.slate.com/id/1001998/>, October 1, 2012.

[26] Evans, Mark, The Final Move Beyond Iraq, 28.

[27] Daniel 4:31-33.

[28] Cardozo, Rabbi Nathan Lopes, "Purim & the War with Iraq," <http:// www .cardozoschool.org/show_article.asp?article_id=362&cat_id=3&cat_ name=Holidays&parent_id=3&subcat_id=31&subcat_name=Purim>, October 1, 2012.

[29] Baxter, Irvin, Politics and Religion, *Endtime*, <http://www.endtime.com/ Radio.aspx>, October 1, 2012.

[30] "Apache Helicopter," *Wikipedia*, <http://en.wikipedia.org/wiki/Apache_ helicopter>, October 1, 2012.

[31] "Mediterranean Union," *Wikipedia*, <http://en.wikipedia.org/wiki/ Mediterranean_ union>, October 1, 2012.

[32] The EU and the Middle East Peace Process," European Union, <http:// eeas.europa.eu/mepp/index_en.htm>, October 1, 2012.
British English spelling.

[33] "Quartet on the Middle East," *Wikipedia*, <http://en.wikipedia.org/wiki/ Quartet_ on_the_Middle_East>, October 1, 2012.

[34] Daniel 7:1-6.
Baxter, Irvin, Politics and Religion, Endtime, <http://www.endtime.com/ Radio.aspx>, October 1, 2012.

[35] "United Nations Special Committee on Palestine," *Wikipedia*, <http://en .wikipedia.org/wiki/United_Nations_Special_Committee_on_Palestine>, October 1, 2012.

[36] Baxter, Irvin, Politics and Religion, Endtime, <http://www.endtime.com/ Radio.aspx>, October 1, 2012.

[37] "Roadmap for Peace," *Wikipedia*, <http://en.wikipedia.org/wiki/Road_ map_for_ peace>, October 1, 2012.

[38] "The Euro-Mediterranean Partnership," European Union, <http://ec.europa.eu/ external_ relations/euromed/index_en.htm>, October 1, 2012.
"European Neighbourhood Policy," European Union, ec.europa.eu/world/ enp/ index_en.htm>, October 1, 2012.

[39] "Iraq War," *Wikipedia*, <http://en.wikipedia.org/wiki/Iraq_war>, October 1, 2012.

[40] Perot, Ross and Wolf, Richard, USA Today, *C-Span*, September 27, 2012.

25. Iraq War III

[1] Perot, Ross and Wolf, Richard, USA Today, *C-Span*, September 27, 2012.

[2] "Tropical Depression Ten (2005)," *Wikipedia*, <http://en.wikipedia.org/ wiki/ Tropical _Depression _Ten_(2005)>, October 1, 2012.

[3] "Ariel Sharon," *Wikipedia*, <http://en.wikipedia.org/wiki/Ariel_sharon>, October 1, 2012.

[4] "2009 Israeli Elections," *Wikipedia*, <http://en.wikipedia.org/wiki/2009_ Israeli_ elections>, October 1, 2012.

[5] "Two-state Solution," Wikipedia, <http://en.wikipedia.org/wiki/Two-state_solution >, October 1, 2012.

[6] "India," *Wikipedia*, <http://en.wikipedia.org/wiki/India>, October 1, 2012.

[7] "Shiite Islam," *Wikipedia*, <http://en.wikipedia.org/wiki/Shiite_Islam>, October 1, 2012.

[8] Ezekiel 38-39.

[9] "China," *Wikipedia*, <http://en.wikipedia.org/wiki/China>, October 1, 2012.

[10] Babbins, Jed and Timperlake, Edward, Showdown: Why China Wants War with the United States, (Washington, DC: Regnery Publishing, 2006).

[11] "Zhu Cheghu," *Wikipedia*, <http://en.wikipedia.org/wiki/Zhu_Chenghu>, October 1, 2012.

[12] "Neville Chamberlain," *Wikipedia*, <http://en.wikipedia.org/wiki/Neville_ Chamberlain>, October 1, 2012.

[13] Daniel 7:1-7, Revelation 13:2.

[14] Matthew 24:15-22.

26. What Kind of People Ought You to Be?

[1] "Doomsday Clock," *The Bulletin*, <http://www.thebulletin.org>, October 1, 2012.

[2] "No Nations Should Have Nukes, Most in USA Say," USA Today, <http:// www. usatoday.com/news/nation/2005-03-31-nuclear-fears_x.htm>, October 1, 2012.

[3] Guzik, David, "2 Peter 3," <u>David Guzik's Commentary</u>, *Enduring Word*, <http://www.enduringword.com/library_commentaries.htm>, October 1, 2012.
Henry, Matthew, "2 Peter 3," <u>Matthew Henry Commentary on the Whole Bible</u>, *Blue Letter Bible*, <http:// cf.blueletterbible.org/commentaries/>, October 1, 2012.
Jamieson, Robert, et al., "2 Peter 3," <u>Commentary Critical and Explanatory on the Whole Bible</u>, *Blue Letter Bible*, <http://cf. blueletterbible.org/ commentaries/>, October 1, 2012.
Scofield, Cyrus, "2 Peter 3," <u>Reference Notes, 1917 Edition</u>, *Bible Study Tools*, <http:// www.biblestudytools.com/commentaries/scofield-reference-notes/>, October 1, 2012.

[4] Revelation 9:13-21, Ezekiel 38-39, Zechariah 12-14, Revelation 16:16-21.

[5] Revelation 1:8.

[6] Guzik, David, "Romans 13," <u>David Guzik's Commentary</u>, *Enduring Word*, <http://www.enduringword.com/library_commentaries.htm>, October 1, 2012.
Henry, Matthew, "Romans 13," <u>Matthew Henry Commentary on the Whole Bible</u>, *Blue Letter Bible*, <http:// cf.blueletterbible.org/commentaries/>, October 1, 2012.
Jamieson, Robert, et al., "Romans 13," <u>Commentary Critical and Explanatory on the Whole Bible</u>, *Blue Letter Bible*, <http://cf. blueletterbible.org/ commentaries/>, October 1, 2012.
Scofield, Cyrus, "Romans 13," <u>Reference Notes, 1917 Edition</u>, *Bible Study Tools*, <http:// www.biblestudytools. com/commentaries/scofield-reference-notes/>, October 1, 2012.

[7] Guzik, David, "1 Peter 4," <u>David Guzik's Commentary</u>, *Enduring Word*, <http://www.enduringword.com/library_commentaries.htm>, October 1, 2012.
Henry, Matthew, "1 Peter 4," <u>Matthew Henry Commentary on the Whole Bible</u>, *Blue Letter Bible*, <http:// cf.blueletterbible.org/commentaries/>, October 1, 2012.
Jamieson, Robert, et al., "1 Peter 4," <u>Commentary Critical and Explanatory on the Whole Bible</u>, *Blue Letter Bible*, <http://cf. blueletterbible.org/ commentaries/>, October 1, 2012.
Scofield, Cyrus, "1 Peter 4," <u>Reference Notes, 1917 Edition</u>, *Bible Study Tools*, <http:// www.biblestudytools. com/commentaries/scofield-reference-notes/>, October 1, 2012.

27. The End of the Beginning

[1] "Handel's Messiah," *Wikipedia*, <http://en.wikipedia.org/wiki/ Messiah_(Handel)>, October 1, 2012.

D. Prophecy Fulfilled

[1] "Diadochi," *Wikipedia*, <http://en.wikipedia.org/wiki/Diadochi>, October 1, 2012.

[2] "Syrian Wars," *Wikipedia*, <http://en.wikipedia.org/wiki//Syrian_Wars>, October 1, 2012.

[3] "Seleucid Empire," *Wikipedia*, <http://en.wikipedia.org/wiki/Seleucid_ Empire>, October 1, 2012.
"Ptolemaic Dynasty," *Wikipedia*, <http://en.wikipedia.org/wiki/Ptolemaic Dynasty>, October 1, 2012.

[4] "Syrian Wars," *Wikipedia*, <http://en.wikipedia.org/wiki//Syrian_Wars>, October 1, 2012.

[5] "Syrian Wars," *Wikipedia*.

[6] "Battle of Raphia," *Wikipedia*, <http://en.wikipedia.org/wiki/Battle_of_ Raphia>, October 1, 2012.

[7] "Syrian Wars," *Wikipedia*, <http://en.wikipedia.org/wiki//Syrian_Wars>, October 1, 2012.

[8] "Battle of Panium," *Wikipedia*, <http://en.wikipedia.org/wiki/Battle_of Panium>, October 1, 2012.

[9] "Syrian Wars," *Wikipedia*, <http://en.wikipedia.org/wiki//Syrian_Wars>, October 1, 2012.

[10] "Battle of Magnesia," *Wikipedia*, <http://en.wikipedia.org/wiki/Battle_ of_Magnesia>, October 1, 2012.

[11] "Heliodorus," *Wikipedia*, <http://en.wikipedia.org/wiki/ Heliodorus_ (minister)>, October 1, 2012.

E. Jewish Feast Dates

[1] Hebcal Jewish Calendar, *Hebcal*, <http://www.hebcal. com/hebcal/>, October 1, 2012.

F. Chronology of Jesus Christ

[1] Bonnett, Bill, "Linear Chronology of Man According to the Scriptures," *Abdicate*, <http://abdicate.net/chron.aspx>, October 1, 2012.

[2] "Hasmonean," *Wikipedia*, <http://en.wikipedia.org/wiki/Hasmonean>, October 1, 2012.
"Antipater the Idumaean," *Wikipedia*, <http://en.wikipedia.org/wiki/ Antipater_the_ idumaean>, October 1, 2012.

[3] "Augustus," *Wikipedia*, <http://en.wikipedia.org/wiki/Augustus>, October 1, 2012.

[4] "Augustus," *Wikipedia*.

[5] Josephus, Flavius, <u>The Antiquities of the Jews</u>, Book 15, Chapter 11, Paragraph 1, *Christian Classics Ethereal Library*, <http://www.ccel.org/ ccel/josephus/ complete>, October 1, 2012.

[6] Josephus, Flavius, <u>The Antiquities of the Jews</u>, Book 15, Chapter 11, Paragraph 6, *Christian Classics Ethereal Library*, <http://www.ccel.org/ ccel/josephus/ complete>, October 1, 2012.

[7] Augustus, Caesar, <u>The Deeds of the Divine Augustus</u>, *Massachusetts Institute of Technology*, <http://classics.mit.edu/Augustus/ deeds.html>, October 1, 2012.

[8] "Star of Bethlehem," *Wikipedia*, <http://en.wikipedia.org/wiki/Star_of_ Bethlehem>, October 1, 2012.
Parpola, Simo, "The Magi and the Star," <u>Bible Review</u>, December 2001, 16-23, 52, 54.
Son of Man, "Triple Conjunction of Jupiter and Saturn," Son of Man, <http://www. sonofman.org /triple.htm>, October 1, 2012.

[9] "Star of Bethlehem," *Wikipedia*.
Parpola, "The Magi and the Star," <u>Bible Review</u>, 16-23, 52, 54.
Son of Man, "Triple Conjunction of Jupiter and Saturn," *Son of Man*.

[10] Steel, Duncan, <u>Marking Time: The Epic Quest to Invent the Perfect Calendar</u>, 330.
Humphreys, Colin, "The Star of Bethlehem">, October 1995, <u>Astronomy & Cosmology</u>, <http://www.asa3.org/ASA/topics/Astronomy-Cosmology/ S&CB%20 10-93Humphreys.html>, October 1, 2012.
Kidger, Mark, "Star of Bethlehem," *Comet and Asteroid Observing*, <http:// www. astrosurf.com/comets/Star_of_Bethlehem/English/ Chinese.htm>, October 1, 2012.

[11] Josephus, Flavius, <u>The Antiquities of the Jews</u>, Book 17, Chapter 6, Paragraph 4, *Christian Classics Ethereal Library*, <http://www.ccel.org/ ccel/josephus/ complete>, October 1, 2012.
"Six Millennium Catalog of Phases of the Moon," *NASA*, <http://eclipse. gsfc.nasa. gov/phase/ phases0001. html>, October 1, 2012.

[12] Josephus, The Antiquities of the Jews, Christian Classics Ethereal Library.
"Six Millennium Catalog of Phases of the Moon," NASA.

[13] "Dionysius Exiguus," *Wikipedia*, <http://en.wikipedia.org/wiki/Dionysius_ Exiguus>, October 1, 2012.

[14] "James Ussher," *Wikipedia*, <http://en.wikipedia.org/wiki/James_Ussher>, October 1, 2012.

[15] "Coponius," *Wikipedia*, <http://en.wikipedia.org/wiki/Coponius>, October 1, 2012.

[16] "Tiberius," *Wikipedia*, <http://en.wikipedia.org/wiki/Tiberius>, October 1, 2012
Note: Because historians exclude years from the reigns of Augustus and Tiberius,

the years are incorrect for Pilate and Caiaphas which delays the ministries of John the Baptist and Jesus Christ.

[17] "Tiberius," *Wikipedia*.

[18] "Caiaphas," *Wikipedia*, <http://en.wikipedia.org/wiki/Caiaphas>, October 1, 2012.

[19] "Pontius Pilate," *Wikipedia*, <http://en.wikipedia.org/wiki/Pontius_Pilate>, October 1, 2012.

[20] "Jerusalem Day," *Wikipedia*, <http://en.wikipedia.org/wiki/Jerusalem _Day>, October 1, 2012.

Appendix G

21st Century
REVELATION

World Wars, Iraq Wars & End Wars

A current understanding of God's plan for our time

21st Century Revelation Online

Visit **www.21stCenturyRevelation.com** for the latest information, questions and answers about history, current events and Bible prophecy with insight into the future. See the Word of God unsealed, revealed and fulfilled in our time. Read the latest information on Bible study classes, prophecy conferences and meeting schedules. God is at work to redeem the world and to prepare the world for the reign of Jesus Christ. His plan for the world includes His Church.

End Time Presentation

Robert Cook is available to speak at churches, schools and civic organizations about Bible prophecy, the End Times and current political, religious and economic events that impact the Church, our nations and the world.

Read the Book Then Pass It on

After you finish reading *21st Century Revelation*, pass it on. Spread this important message of God's plan for our time to encourage other Christians in their walk and ministry. Share this book with your family, friends, your pastor and church leaders, your Christian school principal, leaders and teachers. Knowing and understanding the End Times will change your heart, your life and your ministry to impact your church. Working together, our churches will impact our communities, our states, our nation and the world for the kingdom of God.

21st Century Revelation: World Wars, Iraq Wars & End Wars
A current understanding of God's plan for our time

Volume 1—Creation to Laodicea

A. God
B. God's Word
C. God's Time
D. God's Plan for Our Time

Volume 2—America & the Rapture

A. The United States in the Bible
B. God's Plan for Our Homecoming
C. The Fall of the United States

Volume 3—Tribulation

A. God's Plan for the Tribulation
B. God's Plan for the Great Tribulation
C. God's Plan for the Millennium and Beyond

www.21stCenturyRevelation.com

CPSIA information can be obtained at www.ICGtesting.com
Printed in the USA
LVOW05s2128230813

349211LV00004B/174/P